AMERICAN WRITERS IN REBELLION
From Mark Twain to Dreiser

AMERICAN WRITERS IN REBELLION

From Mark Twain to Dreiser

by H. WAYNE MORGAN

American Century Series
HILL AND WANG · NEW YORK

FIRST EDITION SEPTEMBER 1965
SECOND PRINTING APRIL 1966
THIRD PRINTING MARCH 1968

Manufactured in the United States of America
by The Colonial Press Inc., Clinton, Massachusetts

To DON AND LAUREN BREESE
and JOHN AND BARBARA MARTIN

Preface

FOR TWO GENERATIONS after the Civil War, American literature widened its subject matter and deepened its conclusions. The decades from Mark Twain to Theodore Dreiser, from Realism to Naturalism, were times of re-thinking in American letters. As years of social, political, and economic transition they seem confused and conflicting. It is often easier to see both the unity and variety in great movements by focusing on specific individuals who symbolize a larger change. I discuss men rather than movements in this book and offer a synthesis of critical opinion and general biography of five of the era's most important writers.

Though this book deals with Realism and Naturalism, I am less concerned with the general development of either theory than with how these ideas affected the men involved. By Realism, I mean simply a literary technique based on reporting the facts of daily life within a meaningful humanistic framework. Realists shunned the unusual and decadent, trying to avoid prejudice, false idealism, or sensationalism. Though they believed that literature should teach life's realities, stressing its "good" qualities, they tried to let the reader draw his own conclusions.

By Naturalism, I mean generally the idea that man is at the mercy of biological and emotional drives he does not fully understand. Like Realism, it uses detached observation and relies on specific facts. Naturalism reflects an interest in science and seeks to understand nature's general laws. It denies man's free will apart from nature as a whole, and is often pessimistic in determining his state in life's fullest natural context.

Like all summations, these definitions are inadequate. They are descriptive rather than definitive. All the men in this book departed frequently from the general outlines and specific teachings of the movements and theories they supposedly represent. Creative ability is never bound by orthodoxy, even of its own composition. Both Realism and Naturalism are attitudes of mind rather than techniques of writing.

These essays are not a comprehensive coverage of the period

vii

involved. I discuss only five major figures whose lives and work illuminated their larger world and the general ideas for which they stood. I did not include many lesser but significant people like Sarah Orne Jewett, Henry B. Fuller, Harold Frederic, E. W. Howe, and Jack London. Stephen Crane is the most obvious omission, since I covered his work in a previous book, *Writers in Transition* (1963).

I offer these essays knowing that all who "criticize" or "interpret" works of art are secondhand dealers. Critical judgments are personal and should merely introduce the artistic work. We should try to appreciate a writer's purpose and to judge him for what he did rather than what he might have done. As a nontechnical critic I am frankly more interested in the total quality of a man's work than in his specific weaknesses or idiosyncrasies of style. A relevant human message in a literary work is far more important than strict adherence to a preconceived idea of form.

The finest quality of any creative work is its ability to move different men in different ways. No act of genius has only a single side. I offer here not a final word, but a suggestion, an appreciation, and an introduction to these men and their books which is admittedly highly personal. I will be satisfied, if by presenting my own appreciation and respect for these works I focus some attention on them.

H. WAYNE MORGAN

University of Texas
Fall, 1965

Acknowledgments

Grateful thanks are due the following persons and firms for permission to quote copyrighted materials: the Belknap Press of Harvard University for *The Mark Twain–William Dean Howells Letters,* 2 vols. (Cambridge: 1960); Professor William W. Howells for the works of William Dean Howells; Harper & Row, Inc. for books by Mark Twain, William Dean Howells, and Albert Bigelow Paine; Mrs. Isabel Garland Lord and Mrs. Constance Garland Doyle for books by Hamlin Garland; The Book Club of California for *The Letters of Frank Norris* (San Francisco: 1956); Doubleday, Inc., for Franklin Walker, *Frank Norris: A Biography* (New York: 1932); the New American Library for the works of Theodore Dreiser; the University of Pennsylvania Press for *The Letters of Theodore Dreiser,* 3 vols. (Philadelphia: 1959).

Contents

AMERICAN WRITERS IN REBELLION
From Mark Twain to Dreiser

Mark Twain: The Optimist as Pessimist

Everyone is a moon and has a dark side which he never shows to anybody.

—1897

ONE DAY in 1885, when Samuel Langhorne Clemens, better known as Mark Twain, was fifty and his daughter Susy was fourteen, she began a biography of her father by noting with youth's candor: "I shall have no trouble in knowing what to say about him, as he is a *very* striking character." [1] It was the understatement of the century, for most of the civilized world knew him. And this was only the halfway mark of a fabulous career. In the years ahead, the suns of prosperity and adulation, public acclaim and critical recognition, shone on a fabled head that whitened majestically with time. Shadows of personal tragedy darkened his old age, but they and his temperament only endeared him more to his readers and admirers.

For a whole generation his name was familiar in all corners of the world over which he so freely traveled. He dined with kings and emperors. The world's great societies honored him. His name and fame were on the lips of men everywhere. "As Mark Twain says" commonly prefaced many remarks. His alleged remark on the weather's vagaries entered the language, and his comment that reports of his death were greatly exaggerated was as widely repeated. His humor's edge cut through many of the day's platitudes, revealing an inner man who thought more deeply than other humorists. When he died, surrounded by success, fame, and legend, America seemed to lose her greatest voice. If he seemed a contradiction—a man who began public life as the apparent optimist of travel books and who ended in the cynicism and despair of *What Is Man?* (1906) and *The Mysterious Stranger* (1916)—well, no matter. It was all part of the legend, and eccentricity and contradiction are the coins of genius.

Not many people would have predicted such an illustrious

1

career from his unlikely beginning. He was born on November 30, 1835, in the "almost invisible village of Florida, Monroe County, Missouri." He entered the world two months early, and as he tasted his first breath the light of Halley's comet filled the sky. Always superstitious, he insisted that he came into the world with the comet and would go out with it. When he died in 1910, its light dazzled the skies as if to call his spirit.

Florida was part of the Southwestern frontier, filled with optimism, ruggedness, and provinciality. It boasted few people, and its appearance was not inviting. "Both the streets and the lanes were paved with the same material," Mark Twain remembered, "tough black mud in wet times, deep dust in dry." [2] The village was isolated and lonely, with few advantages for a growing boy or aspiring adult, but it was rich in a kind of life that flowed through the silks of Mark Twain's memory to become the source of his work.

The family was a product of that frontier. His father, John Marshall Clemens, was a frontier lawyer and occasional officeholder. He was a solemn and devoutly puritanical man; but an occasional fancy for speculation offset this grimness, which his son later called "the Sellers complex," and which he himself inherited. The elder Clemens bought a tract of land in Tennessee, which he cautioned his children never to sell. It was his only tangible legacy to them, and their half-hidden lust for speculation rose in later years to a kind of mania in relation to the "Tennessee land." When Mark Twain wrote of Colonel Sellers and his absurd speculations in *The Gilded Age* (1873), he knew whereof he spoke. The elder Clemens was more solemn than harsh. He was a politically conservative Whig, and saw life as a struggle. But he could be affectionate and even indulgent when he thought emotion beneficent.

Mark Twain's mother complemented her husband in both person and attitudes. Though she was devoutly religious and often severe in her tastes and demands on her family, she had a warm heart and an outgoing nature. She became Tom Sawyer's Aunt Polly. She forced the little ones to do their chores, take their medicine, and occasionally punished them, but only out of duty. She often defended the less fortunate and was fiercely independent. She kept a bully from beating his daughter by simply barring his path and was usually at hand in a neighborhood crisis. And legend said that though she drowned excess kittens, she warmed the water first.

Family was not so important to the young Samuel as geography. Unable to prosper in Florida, John Clemens moved to Hannibal, Missouri. Fronting the Mississippi, the town was set solidly in a rustic environment that saw human nature at play in both its best and its worst lights. And so young Samuel came upon the river that shaped his life and that would forever be, to him and his readers, a symbol of lost youth, forgotten innocence, and eternal exploration.

Despite his later assertions that Hannibal was tame, it teemed with various species of humanity and forms of violence. The sensitive eye, even in a child's head, saw much to remember of the conflicting forces that move a man in such a town. He who always found violence fascinating seemed often at hand when it occurred. A man was shot in the streets, and Mark Twain saw witless neighbors place a crushing Bible on his chest while he died. The village jail burned, and the boy blamed himself for having given the hobo inmate matches to cause the accident. He watched in horror one evening as two young men tried to kill their aged uncle while in a drunken stupor. He felt guilt and remorse all his life, and these combined with the frontier's superstitions and the river town's brooding qualities to put an edge of darkness on his outlook. His father was the town coroner for a time, and one evening the boy stumbled into his offices to find a corpse bathed in moonlight in the room's center. He did not know it was there because of an inquest his father was to conduct; he merely fled through the nearest window. "I went out at the window, and I carried the sash along with me," he recorded years later. "I did not need the sash, but it was handier to take it than it was to leave it, and so I took it." [3]

Isolation bred provincialism on this frontier, and the young Mark Twain built up, in his vivid imagination, glorious prospects of the distant world. They were rudely shattered in afteryears when he actually traveled. He could then join perspective with humor to write in *Tom Sawyer* (1876) of the visiting county judge at the Sunday school: "He was from Constantinople, twelve miles away—so he had traveled, and seen the world—these very eyes had looked upon the county courthouse—which was said to have a tin roof." [4]

That isolation prolonged his childhood and bolstered an already active imagination. Its destruction when he was older provided much of the irony, and then pessimism, that denoted developing perspective. But Hannibal's isolation, however real, was easily exaggerated. For that area and era it was a sizable town. It boasted bookstores, law offices, and churches, and aspired to such culture as the frontier permitted. It was not the rude wilderness that the older Mark Twain often criticized.

Always there was the great river to capture a boy's imagination, to take him sailing away on peaceful rafts, or inspire him with terror at flood time. By day it could be a raving torrent, its banks often a mile apart in some places, muddy with the earth of Ohio or Minnesota, laden with the broken fruitage of trees, houses, boats that it devoured in its passage to the Gulf. By night the stars shone on its placid surface as if it were a great ribbon winding down the continent's middle. It was peaceful and beautiful, framed in the green of its shores. But it was also dangerous, as the young man discovered when he later sought to master it with his pilot's skill. The slightest ripple on its surface indicated a sand bar to ground a steamboat. A small snag, deceptive in its swirls, could rip the bottom out of a passing boat. The hungry river continuously ate at its own banks, tumbling houses, animals, and great chunks of land into its depths to be swirled away on the trip to New Orleans.

Through all the river's serenity and terror, light and darkness, beauty and ugliness, the steamboat wound its way, its whistle melancholy, angry, or happy in the early mornings, smoke marking its arrival and departure. This was the golden age of steamboating, when the great freighters and swift, castlelike passenger boats plied from Cincinnati to New Orleans, carrying freight, slaves, fine goods, travelers, and, above all, a fabulous lore. Even the smallest river town such as Hannibal sprang to life in moments when confronted with the call: "Steamboat a-comin'!" That cry and what it symbolized rang through the young Mark Twain's mind like a chorus.

Above all, the river symbolized contact with the outer world. It polluted dank river towns like Natchez with its scum; but it also brought goods, news, a sense of being part of something large and grand. It brought to Mark Twain and his friends a feeling of vastness, of a land without time or cares, a smell and feel of distant places. It was inexhaustible fuel for a sensitive imagination that otherwise might have been stunted or stillborn in such an environment. To Mark Twain it was a highway of romance, and most of his life's peace and meaning would be symbolized by youth floating in that water on a peaceful raft, destination unknown, with no ports of call.

He was an unusual child, but was not a prodigy of intellect. His mother, beset with other worries, found him a great trial, unlike his older brother, Orion, who was more reflective and easily disciplined. He was frail, and seemed anxious to die; like the proverbial cat, he almost drowned at least nine times. In old age his mother once said that he had worried her; not, she noted with a twinkle in her eye, because she was afraid he might die, but afraid he might survive. He kept the child's spirit, adding to it an acute adult's perception. He amazed friends in middle and old age with his charm and vigor and the freshness of his wit and conversation. "He was a youth to the end of his days," his friend William Dean Howells noted, "the heart of a boy with the head of a sage; the heart of a good boy, or a bad boy, but always a wilful boy, and wilfulest to show himself out at every time for just the boy he was." [5]

Mark Twain disliked the formal discipline of schooling—he was his own Tom Sawyer—but he loved to read, literally devouring great quantities of history, biography, and science. The boy who hated lessons would revel in the mechanics' library of New York when working there as a printer. He was a close observer of the men and events around him, making friends easily, full of energy for amusement and more serious projects.

His father died in 1847, leaving his family "a sumptuous legacy of pride in his fine Virginia stock and its national distinction, . . ." but little else except the Tennessee land.[6] Hannibal did not excite Mark Twain, and as he verged on manhood he longed for adventure and worldly success. In 1853 and 1854 he worked as a journeyman printer in New York, St. Louis, Philadelphia, and ultimately went to Keokuk, Iowa, where he worked on a newspaper with his brother Orion. But he was restless, full of nervous energy, eager to see the world; and when he found an unclaimed fifty-dollar bill in the street, he departed for the Amazon, where he hoped to engrave his name on history as an explorer. He immediately got no farther than Cincinnati, where he set type and wrote a few news columns.[7] He did not like journalism. It was too sedentary, and his mind teemed with "Sellerisms."

His trip to South America proved abortive, for upon arriving in New Orleans he discovered that no ships went to the Amazon. Fascinated by the city and its life, the swirl of an elegant Southern civilization with its mixture of French, Negro, and American cultures, Mark Twain decided to become a steamboat pilot. Long rows of the fine craft lay at anchor, discharging or loading passengers and cargo, either ending or beginning the long river trip. It seemed as if the steamboat's golden age would last forever, though some men talked of railroads and a coming war that would sweep the boats from the rivers.

Ignorant of piloting, he persuaded Horace Bixby to train him as an apprentice. After borrowing the necessary money to pay the captain's fee, he embarked on an apprenticeship that made him a well-respected pilot, and which added much to the store of memories for his later writing. For one so disordered and oblivious of detail, Mark Twain rapidly learned the river's many faces. Bixby's eloquent profanity impressed the young cub with the difficulties of the task; and before many months passed, he could read the signs of treacherous or safe water, knew how best to gain speed, and could see the river's marks of change.

Fiercely proud and competitive men piloted and captained the riverboats, and hard races were as much the order of business as carrying freight and passengers. These races often caused terrible accidents and bitter feelings, and tragedy struck Mark Twain when his younger brother Henry was killed in the senseless wreck of the *Pennsylvania*. Twain, who had quarreled with the ship's pilot and gone ashore, blamed himself for his brother's death because of his failure to take Henry along. Like many similar tragedies, this one built a deposit of remorse in the bank of Twain's memory.[8]

No man loved the river or piloting more, nor was it accidental that he chose his pen name from river terms, an expression meaning two fathoms deep and thus "safe water." He gloried in the sense of freedom, in the absolute mastery over his craft which was the pilot's empire, in the life's carefree ease. In later years these experiences poured almost automatically into *Life on the Mississippi* (1883), the first half of which is a nostalgic description of a vanished America. He combined piloting with penetrating observations on the river's life, both in the water and on the shore. But above all, he loved piloting's freedom. "If I have seemed to love my subject, it is no surprising thing, for I loved the profession far better than anything I have followed since, and I took measureless pride in it, . . ." he recalled. "The reason is plain; a pilot in those days was the only unfettered and entirely independent human being that lived in the earth." [9] The exaggeration is perhaps pardonable. He could have returned to the river after the Civil War, but significantly by that time he chose writing as his profession. But the river always haunted his imagination, and there are no greater tributes to it than his. "The piece about the Mississippi is capital," his friend William Dean Howells wrote years later; "it almost made the water in our ice pitcher muddy as I read it. . . ." [10]

His years of piloting preceded the outbreak of the Civil War in 1861, before a new wave of technical progress replaced the steamboat with the railroad train. Mark Twain joined the Confederate ranks, and for a few days in 1861 was an elegant soldier. His military career consisted of poor marching, bad food, and exhaustion. He fell from a burning barn and ended his exploits with a sprained ankle that removed him from the conflict. His heart, to say the least, was not in war, for he disliked anything smacking of organization and control.

Providence or fate entered the scene and set him on the path to fame. His brother Orion was appointed secretary of the newly organized Territory of Nevada, and he took Mark Twain with him as his aide. They left from St. Louis by stage on an exhilarating journey across the great high desert he later immortalized in *Roughing It* (1872). The trip by coach was uncomfortable, but it had the compensation of freedom and an almost dreamlike quality of careless transit. The heavy coach, laden with mail sacks and provisions, was a kind of river raft or steamboat; and the Clemens brothers passed the days and nights smoking, talking, and looking at the scenery and people.

He, whose adult nickname would be "Youth," was a nomad at heart, eager to escape responsibilities and civilization's fetters. "The nomadic instinct is a human instinct," he said; "it was born with Adam and transmitted through the patriarchs, and after thirty centuries of steady effort, civilization has not educated it entirely out of us yet. It has a charm which, once tasted, a man will yearn to taste again." [11] The journey to Nevada, where freedom reigned supreme, mixed with adventure and excitement, was a prelude that he long remembered. "Even at this day it thrills me through and through to think of the life, the gladness and the wild sense of freedom that used to make the blood dance in my veins on those fine overland mornings!" [12]

Mark Twain came upon the West as did few later men. The railroad and peace, which came after him, would "civilize" the mining frontier. To a man accustomed to the lushness of the Mississippi River Valley, Nevada was barren and desolate, but this landscape captured his imagination. He often hated the physical discomforts of roughing it, but he loved the land's vast cleanness and its sense of freedom.

He could stand, as he wrote his mother, in Virginia City at the foot of the Sierras and see in one direction nothing but the sagebrush that clawed at his legs when he tried to walk through it. It was rooted lightly in sucking sand that blew in his eyes, and its shiftiness symbolized the transitory nature of the life artificially planted in it. But he could see the great mountains, wreathed in snow, glittering on bright days against blue skies like something extra-terrestrial. What food for memories it all was, and how it would come back cloaked in nostalgic magic in after years![13]

When he tired of the town or the cares of mining, he escaped to Lake Tahoe's sylvan wilderness, whose very taste and tang were freedom. There "the pipe-smoking, song-singing, and yarn-spinning around the evening camp-fire in the still solitudes of the desert was a happy care-free sort of recreation that seemed the very summit and culmination of earthly luxury." [14]

The life he confronted matched the scenery, for both came from heroic molds. Loneliness was endemic, but friendships were quick and strong. The amenities taken for granted in the East were at a premium here, and though men could be grasping and hard, they could also be gentle and sentimental. Over all of life lay the lure of mining, and the desire to get rich quick filled almost every man in the Territory as the steady stream of precious metal poured from the earth. The mining frenzy captured Mark Twain, for he had few duties with his brother. His lust for riches flared out, and he dug with the rest. But he discovered that his hands did not easily fit a shovel; he was quickly discouraged. For a few days he thought himself a millionaire, but failure to file his claim put him back in poverty. He abandoned one shaft just when gold came to light and risked his life chasing the elusive metals that made other men millionaires. In desperation, he worked for a quartz-milling company but found the laborer's lot too hard; he could never learn how to shovel sand correctly with a long-handled spade. He made no money and, as he put it, the company could hardly pay him to shovel dirt down his shirt. He quit. It was the end of his mining career.

He was depressed; he seemed to fail at everything he touched. Always given to fits of melancholy and acute depression, he knew his own faults. On leaving home, his mother's emotional legacy was all too apparent in her forcing him to promise not to drink or gamble,[15] an injunction to which he was more faithful than might be expected. His letters from Nevada revealed a split personality, a man given to external cheer and internal doubt. "Don't you know that it's all talk and no cider so far?" he wrote his sister, who was unduly impressed by his reports.[16] Guilt often gnawed at his conscience. He was naturally lazy, but obsessed by the necessity to work. He thought he was worthless, but loved fame and frankly gloried in the respect of his fellows. He considered his talents limited, but "I am proud to say I am the most conceited ass in the Territory." [17] He recognized the dark strain beneath his cheerfulness, casting gloomy doubts over worldly success and the meanings of life. As his literary fame burgeoned in the Sierras, he wrote his mother honestly: "You observe that under a cheerful exterior I have got a spirit that is angry with me and gives me freely its contempt." [18]

His real riches lay elsewhere, and he mined them with a pen rather than a pick and shovel. Disgusted with mining and its false lures, he took a job in 1862 with the rather bohemian group that published the Virginia City *Territorial Enterprise*. Given to truth, its publisher said, the *Enterprise* was a remarkable paper for such a wilderness. It dealt in the sordid facts of frontier life, had strong interests in politics, and attempted to bring outside news to its readers. It also provided an outlet for Twain's sense of humor. He covered shootings, hangings, strikes, and politics; and he became a potent journalist. For a time he was "governor" of the Territorial legislature's mock "Third House," and gained some political influence.

He met traveling entertainers and humorists who passed through Virginia City, and the amusements of San Francisco were not far away. Above all he developed a fine literary style savoring of frontier candor and rustic wit, coupled with an innate common sense and an occasional outburst at injustice that set him above ordinary journalists. Here he first used the pen name that become immortal: Mark Twain. Here he first mined the veins of memory and perception that made him more than a mere humorist.

In 1864 he left for San Francisco and another reportorial job. He met Bret Harte and other local colorists whose wares and styles were in vogue. Though he afterward pilloried Harte's effete style, Mark Twain always acknowledged the debt he owed the Bay City editor and writer, who taught him how to use the language in truly finished writing. Twain was an eager student, but was restless and tired quickly of the city. Poverty dogged his footsteps, and at last he secured a job from the Sacramento *Union* reporting a tour of the Sandwich Islands, as Hawaii was then called. His recollections of that trip later filled out *Roughing It,* and while they were unequal to the prose and humor of the book's first part, the letters revealed a keen eye for detail, a fascination with topography and humanity, and social consciousness.

He attained sudden national fame in 1865 through the publication of his short story "The Celebrated Jumping Frog of Calaveras County." His friend, the widely known humorist Artemus Ward, whom he had met in Nevada, wanted the article for a book, but it arrived too late and was published in the last issue of a dying

Eastern magazine. Its piquant frontier quality of language and fine humor caught readers' fancies, and in a matter of weeks it was pirated and reprinted in dozens of newspapers. The story was insignificant in itself, a secondhand telling of how a man won a frog race by loading the opponent's entry with buckshot. But Twain's style was captivating, and the narrator he created to repeat the tale was as funny as the story itself. Readers sensed that the story came from a first-rate eye.

He was now a celebrity and departed for home and the East in triumph. He found to his amazement that people would pay to hear him lecture, an experiment he first hesitatingly tried in San Francisco, where he was a sensation. His appearance, his slow, carefully cultivated drawl, his dead-pan humor that innocently cut the ground from hypocrisy, pomposity, and self-importance, captured audiences. Though he later hated the thought of lecturing, he enjoyed the public recognition as well as the money it produced.

How to fulfill his developing career? In 1867 he accepted an assignment for the *Alta California* to report on a world trip and embarked on the *Quaker City*, a new excursion boat, for a grand tour that became famous as reported in his first widely read book, *The Innocents Abroad* (1869). Equipped with the narrow prejudices of tourists in all ages, fortified in this instance by the rawness of their American background, the latter-day pilgrims in Twain's company swept across Europe. They ransacked museums and churches, and penetrated into Egypt and the Holy Land, chipping pieces from famous statuary, scribbling their names on ancient ruins, and leaving in their wake hilarious accounts of the conflict of old and new.

As a travel book, *The Innocents* was a masterpiece. It was both a perceptive and amusing account of the journey and its pilgrims, and a parody of the awful travel literature that blossomed during the Gilded Age. Twain's own inexperience and questionable taste flowed through the book to bolster his criticisms of Europe's dirt, the Holy Land's absurd religious fakery, and the questionable nature of mankind in general.

Written in a forthright style, spiced with anecdotes, and fortified by shrewd insight, *The Innocents* was bound to capture a large audience; for it reflected the smug prejudices in which that day's provincial America gloried. Highly critical of "old masters," Mark Twain saw value in other things that appealed more to his compatriots. The miles of stilted saints, faded landscapes, crooked madonnas, and dull tapestries did not impress him so much as the fast and efficient railways in France and Italy, the orderly government in Germany, and the backwardness he saw in the poverty-stricken and ignorant peoples who crowded around him. The old masters left him cold; he preferred prints to the originals because they were brighter. To him, medieval art only reflected religious bigotry, and he deplored painters who glorified base subjects like Catherine de' Medici. His American moralism showed through all his judgments on the arts.

He did not dislike art, but he hated the posing that went with the standard appreciation of the masters. "It vexes me to hear people talk so glibly of 'feeling,' 'expression,' 'tone,' and those other easily acquired and inexpensive technicalities of art that make such a fine show in conversations concerning pictures." [19] Though he was neither critic nor connoisseur, he did like art. His tastes were what a later era called bourgeois; but he was not dead to painting, statuary, and music. He loved singing, but hated opera. The stiff absurdity of the average operatic production bored him, but he liked the "airs" from *Il Trovatore* or other works once they passed through the hurdy-gurdy or melodeon. [20]

The Holy Land's religious quackery enraged him. The Biblical sites—Adam's tomb, the grave of Lazarus, the manger of Christ's birth—left him cold, for it was patently absurd to his rational eyes that such things existed. This fraud, coupled with the squalor and misery of the Holy Land's peoples, proved to him that the iron hand of superstition and priestcraft was still too strong in the Old World.

Beneath his criticism and reports flowed more substantial impressions. He saw everywhere the temporal quality of fame and the pettiness of man's achievements, the beginnings of the personal perspective that expanded and darkened with age. He was not insensible to the past's grandeur, either in human or artistic terms. The deeper lesson of *The Innocents* lay, however, in Mark Twain's measurement of progress in material terms. That country was progressive which gave its people the best material standard of living, and not all the cathedrals and masters could compensate this lack. Filled on his tour with an honest disgust at the misery and poverty he saw, Twain found no value in galleries, villas, and churches if the nation that produced and treasured them wore rags. In these attitudes he spoke for his country as well as himself, a culture that savored facts over theories; that liked tangible things of life rather than dead traditions; that looked forward rather than backward.

Though Twain referred to *The Innocents Abroad* as apprentice labor, the book was important in his career. It brought him fame and money and saw the first development of the pessimism and detached world view that dominated the end of his career. *The Innocents* was at least an early germ of the international novel, depicting the clash of old and new cultures, that developed in the abler hands of Henry James and Edith Wharton. The book ·was and still is funny; but an honest indignation spiced its humor, a deeply felt anger at misery, poverty, and superstition that kept millions in mental chains.

What he saw frankly shocked him, and his undeveloped perspective and youthful hardness bred a distaste for people that later became contempt. With customary Yankee bluntness, he argued in effect that the rabble who confronted him in the streets of Rome or Jerusalem, displaying their sores and misery for his pity and money, could blame themselves as well as their masters for their plight.

His immediate personal legacy from *The Innocents* was not fame and riches, or even the broadened view it gave his writing and personality, but the wife who became the center of his life. As in a fairy tale, he fell in love with her picture in the locket her brother Charles Langdon carried on the *Quaker City*. He wangled an introduction into her sedate Victorian home in Hartford upon his return and contrived through a false illness to have her nurse him. They married in 1870 after a long courtship. The match was curious. The Langdons were rich and middle class in their tastes and standards; and not all the family approved of this wild man from the West, whose only asset was his dubious pen, and whose tastes seemed not merely uncommon but often outlandish.

In many ways, Olivia Langdon Clemens was an ideal mate for Mark Twain. Gentle, patient, kindly, she counterbalanced many of his faults. Her smoothness offset his roughness. Her patience complemented his quick temper. Her refinement was a welcome antidote to his boisterous nature; and she understood many of his needs. She could be outgoing and deeply affectionate, which surprised Twain, who had never seen his parents embrace, and whose stern father had kissed his daughter only on his deathbed.

She was his constant critic, but she was not an especially sensitive or astute person. Her chief concern was his profane lapses, and to eliminate whatever evidence of barbarism remained in his writing. He published nothing in her lifetime that she did not read and approve. She was not the prudish tyrant some critics thought, but she was determined that her husband should not offend the standards of his age. And there was nothing he would not do for her. Of church, which he hated, he once said: "Oh yes, I go. It 'most kills me,' but I go," obviously to please Livy, until she too lapsed into the freedom of thought that eliminated church.[21]

But Mark Twain needed no censor. His own squeamishness assured his work's moral probity, and neither Howells nor Livy emasculated his writing or stunted his growth as an artist. If Realism meant presenting every particle of life, the sordid as well as the happy, then he was never a realist. If it was an honest presentation of the materials of life in the context of a larger world view, then he was a realist. Howells or Livy might have objected to an occasional "hell" or "damn," or veiled reference to sex in *Tom Sawyer* or *Huck Finn,* but Twain would have excised them without urging. He often left them in merely to gauge Livy's reaction.

An age now accustomed to the candid clinical treatment of sex in both the best and worst of its reading matter finds this difficult to understand. Twain's puritan heritage, which superimposed rigid personal control over his naturally ebullient and outgoing nature, accounted for much of his distaste for sexual realism. He matured on frontiers and in situations that held women in special awe, and would have been the last to besmirch that standard. He knew that young people read his books, and he knew also that in America women controlled public morality. He was acutely conscious of his public role and would not risk it by such offense. But this lack of candor merely reflected the fact that such matters were not central to his life or his work. He might compose an occasional bawdy story like "1601," and few enjoyed or told a better story, off-color or otherwise; but such topics were not his special interest.

Still, the omission was striking in a man who never hesitated to assault moral standards or public opinions in other spheres. He reported with innocent candor how he covered his face for shame during a cancan dance in Paris, and he disliked the French and other continental peoples for their supposedly loose sexual conduct. This from a man who grew up on the Mississippi and lived on the rough and ready Nevada mining frontier! In none of his books did he develop a female character beyond a one-dimensional frame. He was the child and the reflection of his age where the sacred cows of middle-class morality were touched. Like Howells, perhaps he wished basically to write books and present a life that young people in particular might read with a sense of identification and understanding.

Aside from his wife, Twain found his greatest comfort in Howells' friendship. He was an excellent editor and advisor for a man of Twain's mercurial temper and haphazard methods. He was calm but not stuffy, authoritative but not pompous, a writer himself familiar with the craft's problems. He flavored his talk and his friendship with the saving grace of humor. His almost feminine understanding of how to manage men would have made him a great politician, and Twain recognized his debt. ". . . I owe as much to your training as the rude country job printer owes to the city boss who takes him in hand and teaches him the right way to handle his art," he wrote in 1878.[22]

In middle life, Mark Twain was famous, wealthy, happy in his personal life, already an American institution. The Western writer now became the settled figure of Eastern society and probity. And what a figure he was! Prosperity and fame did not until old age change his youthful form, nor did acceptance into staid Eastern circles ever banish the edge of Western roughness. He was a magnetic speaker and compelling figure. Howells caught him in a fine snapshot:

He glimmered at you from the narrow slits of fine blue-greenish eyes, under branching eyebrows, which with age grew more and more like a sort of plumage, and he was apt to smile into your face with a subtle but amiable perception, and yet with a sort of remote absence; you were all there for him, but he was not all there for you.[23]

He loved socializing and smiled when his friends dubbed him "the Belle of New York." Where he sat was the table's head, and the sharp edge of truth lay just beneath his banter. His closest friends suffered most from his gregariousness; for he impulsively wrote them endless letters and descended on them for long visits without warning, clad perhaps in an outrageous costume, filled with plans and fulminations. "Your visit was a perfect ovation for us," Howells once wrote; "we never enjoy anything so much as those visits of yours. The smoke and the Scotch and the late hours almost kill us; but we look each other in the eyes when [you] are gone, and say what a glorious time it was, and air the library, and begin sleeping and dieting, and longing to have you back again." [24]

His habits were irregular and he was given to nostrums, inherited from a mother who had practiced the water cure, diet fads, and electromagnetism on him. For years he slept poorly, hence his love of lying abed till noon, and he tried various soporifics to cure the malady. Now it was champagne drunk at bedtime; this gave way to heated Scotch, which in turn surrendered to an evening glass of lager beer as insomnia's cure. These finally availing little, he lay on the bathroom floor, which he pronounced ideal for inducing sleep. And then to his surprise, he discovered that simply by retiring early to his own bed he could fall fast asleep.

His prodigious energy was a natural phenomenon, like a great waterfall, but it was the vitality of nervousness rather than disciplined purpose. His variety of interests and gusto of attack explain much of the apparent inconsistency of his thought and work. He might lay aside a project and return to it for the same purpose but from a different angle, giving a false notion of where he had been or what he intended to do. His work like his life was a series of brilliant fragments—some flawed, some crystal clear, most disordered—with light falling on them in bright flashes rather than in steady streams.

His worst habits, smoking and swearing, sorely tried those around him, but were a release for his volcanic energy, and became part of the legend around him. He loved a bad cigar and could smoke dozens a day. Whatever he touched was grimed with ashes; wherever he went a trail of smoke followed. "Children of twenty-five, who have seven years of experience, try to tell me what is a good cigar and what isn't," he said. "Me, who never learned to smoke, but always smoked; me, who came into the world asking for a light." [25]

His swearing reflected the rich vocabulary of the river and the mining frontier, and was as harmless to those around him as it was colorful. Though he tried not to offend Livy, "the soothing consolation of swearing" was his chief safety valve.[26] It seemed so natural in him that his daughter, shocked at hearing another man swear and being told that her father did it all the time, innocently excused the habit as part of his joking.

The child in him loved display and show. "He had always a relish for personal effect, . . ." Howells remembered. He ended his days clad all in white, a stunning effect, and never missed the slightest occasion to don his scarlet Oxford degree, "which he said he would like to wear all the time." [27] He avoided no crowd that might admire him, nor would he take an unfrequented route, whether to a hotel dining room or across an international border. He was acutely conscious of his status, and loved plaudits; and yet he covered all his vanity with a simple charm, until it seemed only his due and not vanity at all.

Whether in his country home near Hartford, his villa in Florence, his New York apartment, or the last great house, "Stormfield," he lived lavishly. He enjoyed the finest foods and wines, the best furnishings, and an expensive level of hospitality. In his last years, in retirement, his household cost fifty dollars a day. Like his own Connecticut Yankee, he might have said: "For I never care to do a thing in a quiet way; it's got to be theatrical or I don't take any interest in it." [28]

Over all this lay the comforting web of family love. No father was more thoughtful or patient in playing charades, reading aloud before the fireplace, or tramping over the countryside. He was attentive and faithful to his wife's smallest wants. To a world accustomed to mad geniuses and deranged artists, this love of domesticity is striking. But the darker side of his moon was always there, and in a moment he might turn from happy reading to morose speculations or silence. The genius in him may not have warred with the world in open and defiant rebellion, but it struggled with itself.

This establishment, and the whole role of public figure, cost a great deal of money, and Twain rapidly became a businessman-author. He was an owner in, as well as an author for, the Charles L. Webster Company, which specialized in the subscription books the Gilded Age loved. The pressures of business and writing hounded him and ended in a great crash in his later years that nearly killed him. To feed his presses and maintain his reputation, and on a dare from their wives, he and Charles Dudley Warner wrote *The Gilded Age* (1873), whose title came to designate that era.

This was in effect Mark Twain's only extended piece of fiction. His other novels were escapes into the past of *Tom Sawyer* or into the mordant speculation of *The Mysterious Stranger*. As a novel, *The Gilded Age* had little to recommend it. Its contrived plot dealt with political corruption based on an actual episode in the era's politics, and a pasteboard love affair. But it produced a great character, Colonel Beriah Sellers, modeled on a distant cousin of Twain's, whose gift for words and unabashed but unfulfilled frontier optimism kept his family poor all his life. No project was too large or too small for the Colonel's attention, and he could persuade wooden Indians to do his bidding. "The Colonel's tongue was a magician's wand that turned dried apples into figs and water into wine as easily as it could change a hovel into a palace and present poverty into future riches." [29]

Though a failure as a whole, the book abounded in sharp vignettes and moving scenes, for pity was the underside of Sellers' unconscious humor and verbal flatulence. Few readers could forget the opening scenes of rural idleness and intellectual starvation. Or the fine scene in which the Colonel built his air castles of riches and fame while his family froze in the pitiful warmth of a candle in the parlor stove. Who could deny both the pathos and the humor of the scene where the bankrupt aristocrat grandly prescribed his only food, turnips and water, as a cure for the cholera then supposedly raging in the countryside?

If the novel failed structurally, it had an important place in

Twain's work. He showed the poverty of country life and the intellectual starvation that went with the false optimism of the frontier. Men often did not work because they counted on the future and automatic progress. Neither ever came due, but the human animal loved false optimism.[30] His sharp comments on public morality and politics revealed that the moralist in him was not dead. In this book as in all his early work he belied the facile theory that the tragedies of his old age made him a pessimist. In *The Gilded Age,* men were vacuous and depraved, and their society was absurd and often evil. Death was a welcome release from life for the tarnished heroine, and the work savored everywhere of a sharp bitterness and determinism.

Mark Twain was far more interested in contemporary politics than he seemed. Though he was never an avid reformer, preferring to feel that little could be done against man's folly, injustice rankled him. In *The Gilded Age* and *A Connecticut Yankee* he showed basic reservations about democracy and the American political system. He attacked corruption and bossism in *The Gilded Age,* but he also held no brief for the mass indifference and ignorance that let them flourish. He was a staunch Republican, reflecting a family political bent that stemmed from a Whiggish concern for property protection and social conservatism evidenced in his father's name, John Marshall Clemens. But he left the party to vote for Grover Cleveland in 1884 because he disliked James G. Blaine's questionable public record. He displayed a growing suspicion of universal suffrage, the foreign born, the easily tainted ballot of representative democracy, and a basic feeling that perhaps the propertied ought to run the country they caused to prosper. He was often caught in the snares of antiforeignism that complemented a consistent anti-Catholicism whose literary tools were his hatred of monarchy and an established church, depicted so savagely in *A Connecticut Yankee.* He mixed widely and easily with the economic and social elite. He counted the Standard Oil tycoon Henry Rogers not merely his personal financial savior, but a trusted and honored friend. He never quite lost a lingering notion that a man prospered because he revealed the talent for success and that the poor often deserved poverty.

Yet he was no more consistent in this than in other things, for social snobbery and injustice angered him. He may perhaps be forgiven for much of this when one remembers that he confronted first-generation immigrants too often manipulated by political bosses. He shared his fear of a revived Romanism with a whole generation. And in view of his own personality, origins, and success he was bound to echo much of the rhetoric of self-help and rugged individualism.

The public did not love him for these themes, even if it detected them, but for his humor. His readers reveled in *The Innocents* and *Roughing It* because though they laughed at the narrator's experience, he laughed with them. Twain's humor had little in common with the absurd spelling, puns on large words, or the tall tale. Though he knew Artemus Ward, Orpheus Kerr, and Josh Billings —the rustic frontier humorists—he did not follow their pattern. His humor had a two-dimensional quality. It did not merely repeat funny stories, but took the reader into its confidence as both observer and participant. In his best pages Twain's humor was spontaneous, hilarious, often filled with pathos, and just real enough to seem logical. In the mind's eye of most readers the pictures he painted might have happened to them.

In his comedy's shadow, whether in his descriptions of tourists defacing art works, or of Tom Sawyer in Sunday school, or of himself in his mining days, lay an understanding that humor should enlighten general principles. "The grotesque exaggeration and broad irony with which the life is described are conjecturably the truest colors that could have been used," Howells remarked of *Roughing It,* "for all existence there [in Nevada] must have looked like an extravagant joke, the humor of which was only deepened by its netherside of tragedy." [31]

Lightened by an honest anger at injustice that revealed his moralistic view, flashing with a wit that delved into men's motives, his fun was seldom cruel. Though many of his comments were acid, Twain never used men as pawns in his humor. He had an eye for men at work, whether glorious or absurd. As Howells said in reviewing *The Innocents*: ". . . we do not remember where it [humor] is indulged in at the cost of the weak or the helpless side, or where it is insolent, with all its sauciness and irreverence." [32]

Behind his bright front of pleasure in success lay the haunting suspicion that wit had cost him the creative genius that would have flowered under adversity or for different audiences. In after years, when all seemed dark, he said to Helen Keller: "I have only amused people. Their laughter has submerged me." [33]

He used his humor as an honest blade to cut the supports from intolerance and sham. His perception of the gulf between what men preached and what they did was the center of his work. His Western gusto and the demands of his own personality required an independence from control that made him attack the false values and ideals his era cherished, simply because they threatened individuality. He was always a moralist, if not a reformer, using his talent to show man's condition by pointing out flaws. As a young reporter, he raged at mistreatment of the Chinese and left San Francisco because of police brutality. This despite his lack of deep respect for "coolies" or the "natives" he saw as decadent peoples in Hawaii. *It was the principle, not necessarily its application, that mattered.* He combined this sense of injustice with a sympathy that made him secure the dismissal of a cab driver for rudeness to his housekeeper and then urge his re-employment lest his family starve.

As a young man, Mark Twain was often a snob, condescending to the foreign born, doubtful of the virtue of mass participation in government, castigating frontier juries composed of rubes, jibing at legislatures elected by morons, a trifle cold in the face of want. He betrayed his own Whiggish origins in a desire for money, a drive for prestige, a deferential respect for propertied men. In his prosperous middle years he mixed with an easy awe among Hartford's and New York's business elite. He had an eye for the main chance, seizing easily on the glittering catch phrases of material well-being that justified his own rise as a literary tycoon. He sometimes subordinated art and his beliefs to business, suppressing many things that would have hurt his sales.

But he lived too long and saw too much ever to abandon his belief in the goodness and worth of some individual men, if not of the species as a whole. He had the capacity to grow that marked not merely the attractive personality but the artist's mind. He lived to repudiate the errors of his early snobbery and narrow view. The better master of his final years, tempered in sadness and sober observation, found room in Captain Stormfield's heaven for men of all colors and stations. He came to see that a view which excludes or patronizes a man for the accidents of his birth or upbringing is not wide enough for personal growth.

If he was not a temporal crusader, he used his work for frankly moral purposes. "There are those who say a novel should be a work of art solely, and you must not preach in it, you must not teach in it," he said in his memoirs. "That may be true as regards novels but it is not true as regards humor. Humor must not professedly teach, and it must not professedly preach, but it must do both if it would live forever." And he shrewdly added: "By forever, I mean thirty years." [34]

Satire demands detachment from the subjects it criticizes and seeks to change, and Mark Twain lacked that all-important quality. He was never aloof. He was always a part of the things he criticized, and this limitation kept his best humor from rising to true satire. He was familiar with the weakness: "I wish I *could* give those sharp satires on European life which you mention," he wrote Howells in 1879, "but of course a man can't write successful satire except he be in a calm judicial good-humor—whereas . . . in truth I don't ever seem to be in good enough humor with ANYTHING to satirize it; no, I want to stand up before it & *curse* it, & foam at the mouth,—or take a club and pound it to rags and pulp." [35] Despite this, his best pages remain vital and alive precisely because they seem real to any reader, and because they illuminate, for better or worse, some aspect of universal life.

These were the "flush times" of Mark Twain's life, the rich middle span when he turned from travel books and humorous memoirs to deeper soundings in a memory that turned the water of facts into the wine of nostalgic fiction. Two books from these years marked not only the best of his own work but remained landmarks in American literature. They were *Tom Sawyer* (1876) and *Huckleberry Finn* (1884).

Howells, who read the manuscript of *Tom Sawyer,* was enchanted, and the book's popular success was predictable and quickly fulfilled. Who was not stirred by this boy's tale for adults, filled with humor and pathos, success and failure, triumph and tragedy, and savoring everywhere of a knowing innocence and a childish wisdom that appealed to an American sentiment that mixed practicality and idealism in life? Its philosophy aside, the book was good reading. There was the tale of Injun Joe and his grisly crimes, and his equally grisly end. What of the days spent in carefree boyish indolence on the river bank or in the swimming hole? Who has forgotten the horrors of school, the pangs of first love, the cunning tricks of childhood, depicted in these pages? And what sharp vignettes rise from it: the whitewashed fence, the Sunday school scholar and his false disciples David and Goliath, Becky and the terror of the cave. Written with charm, grace, and simplicity, the book was an instant success and remains an American classic.

Tom Sawyer brought to the generation that first read it a compelling charm, for in many instances the readers of Twain's middle years had spent their childhoods in similar circumstances. He voiced their mute feelings. America was still rural, oriented toward small-town life, and Tom Sawyer seemed both realistic and fictional. The book's beauty for a later generation which has left the farm for the city lies elsewhere. It is covered with nostalgia. It presented a vanished America, but it also offered a boyhood that most men like even if they did not have it. Speaking from a child's viewpoint in an adult's world, Tom Sawyer voiced every man's complaints against authority, the outmoded and absurd, the insignificant and useless. He offered in their place, with the wisdom of the child-man, those things in life that seem both happy and important—freedom, irresponsibility, ease. *Tom Sawyer* was a paean of escape, not merely from an ordered world with rules and responsibilities, but from adulthood and its cares and fears to the innocence of childhood. It was a book and a viewpoint seeking a lost Eden.

It was an Eden ringed with darkness, for violence abounded in the story—murder, grave-robbing, starvation in an empty cave, fights, and the raw forces of nature. But the book's violence was not very real because it added no dimension to the boys' consciousness. It was seen with a child's perspective that gauged such events only in the form of transitory fear rather than in added perception.

Though it continued the theme, setting, and characters of *Tom Sawyer, Huckleberry Finn* was a more profound work. Breaking in two at the end and overly long, it still offered two great heroes, Nigger Jim and Huck Finn. The saga of their escape from violence and convention was finely wrought. For Twain, these two books were miracles of clarity and construction, despite the difficulties of composition that placed a gap of seven years between finishing the two halves of *Huckleberry Finn*.

In *Huck Finn,* Twain began to focus many of the ideas that ran through his earlier work. His search for escape, his sadness at innocence lost to reality, formed the book's core. But he was also deeply concerned with violence, and the story abounded with cruelties and jolting experiences which, unlike *Tom Sawyer,* added to the depth of Huck's already old consciousness. Huck was not a child at the book's end. He matured through living; and he knew that men were often weak, evil, foolish, and stupid. He saw the folly of the Shepherdson-Granger feud. He saw the beast rise in the mob that Colonel Shelburn turned from his door with contempt. He saw the awful inhumanity of slavery in the form of unconscious acceptance. Men preyed upon each other, as his charlatan companions, the Duke and King, proved all too clearly. There were good men with good motives, but in a world of hard knocks it paid to be ready to run.

The book was a burning indictment of slavery, as if Twain wished to erase his earlier halting judgments of the Negro. *Huck Finn* preached that until they learned sympathy and respect for each other, all men were slaves. Huck's emergence to life lay in such simple revolutions as his understanding that Jim was a person; in apologizing to the former slave without remorse; even in his sorrow for the well-merited punishment of the Duke and King.

The label "children's books" on these works irritated Twain. "It is *not* a boy's book, at all," he wrote Howells about *Tom Sawyer*. "It will only be read by adults. It is only written for adults." [36] These books were the finest of Mark Twain's creative talent. Nothing he did afterward matched either their tone or content, and all he did prior to them pointed toward their fruition. They were his best works because in their pages he momentarily solved his bifurcated vision. In them he saw life as a whole, through the boy's nature with the man's perception.

In the mid-1880s he was at the height of recognition and ability. The public knew him as a writer, and he saw himself as an author. He might complain about imagined and real fetters, threatening to go back to the river as a pilot, and actually taking a nostalgic river journey to complete *Life on the Mississippi;* but his lot was cast with pen and ink. "To me, the most important feature of my life is its literary feature," he would say in old age, and even in his last years he wrote for his own amusement if not for publication.[37]

His method of writing, like his method of sleeping, was erratic. He maintained no fixed routine and wrote upon whatever entered his mind. He might fall in a given day upon a dozen projects, few of which mercifully ever bore fruit. He passed whole days and nights at his desk without rest, conversation, or food once the demon rose within him. He believed that he was merely an amanuensis, transcribing a kind of spirit writing pouring from a hidden "tank" of memory that filled up from time to time. What a mystery it all was to him! "Indeed I am a mud image, & it puzzles me to know what it is in me that writes, & that has comedy-fancies & finds pleasure in phrasing them," he wrote Howells in 1897. "It is a law of our nature, of course, or it wouldn't happen; the thing in me forgets the presence of the mud image & goes its own way wholly unconscious of it & apparently of no kinship with it." [38]

He believed that no man created anything new. No one ever had an original thought, merely the disposition and facility to set down ideas engendered from outside him. All men were merely the sum of all their ancestors and the past. An author could therefore write only of what he knew first hand. "I confine myself to life with which I am familiar when pretending to portray life." [39]

All the logic of his own career sustained this view of automatic composition. His own work for the most part flowed from him automatically, like water from a rock stricken by some magic staff. His poorest work—*Tom Sawyer Abroad,* "Those Extraordinary Twins," *Following the Equator,* the last half of *Life on the Mississippi*—was the product of duty rather than desire.

Memory was the ore-bearing precious metal, and its refining baffled him. But he was not blind to the tricks of nostalgia. "Schoolboy days are no happier than the days of after life, but we look back upon them regretfully because we have forgotten our punishments at school, and how we grieved when our marbles were lost and our kites destroyed," he wrote in *The Innocents Abroad,* "because we have forgotten all the sorrows and privations of that canonized epoch and remember only its orchard robberies, its wooden sword pageants and its fishing holidays." [40]

He longed to recover not the facts of yesteryears, but the impressions, and their meanings. As time went on, he believed that life was mental for every man, "and his *thoughts,* not those other things [events], are his history." [41] But he knew how tricky it all was: "It isn't so astonishing the things that I can remember as the number of things I can remember that aren't so." [42]

Though aware of the faultiness of recollection, he strove for truthfulness in his own work, adding to the past's facts the dimensions of perception that came with time's perspectives. He hated sham and the sugary fiction of his own day. Though he was never an avowed "Realist" of any formal school, he was a realist in his views. "Homely truth is unpalatable," Tom Sawyer said, and Twain spoke out regularly against fictional romancers and sentimentalists.[43] He always deplored the "sham sentimentality" of what he called schoolgirl compositions.[44] His whole literary development, whatever its inconsistencies, was a plea for honesty and realism.

Twain combined his hatred for sham and his knowledge of frontier life in a famous assault on James Fenimore Cooper's "literary offences." Cooper's bloated prose, absurd plots, stilted characters, fatuous dialogue, and general incredibility were almost too easy a mark. It was child's work to condemn bullets that followed each other through the same hole without leaving marks, Indians who talked at a paragraph's beginning like Harvard men and like hillbillies at its end, frontiersmen who started one page with disquisitions on Life and Love and ended sounding like riverboat pilots, absurd coincidences, divine interventions, and superhuman powers that contrived to help an already overworked plot. All that Twain hated in bad prose and unreal literature focused in Cooper's spurious frontier years, and provoked his famous dictum that the author of *Leatherstocking* "saw nearly all things as through a glass eye, darkly." [45]

When he tired of beating the straw man of Cooper's faults, Twain leveled his critical sights at Sir Walter Scott. "Lord, it's all so juvenile!" he exclaimed to Brander Matthews while reading a Scott novel, "so artificial, so shoddy; and such wax figures and skeletons and spectres." [46] Hating the Middle Ages, he easily blasted Scott's mannered romanticisms, even blaming him for the American Civil War. Had Scott's novels not buttressed dead Southern institutions and given the South a false notion of chivalry, the war would never have come.[47]

In cataloguing these literary sins, Twain revealed more of himself than of the things he attacked, for he showed quite clearly that he followed a logical creative standard. He was not the occasional or accidental talent that many people thought they saw, or that later critics explained away. He wrote easily and hurriedly, and hated revision, but he had a keen sense of the good and bad in his own work. His desk and library shelves were packed with manuscripts he never finished, and he carefully revised his best work.

He assaulted the "romancers," but he himself was a natural romantic with an important difference: his nostalgic tales dealt with facts and added a vital dimension to experience in the telling. As usual, Howells was shrewd: "At heart Clemens was romantic, and he would have had the world of fiction stately and handsome and whatever the real world was not; but he was not romanticistic, and he was too helplessly an artist not to wish his own work to show life as he had seen it." [48]

Not even trips abroad, excited conversation, or sustained writing dampened Twain's nervousness and energy. He was always alive to new ideas and was fascinated by machinery; and though he knew nothing about it, his willingness to invest in it cost him dearly. It figured prominently in his books and conversation. *The Innocents Abroad* teemed with allusions to the beneficent effects of machinery, technology, and new ideas. Though this view of technical progress was more apparent than real in Twain's beliefs and writings, it was nonetheless there. By mid-life, he began to turn from it in *A Connecticut Yankee at King Arthur's Court* (1889). That book's chief moral, as the well-meaning Yankee discovered to his chagrin, was that the apparatus of material well-being did not insure human progress. It was a major step away from Twain's easier view about society in his early works and travel books. He spent his remaining years plumbing the deeper subject of moral progress.

Like his own Colonel Sellers, or his brother Orion, he had great visions of the wealth to come from inventions. Try as he might he could not suppress the frontier optimism and castle-building that devoured the good Colonel, leaving him poorer but none the wiser. Twain was the first person to have a private telephone in his home. He was among the first authors to write on the typewriter, among the first to use a dictaphone, which he loved because it allowed him to ramble endlessly. He was an early user of the fountain pen and was so fond of such musical gadgets as the melodeon and teleharmonium that he had them moved from house to house with him. He early mastered, if only temporarily, the high-wheeled bicycle, producing along the way that comic masterpiece, "Taming the Bicycle."

A machine finally ruined his bright worldly prospect and cast shadows on his whole philosophy of life: the infamous Paige Typesetter. The invention easily ensnared Twain, for he saw greater book production and millions of dollars in an instrument that set more type in a day than a dozen men. He purchased shares of the company, subsidized the inventor, James Paige, and finally underwrote the project that absorbed money like desert sands drinking water. As he fell into the technical details of manufacturing, perfecting, and selling the machine in the mid-1890s, the old Sellers complex rose from its natural resting place and painted a lurid picture of the millions to be made. Vistas of nervous idleness, freedom from publishers' schedules, and the slave labor of copy reading rose before him, with his own name forever secure in the annals of both literature and industry. Then the bubble burst, and life turned upon its darling. He who had known little but success saw before him nothing but failure, financial insecurity, and personal tragedy that helped turn him from the jaunty pioneer of *Roughing It* into the bitter cynic of *The Mysterious Stranger*.

The Panic of 1893, whose tremors reached into nearly every business establishment, spelled his ruin. The typesetter failed, and the firm of Charles Webster, in which Twain was a major partner, collapsed disastrously. Webster had published Twain's own works and the fantastically successful memoirs of General U. S. Grant. But high overhead, the dying subscription book industry the firm fed, and the Panic spelled doom. In 1894 Twain was insolvent and embittered, with his whole reputation at stake. "All through my life I have been the easy prey of the cheap adventurer," he remembered. "He came, he lied, he robbed, and went his way, and the next one arrived by the next train and began to scrape up what was left." [49] But Twain and his haphazard methods invited confusion. He was only too eager to risk his funds for a quick killing, and it was not always the inventor's fault that the invention failed. Nor was Twain cheated by his publishers and partners. His own private desire, lusting after wealth and power, ending in disastrous "Sellersism," was at fault.

The fact remained that verging on old age he was captured in a world-wide depression and saddled with huge debts. His creditors would have taken partial payment, but an innate honesty, and a refusal to hazard the integrity of his name, made him pay his debts in full. But how? He returned to the lecture circuit which he had once loved and then loathed. The choice was made harder by his age and family obligations, but he embarked on a world tour that solidified his fame to the masses of America and the world. Across the United States, to Hawaii, Australia, India, the Near East, and Europe his trail unwound. He repeated the same ideas, the same style, and same lectures until at last he sickened and went no farther. For four years he slaved to pay his debts, his personal view of life darkening, his energy failing, only grim persistence sustaining him. In 1898 he paid the last bill and was free.

As if to emphasize a mysterious punishment, life dealt him its hardest blow in the death of his beloved daughter Susy in 1896 while he was abroad. The thought of her dying alone, of the loss of her splendid talents and beautiful youth, turned Twain inward in a search from which he never emerged. The events yet to come only made that inner quest more bitter. No wonder he wrote his closest friend in 1897:

You have seen our whole voyage. You have seen us go to sea, a cloud of sail, and the flag at peak; and you see us now, chartless, adrift— derelicts; battered, water-logged, our sails a ruck of rags, our pride gone. The vanity of life was all we had, and there is no more vanity left in us. We are even ashamed of that we had; ashamed that we trusted the promises of life and builded high—to come to this! [50]

The brooding master returned to America and lived for a time with his wife and remaining daughters, the musically gifted Clara and the sprightly but fatally marked Jean. Nervousness and grief drove him aimlessly from house to house. He wrote acid scribbles in his notebooks for works he never finished, or diaries committed only to his memory or his safe. His only recent fiction was the favorite among his own books, *The Personal Recollections of Joan of Arc* (1896), a flat, deadly, one-dimensional escape from reality into a false purity. He finished one more book, a report of his world tour, *Following the Equator* (1897), the tired journal of a man committed to introspection. Though once more prosperous because of a better publishing arrangement, he was again beset by agony; Mrs. Clemens died of heart disease in Italy in 1904. Only a year before his own death, Jean died of heart failure, com- pounded by epilepsy. He despaired of all but death, saying in *Pudd'nhead Wilson* that it was Adam's great gift to his successors. He remarked in his journals: "The human race consists of the damned and the ought-to-be-damned." [51]

The pessimism that had always flowed through his work focused now in a bitter view of life and ended in a despairing notion of man's nature. Knowing himself, he often said, he knew that the species was depraved. Look around, he would say. Does not man prey on his fellows, doing evil instead of good, looting the globe, torturing animals, cheating, lying, swindling? And did this not prove that, all his pretentions aside, man was only an animal— worse, for he knew better. "Of the entire brood he is the only one—the solitary one—that possesses malice." [52] Man's fault was the Moral Sense that showed him right and wrong, for he easily and often chose wrong. [53] How petty it all was, life, mankind, and the world! That lovable hero, Captain Stormfield, found on his way to heaven that the earth counted for little in celestial bookkeeping. A comet that raced past him carried brimstone to Satan equal to

"Eighteen hundred thousand billion quintillions of kazarks," and a kazark equaled *"a hundred and sixty-nine worlds like ours!"* [54]

Around all this bitterness at man's smallness lay the sharp edge of selfishness. Man did nothing, Twain insisted, save for self-glorification. "The symbol of the human race ought to be an axe," he declared, "every human being has one concealed about his person." [55] The false fronts of convention, morality, culture, only partly hid the sham creature beneath it. God created mankind, he said, because the monkey's antics disappointed Him, and human history richly rewarded His efforts. [56]

It was not a new view. The misfortunes of old age, bankruptcy, overwork, and deaths in his family merely focused his final recognition of life's essential darkness. He had never really believed in progress or man's goodness. As early as 1884 he wrote Howells in a fury over a minor matter that man was not "really fit for anything but to be stood up on the street corner as a convenience for dogs." [57] In the brooding despair of old age that almost made him insane, he reinforced all these notions by turning inward. His guilt, remorse, avarice, weakness, mounted up. Was he not mankind writ small? "Every human is in his own person the whole human race, with not a single detail lacking," he told his suppressed journal. "The human race is a race of cowards and I am not only marching in that procession but carrying a banner." [58] Nothing better delimits his vision or highlights his lack of central philosophy than this homage to darkness. Nervous, excitable, disordered, he lacked the formal education that might have systematized his thought and stabilized his person. At the mercy of clichés used to explain his own and man's follies and shortcomings, caught in the complexities of a world in transition, Twain naturally fell back on the easiest and most logical explanation of his situation, the mordant determinism of *The Mysterious Stranger.*

Always restless, crossing oceans, moving in and out of villas and town houses, Twain's mind teemed with fantasies that old age and retirement turned to nightmares. For a time he fancied that the universe was God and that men were bacilli in some vast creature's blood, bearers of disease and pestilence. He proposed a history of microbes by one of their number. Two such schemes matured in the rollicking "Captain Stormfield's Visit to Heaven" (1909), which Twain suppressed because he mistakenly thought it shocking, and *The Mysterious Stranger*. Captain Stormfield found how small human life and the world were in the sum of things. The beautiful Satan of *The Mysterious Stranger* showed that man was at the mercy of forces beyond his control, the prey of superstition and folly, and prone to do evil because it was attractive.

There was no progress, and the future held more horror than anyone dreamed of. The sum total of human misery kept pace with the sum total of human material progress; the balance remained the same. Man was the same as in ancient times; only the costumes changed. The material progress Twain once thought beneficent and which he praised in the form of railroads, steam engines, and sanitation might be fatal after all. The more opportunity it gave for prosperity the more it fed man's base desires. Perhaps progress, like revolution, ate its own children.[59] A man might be optimistic in youth, but only a fool was hopeful after middle age.[60] And it was all predetermined, for no one mastered either his own fate or his own self. He was at the mercy of the sum of his past, his environment, and a biologically endowed temperament that made him sanguine or gloomy, good or bad. He could overcome nothing, and in the end everything was all an illusion.[61] As Satan told his young charges in *The Mysterious Stranger:*

"It is true, that which I have revealed to you; there is no God, no universe, no human race, no earthly life, no heaven, no hell. It is all a dream—a grotesque and foolish dream. Nothing exists but you. And you are but a *thought*—a vagrant thought, a useless thought, a homeless thought, wandering forlorn among empty eternities."

He vanished and left me appalled; for I knew, and realized, that all he had said was true.[62]

It was the darkest view in contemporary American letters, the more surprising for its source. His works had always been filled, for the public at least, with the jauntiness of youth. He was the apparent celebrant of American ideals and technical progress, the dreamy storyteller of the American past in the form of childhood idylls. His public did not read these bitter musings, for Twain published little after *Following the Equator* except occasional notes, articles, and pieces of memoirs. *What Is Man?* (1906), however, outlined his determinism and pessimism. But the public, in any event, had always paid homage to the man as well as his work, and presumed now that these patches of darkness were irrelevant or an idle whim.

Always a bundle of contradictions, Twain was never more complex than in his dealings with the philosophy of darkness. Infuriated by sham, railing at hypocrisy, he could easily refuse to publish such thoughts on the grounds that he was an admitted coward. He preferred to leave his testament of pessimism for his literary executors and referred idly to an edition of his suppressed works scheduled a hundred years after his death. In the meantime, he deemed his private thoughts heretical enough to merit suppression. He could not risk his reputation, he could not threaten the moral code, he could not reveal his inner self. What good would it do anyway? he asked. No one would understand or listen.

Twain's pride in *What is Man?*, the private "Bible" which he long suppressed because of its bleak determinism and assault on accepted morality, well defined the limits of his critical and philosophical faculties. It was little more than a tedious and often sophomoric disquisition on free will. It was significantly long in composition, indicating Twain's confusion and doubts. Cast in the form of a dialogue between Old Man and Young Man, it belabored such topics as pure motivation, selfishness, optimism, and original thought with a zeal that seems both pathetic and quaint to modern readers. That he thought it revolutionary makes one wonder about his standards. It will not surprise or depress anyone who has lived in the twentieth century.

His philosophical discoveries were not very amazing. Many men at twenty arrive at the viewpoint that Twain polished at seventy, and without his personal loss. Not all raise pessimism into a law of life; but seen in perspective, these harried reflections, however they blighted his thinking, were not the sum of Twain's legacy. Though aged and in seclusion, he found joy in life. His daughter Clara was still his heart's delight; and though his pace was slower, life still interested him. So vivid were the contradictions in his thought and person that he could write with ease shortly after Jean's death: "A man's temperament is born in him and no circumstances can ever change it. My temperament has never allowed my spirits to remain depressed long at a time." [63] As always, Howells was shrewd in his assessment of Twain's darkness: "Life had always amused him, and in the resurgence of its interests after his sorrow had ebbed away he was again deeply interested in the world and in the human race, which, though damned, abounded in subjects of curious inquiry." [64]

No man who knew Mark Twain doubted his kindness, or his love of his fellows, despite his occasional acidulous outbursts. His view of the human dilemma was deep but not broad; he found much to save and admire in some men, but not in the race. He might love, assist, praise many men; but he could not forgive the race for its folly, or understand how any animal so endowed with individual intelligence and beauty could remain in sum so stupid.

His concern with the human dilemma saved his pessimism from mere misanthropy. His protests aside, he was and remains a great humanist in literature, more bitter at man's failings precisely because he expected more of him. Man's refusal to become what he might angered the moralist in him. The determinist in him was enraged at the universe or system that prevented this fruition. The war between these two attitudes explained the weakness of most of his early work, and only in *Tom Sawyer* and *Huckleberry Finn* did he solve this technical dilemma by combining past and present in two levels of perception, those of child and man. Torn as he was between these two poles of dark and light, Twain failed to rise in his philosophic musings to the level of tragedy, for he lacked the all-important detached stance. This was his personal saving grace, for he could then love some and despise the mass. But the old humorist would never completely die, for in his deepest gloom his assaults on man aimed at purification of the species by exposing these faults. Even the fantasies of *The Mysterious Stranger* were not very real, for Twain here searched for a kind of salvation, blaming mankind's faults and his own on some supernatural system. [65]

It would be foolish to dismiss or minimize Twain's pessimism and determinism. But their hidden purpose weakened them; it was always that of the humanist, to lift, to cleanse, and to create as well as to criticize. The apparent paradox of Twain's thought is explained when seen as a whole, for the shock of his losses late in life did not make him a pessimist. He had never wholly believed either in the mechanical and social progress which his era and country praised, or the goodness of man. He was always the social critic, the moralist, the man honestly indignant at life's follies and pains. His deathbed gloom was merely the logical extension of these thoughts.

He was that kind of pessimist in old age because he had been a free thinker in youth, and because he felt the profound social changes of his lifetime. Reared in an environment that counted all things possible to him who tried, and having fulfilled that ideal in his own life, he lived to see it thrown into doubt. In his old age he saw his country in the grip of empire and international entanglements that no one in the Hannibal of his youth dreamed possible. True to his role as a social critic as well as artist, Twain saw the trends of his country and the whole future of man toward bigness and impersonality, both of which allowed free play for man's innate weaknesses. Because he feared that America's historic social and moral goals might be swallowed up in these seas of materialism and the fast pace of events, he never simply resigned himself. He wrote until he died. He did not publish his writings, but the gift in him could not simply wither and die.

Born in peace, he lived to see war. Growing up in an America of isolation and security, he saw her acquire an empire with means he opposed and be threatened herself by new forces. Raised on the assumption that men could do good, he lived to see them do much evil. Always baffling in his inconsistencies, alternating between violence and placidity, he was an amazing figure in American history. His best work will endure and be read as the testament of a great heart and gifted imagination. Perhaps Mr. Howells should have the last critical word. His was "a nature whose tragical seriousness broke in the laughter which the unwise took for the whole of him." [66]

Old age and death could not rob him of a life he said he did not value. "Life was a fairy tale then," he wrote an old friend as the shadows closed; "it is a tragedy now." [67] But there were full days and honors yet to come. He lived in hushed elegance in his New York apartment, amused by Clara and a few old friends, sallying forth occasionally for an honorary dinner or to make a sharp comment. The white head grew leonine, the eyes twinkled, and if the drooping mustache whitened and seemed sorrowful, it still sat atop a mouth filled with wit and wisdom. Oxford honored him with a degree in 1907 and provoked his last trip abroad in a final triumphal tour. He wintered in Bermuda, summered in Connecticut, and still had abundant energy for the billiards he never ceased to love, and the dictated autobiography that was the toy of his later years.

Howells' son, a promising architect, designed a great country house for him, aptly named "Stormfield," where he died on April 21, 1910. His forebodings mounted as the sky blazed with the comet that had ushered him into life and which he knew would take him out. He lay in his immense Renaissance bed whose posts were singing cherubs, his hair awry, his eyes shrewd, and grew restive as he watched the sky. Peering over his spectacles, he would rub his great mane, mutter a heresy, chomp a cigar.

William Dean Howells: The Realist as Reformer

But I am not sorry for having wrought in common, crude material so much; that is the right American stuff; and perhaps hereafter, when my din is done, if any one is curious to know what that noise was, it will be found to have proceeded from a small insect which was scraping about on the surface of our life and trying to get into its meaning for the sake of the other insects, larger or smaller.

—1903

THE OLD MAN loved to reminisce in the twilight years before the First World War when he seemed to be a gentle anachronism. He would slump down in his chair, hook his right thumb in his vest, put his left hand aside his head, and, thus tilted, look at his visitor with a glance of kind shrewdness. His clothes were old-fashioned, his hair gray, and though he did not look it because of the genial authority his figure exuded, he was short and stout. He looked like anyone's grandfather or a kindly parson. But the moment he began to talk, spicing his conversation with a quick humor that lighted up his eyes, shaping his mouth in a puckish curve as he made a wry point, or stiffening slightly as he remembered his literary and social wars, he at once became much more.

As he talked his listener might reflect that he was a national institution. He had shaped a whole generation of American letters, had devised and fostered a school of writing called Realism, and had generously supported the work of dozens of younger men, themselves now well known. It was hard to conceive of the wrath he had brought down on his head by mixing politics and social reform with writing. He seemed the last man to be concerned with the sweat and grime of the working world. But he had been a major social critic in the 1890s, an era which, in view of all that had succeeded it, seemed several geologic ages away. He might straighten

37

up, alive with memories of famous men he had known and crusades he had mounted, now against the walls of Romance, now against the battlements of economic privilege. He would talk a while longer and then leave a final word of advice. No visitor could help respecting him, for he had a fine mind, and was still at this late date the Good Gray Dean of American letters, William Dean Howells.

It was not always thus. Who would have thought in those rustic pre-Civil War days that a slight, frail, and somewhat dreamy young man would come to this position? The Ohio of his birth was vital, colorful, and exciting; but it did not produce literary lights or cultural arbiters. He was born on March 1, 1837, in Martin's Ferry, Ohio, the son of William Cooper Howells, itinerant newsman and country editor. The elder Howells was an amalgam of personal toughness and emotional kindness. He tempered his hard labors and rustic background with mystic religion. The humanism of "conscience Whiggery" led him to detest slavery, and he often risked his meager living and the fortunes of his large family for his principles.

Fortunately, the West of that day was a melting pot of emotions as well as races. The Howells family, though moving frequently and never overly secure economically, was not persecuted. William Howells became a figure of some importance in local Republican politics as that party's fortunes began their meteoric rise to national dominance in the late 1850s. Though Ohio was isolated, and its people at the mercy of poor communications and the emotional hazards of loneliness and hard work, it was not an intellectual wilderness. The country editor, like the country doctor and lawyer, was usually a man of stature and influence in the community. Printing was almost a disease with such men, and they risked hardship to continue their trade. They were often interested in literature, and William Cooper Howells encouraged his son's literary tastes.

In after years, William Dean Howells recaptured much of his youth in a delightful memoir, *A Boy's Town* (1890). While nostalgia never covered the rough spots and steep places, he recalled that his neighbors had tolerated almost any kind of thinking. All things considered, it was a free and stimulating environment for a young man who wished to grow into a life of letters.[1] The villagers could not go to culture, but it came to them. Some of the greatest names in American life made regular pilgrimages through the Ohio Valley. "That was the heyday of lecturing," Howells said, "and now and then a literary light from the East swam into our skies." [2]

The Howells family required the labor of all its members, and William Dean set type before he was ten. He remembered with chagrin the cold mornings when he warmed his fingers patiently before the fire until they would pick up the type. He delivered papers and collected subscriptions, often paid for "in kind," a pig or brace of squawking chickens that ultimately graced the Howells table. As an old man, heavy with honors, fame, and the economic comfort denied him as a youth, he looked to that daily grind of labor with pain. ". . . when I think of it, and of the wide-spread, never-ending struggle for life which it was and is the type of, I cannot but abhor the economic conditions which we still suppose an essential of civilization." [3] He was not bitter that he could not attend college, though he later regretted his lack of formal learning. The world would be his school and the source of his literary output.

Literary ambitions consumed him as he entered his teens, for he had already discovered the magic of books in his father's attic, and spent every hour when not at work reading. "What I wished to do always and evermore was to think and dream and talk literature, and literature only." [4] Obsessed, like many youths, with a fear of time, he burned to see his name in print, feeling that he was always "in a continual strife with time and fate. . . ." [5]

This ambition and fear combined with nervousness to make him what the frontier called "morbid," given to deep introspection and a darkness of the spirit that for a time almost killed him. He suffered from recurrent dreams and a pathological fear of death from hydrophobia that made him hate dogs. The natural setting, filled with darkness and distance, the very ground seeming to reek with tales of Indian horror, the loneliness and isolation—all heightened his fears and founded his lifelong interest in psychic phenomena and the supernatural.

His father, having passed through the same crisis as a young man, understood and applied the best therapy, long walks in the woods and rich conversations over things spiritual and literary.

A dry wit and deep-seated honesty made the elder Howells a perfect companion. An edge of these neuroses remained on Howells' life and work, but he emerged into young manhood with a wholesome and well-integrated view of life. He showed from the first the thoughtfulness of others, the easy smile, and the calmness that marked his whole adulthood.

He was a romantic youth, devouring in great gulps the poetry of Heine, then a fad in the United States, reveling for a time in the romanticism he would soon renounce. He carried this love so far that James Russell Lowell wrote him in 1864 to "sweat the Heine" out of his system "as men do mercury." [6] But he also read Cervantes and other realistic writers. They offered a kind of romance but tempered their view with a basic honesty in dealing with human events that helped set him on the road to his own literary realism.

Howells combined writing with reading, claiming poetry as his first love, a delusion that lasted until the success of his travel books and fiction after the Civil War. His father used him as a reporter as well as compositor and delivery boy in Ashtabula, Jefferson, and finally Columbus, where he settled in 1857 as a legislative reporter and contributor to the *Ohio State Journal*. Young William Dean's poetry impressed his father, who circulated it among country editors, launching him on a gratifying if modest career. This career both culminated and ended in 1860, when he published *Poems of Two Friends* with his close friend John J. Piatt.

In 1858 and 1859, he was a reporter and editorial writer for the *Ohio State Journal,* which took him to the city's low as well as high life. He dined with Governor Salmon P. Chase, then on the threshold of his national career in Lincoln's administration. But the next day he was in the local police station, surveying a motley collection of drunks, hoboes, wife-beaters, and swindlers, seeking material for his newspaper. His sensitive nature rebelled against the procession of misery and dreariness, and he fled from reporting. ". . . I renounced the opportunity offered me by that university of the streets and police-stations, with its faculty of patrolmen and ward politicians and saloon-keepers." [7]

In 1861, the sectional crisis over slavery sharpened into war.

But before those climactic events, Howells wrote a brief campaign biography of Abraham Lincoln, a task of which he thought so little that he did not even interview the candidate himself. A traveling secretary returned the necessary information and impressions to Howells, who turned the material into a lucid essay that Lincoln himself later approved.

Strangely enough, the election's excitement and the threatening events of the "Great Secession Winter" did not affect Howells. Restless and eager to see the world, he took his meager proceeds from the campaign biography, and a vague commission to write articles on eastern industry for western newspapers, and went to Boston and New York.

Boston enchanted Howells, who later made it and Cambridge his home, for its very name was a tocsin of learning, culture, and society. To any Westerner, eager for adventures of the mind and pen, it was the hub of the universe, as it styled itself with a permissible arrogance and charming naïveté. Basking in the lights of wealth, prestige, and a vitality of men and goods, the city was arresting in its strength and symbolism. Softer lights clustered around the names and works of a generation of men remarkable for their productivity and influence in culture and politics. Longfellow, Whittier, Thoreau, Holmes, Lowell—these were the Brahmins, and though aging they were still fascinating and powerful in cultural circles.

Howells' first pilgrimage to Boston and Cambridge brought him to the Brahmins' attention, for he had already contributed poems to the august *Atlantic Monthly*. Perhaps they recognized something in the callow youth, whose shyness was such that he could hardly ask the way to Whittier's house or talk intelligently with the brooding Hawthorne. He was a curious combination of shyness, kindness, naïveté, and confidence; and they treated him almost as one of themselves. In the presence of Holmes and Lowell, nervously drinking tea and talking poetry, he was astonished to hear the Autocrat remark with a chuckle: "Well, James, this is something like the apostolic succession; this is the laying on of hands." [8] The great men were fascinated by the West, confident that from its rustic vitality a literature and culture of depth as well as breadth would come. The young Howells did not share their optimism, for to him and his peers the East meant culture. Time changed his view, but for now he wished to enter the charmed circle.

A trip to New York, so unlike Boston in its frank brashness and celebration of wealth, only assured Howells that the older milieu was his own. He took in the city's vitality, alive in many sections with the colors and conversation of its foreign-born population, toured the teeming wharves, noted the city's impersonality, and sensed tensions that were the stuff of both life and literature. Newspaper friends wined and dined him in a fashionable Bohemian atmosphere, which though interesting was tiresome. He might watch and smile; but he could never join the carefree abandon, excitement, and mild hedonism that combined with irresponsibility to make the Bohemian life. "The bohemians were the beginning and the end of the story for me, and to tell the truth I did not like the story." [9]

Hungrier than ever for the literary life, Howells returned to Columbus, the taste of Boston lingering on his palate. He determined to escape the frontier isolation and provinciality that could never again satisfy him. Spring brought war, and he went East to Washington, seeking a political appointment from the new administration. He preferred a consulship; the foreign environment was stimulating, and there would be time to write. His contacts with the *Atlantic Monthly* and publishing firms in Boston might start his literary career despite war's disadvantages and discomforts.

Rome was available, but the post carried no salary and the fees were small. Howells used friends such as John Hay, Lincoln's secretary and a future writer, to get the consulship at Venice, which carried a small but adequate salary and light duties. Again he missed his chance to talk with Lincoln, though the harried President smiled in his direction and seemed to invite conversation. Howells was too shy to approach him, missing for the second time the priceless chance of personal conversation.

He left for Venice as quickly as possible, but not before making at least tentative and hopeful arrangements to marry his sweetheart, Elinor Mead, of Brattleboro, Vermont. In 1862, accompanied by her brother, she met him in Europe; and after a hectic interval they were married in Paris, beginning a long wedded life.

Venice, sitting like a crown on the Adriatic, fulfilled his dreams of foreign charm and exotic settings. He learned the language so well that he was often mistaken for a native. He spent most of his time either reading or observing the life around him. True to his later literary Realism, he noted the small, human details of daily existence. A head thrown back in laughter, a vivid gesture on the street, a mocking glance, an impulsive display of affection—all caught his eye like photographs that he could transmute into paintings of reality. He went to the opera, the puppet show, the theater, the churches, and museums. But the painted Madonnas did not intrigue him so much as the human ones who knelt before them. The museums' paintings were lifeless compared to the subjects he saw on every hand. And no puppets could compare with those on the streets.

He came to Venice filled with the romantic visions that afflict most tourists, fortified in his case by a traditional American inferiority in the things of time and history. But he rapidly abandoned this view, seeing the city with eyes that his friend Mark Twain would shortly duplicate. He "had set my face against that romantic Venice which Byron and the Byronic poets and novelists had invented for the easy emotioning of the newcomer." [10] Venice and all of European life made him re-examine his views of America, and in the end were major forces in turning him toward his own country as a source of art. His attitude toward Europe and his view of America had been ambivalent, but the years in Venice assured him finally of his country's superiority. He wrote his sister and father often, praising America, saying as his term closed that he wished to go to Oregon or some place equally remote from Europe, to appraise and present American life. [11]

But Italy gave him much: a fresh view of humanity, the perspective of travel, insight into an old culture, a sense of the past, and contrast for his own life and work. He enjoyed the people and their pace of life. His experiences made him a leading American authority on Italy and provided the setting for half a dozen of his early novels. Above all, it gave him a foundation in literary realism, for he read and attended realistic plays, especially those of Carlo Goldoni. Concerned with the quiet drama of normal human activities and passions, they were a reaction against sentimentality and immediately caught Howells' fancy. His knowledge of Italian writing produced an essay for the *Atlantic Monthly* that refreshed his contacts with the Brahmins. Returning to America, he finally settled in Cambridge as a younger member of Longfellow's Dante Club, with recognition among the elder statesmen who still dominated American letters.

As his consulship ended in 1865, Howells' future was undecided. He wished to break the bonds that held him to Ohio, but he felt a natural responsibility toward his family. His father asked him to return to the newspaper, which had fallen upon hard times. Though the thought filled him with horror, he dutifully agreed. ". . . but I confess that the thought of subscription, advertising and stationery fills me with dismay," he wrote bluntly.[12]

Fortunately, he did not need to comply, and went to New York, wife and baby in tow, to work as a contributing editor to *The New York Times, The Nation,* and other newspapers. Destiny shone on him in 1866 when he became assistant managing editor of the *Atlantic Monthly*. His lack of funds and the often dreary clerical work did not dull the edge of his satisfaction at being in America's cultural bosom. As Brete Harte exclaimed in awe at the Hub: "Why, you couldn't fire a revolver from your front porch anywhere without bringing down a two-volumer!" [13]

Howells' duties at the *Atlantic Monthly* could merely have been clerical, had he not chosen to make them something more. The magazine's publisher, James T. Fields, hired him because of his background in printing, which somewhat disappointed the young applicant. He had hoped that his literary potential was his best recommendation. He read proof, checked facts in articles, reviewed books, and pulled the whole issue together each month. He performed these often delicate missions (who could better have reminded Lowell of a factual error in one of his articles?) with a tact and efficiency that made the magazine a model of good journalism. For most of the rest of his life, Howells faced editorial chores; first in this capacity, then as managing editor of the *Monthly* from 1871 to 1881, as author of the "Editor's Study" in *Harper's New Monthly Magazine* after 1886, and finally in the long twilight of his life as the occupant of the "Editor's Easy Chair." These duties took time and endless energy, but he was an avid and constant worker, writing wherever and whenever he could, trusting to industry rather than transient inspiration. In his long lifetime, he wrote over fifty books of fiction, belles-lettres, travel memoirs, criticism, and biographical essays. The discipline of journalism, his even temper, and natural industry made it all possible. How much of his creative ability he sacrificed to editorial work is another question. Free from such burdens he might have produced finer, if less voluminous work.

He entered the world of letters in 1866 with *Venetian Life,* a re-creation of his tenure spent there, told in a simple, easy manner, dealing with both the picturesque and the commonplace. It was a charming book, warm with the author's humanity and its Italian setting, full of an easy tone that finally carried it through seven editions. It was not profound, though it revealed his keen observation and interest in life, but it was far above the era's standard travel book.

These were busy years. Writing books and managing a powerful national magazine were demanding enough, especially when he became editor-in-chief in 1871, but to this his growing literary reputation added academic demands. In 1867 Harvard awarded him an honorary M.A., and from 1869 to 1871 he lectured there on Italian drama and poetry. Though flattered by scholarly attention and gratified at the chance to display his learning, Howells was not academically inclined. He declined a professorship at Harvard and one at the new and influential Johns Hopkins University in 1882 on what he considered the excellent grounds of incompetence. He could have been a successful professor, but preferred writing fiction, where his fancy had larger rein.

Howells produced his first novel, *Their Wedding Journey,* in 1872. He embarked on his career as a novelist with only a vague theoretical basis for his fiction, and with many conflicts still unresolved in his mind. But he wrote of the life he knew in a truthful manner, rejecting romance and the improbable fiction that his generation loved. He would cling to the ideals of neither sentimentality nor costumery but would make a new position for himself, confident that there was not only a market but an appreciative audience for such work. "If I succeed in this—and I believe I shall—I see clear before me a path in literature which no one else

has tried, and which I believe I can make most distinctly my own,"
he wrote his father while composing *Their Wedding Journey*.[14]

The book's theme was set early. "Ah! poor Real Life, which I
love, can I make others share the delight I find in thy foolish and
insipid face?" [15] The book was simply a thinly disguised account of
Howells' own wedding journey, cast as Basil and Isabel March's
tour from Boston to Quebec. Howells, as narrator, wished only "to
speak a little of well known and easily accessible places, to present
now and then a bit of landscape and now a sketch of character." [16]
It was not very romantic, but it was honest. The book was dotted
with sharp comments on American institutions: the railroad-station
food, the porter's insolence, the behavior of tourists at Niagara
Falls, the rude hotel clerk, a snap now and then at politics, and a
steady stream of wise and witty remarks on women.

It also contained germs of social thinking and reflections of
deeper thoughts that Howells would later develop. Vulgar riches
disgusted Basil March, who would return with the same theme in
Howells' most powerful novel. However, he voiced doubts about
American economics and the idle rich who infested the fashionable
hotels where the newlyweds stayed. "The almighty dollar defeats
itself, and finally buys nothing that a man cares to have. The very
highest pleasure that such an American's money can purchase is
exile, and to this rich man doubtless Europe is a twice-told tale." [17]
The Marches noted the impersonality of New York and man's
often unconscious cruelty to his fellows, stating for the first time a
major theme in his subsequent work, the interdependence of individuals. Seeing the lack of interest with which passers-by viewed
a victim of sunstroke, March noted rather sadly the book's real
point: "Nothing is so hard as to understand that there are human
beings in this world besides one's self and one's set." [18]

Their Wedding Journey was technically imperfect. The narrator
too often interrupted the action to preach. But the book was deceptive in its very quietness and lack of pretension. In his early works,
Howells created a view of life and philosophy of action that was
more real than apparent. It rose from the small, seemingly insignificant, unexciting details of daily living with which he worked so
patiently. It rested on the idea that was the basis of all his work:
the particulars of life make up its general sum, and great truths

may lie in the smallest of situations and events. Any man and any action might give the clue to the general principle behind all men and actions. As he said in his last years: "I have my little theory that human nature is elementally much the same always and everywhere, and that if the man of intelligence will study this in his own heart he will know pretty well what all other men have been in essentials." [19] No man grew without participating in these seemingly insignificant things. Commitment was necessary for life. "That's the nature of worlds, big and little," he wrote in *The Undiscovered Country* (1880); "you can't be at home *near* them; you have to be *in* them to be comfortable." [20]

His reputation now firmly begun with *Their Wedding Journey,* economically secure, and fascinated by the process of realistic writing which he had begun to define, Howells embarked upon the series of novels that made him a major figure in American letters. He began his career essentially as a writer of travel books, both fact and fiction, and travel figured prominently in his early work because it confronted people with events and situations that tested their character. "At any rate, if I were to write a story, I should want to take the slightest sort of plot, and lay the scene in the dullest kind of place, and then bring out all their possibilities," he wrote in *A Chance Acquaintance* (1873).[21]

Beneath this avowed purpose of realistic writing lay a growing insistence on the importance of the American scene. *A Chance Acquaintance,* so called because of the chance flirtation between the stuffy Miles Arbuton of Boston and the innocent but shrewd Kitty Ellison on a trip to Canada, showed Howells' sharpening awareness of the richness of the American landscape. The story involved conflicts of old and new, East and West, American and Europeanized customs, and above all, innocence and experience.

Miles Arbuton, a typically stiff and narrowly provincial Bostonian, had nothing on his horizon but proper social conventions and was Europeanized in all his values. Comparing every scenic wonder on the trip to something abroad, he was chagrined to hear Kitty snap: "Then you've really found something in an American landscape. I suppose we ought to congratulate it." [22] On the whole, Arbuton was "at a loss with these people, who looked at life in so bizarre a temper, yet without airiness or pretension, nay, with a whimsical readiness to acknowledge kindred in every droll or laughable thing." [23] He fell back only on the conventions he knew, disregarding the worth of individuals, provoking Kitty to lambaste his ideal of a gentleman: "I wasn't taught to respect the idea of a gentleman very much. I've often heard my uncle say that, at the best, it was a poor excuse for not being just honest and just brave and just kind, and a false pretense of being something more. I believe, if I were a man, I shouldn't want to be a gentleman." [24]

In this early stage of growth, Howells' view of America was not yet stabilized. He loved his country's color, vitality, and richness of character. He also disliked its provinciality and its sharp class consciousness, all the more obvious in a supposedly equalitarian country. He detested snobbery and sham culture, symbolized by the very Boston he prized so highly. He could tolerate an aristocracy of the arts and intellect, but he could not suffer one based on money or artificial position. He devoted the remainder of his life to developing the idea that an individual's greatest responsibility is to respect others for what they are, not for where they reside on any artificial social scale. While this theme may now seem commonplace, to his generation it was "realistic" enough. Class lines were then much more sharply defined, and the America of that day patterned itself on European models.

Howells won quick praise for his portrayal of women, and he created moving and believable heroines. No swooning ladies, waiting in flowered bowers for romantic knights, peopled his pages. He portrayed society women, working girls, professional women, divorcees, reformers, and schoolgirls with an appealing accuracy, displaying a great understanding of the subtleties of female psychology.

It was easy to satirize conventional attitudes toward American women. "They were Americans," he remarked of the fawning male passengers of the *Aroostook,* "and they knew how to worship a woman." [25] How fascinating women were in their contradictions! Emotional on the one hand and supposedly weak, in times of crisis they could be made of iron. Living in small worlds, surrounded by petty problems, they could also be ruthless in having their way. Flighty and irrational, none could be more coldly rational than a woman scorned. Howells could have said with Ferris in *A Foregone Conclusion* (1875): "He mused in silence his wonder that so much addlepatedness as was at once observable in Mrs. Vervain should exist along with so much common-sense." [26]

Though the accusation that he wrote for a female audience, which in turn restricted his range, was untrue, Howells knew the influence women wielded in America. "It often happens in the country that you find the women practicing some of the arts of civilization, while their menfolk are still sunk in barbaric uses," he noted in *The Lady of the Aroostook* (1879).[27]

Howells drew one of his major feminine characters in Lydia Blood, the Lady of the Aroostook, in a book full of subtleties and charm. It requires a stretch of the imagination to comprehend its plot, for who can remember an America in which a country girl crossing the Atlantic could be morally suspect because she was unescorted? Howells used the book to explore the sham social code that made this state almost unspeakable, to satirize expatriate Americans, and to elaborate his theme of innocence meeting experience.

Howells pilloried the stuffy Dunham, who mocked the country girl's purity and innocence, and who posed as a man of the world. He had never been abroad before, but he regularly read English periodicals, "and this gave him the foreign stand-point from which he was fond of viewing his native world." [28] Once in the Venice he knew so well, the author spoke with perceptive irony of Lydia's aunt, who proposed "to show them that an American can be more European than any of them, if she chooses!" [29]

Howells was among the first American writers to give flesh to the bones of the international setting in fiction. Not because he liked exotic settings, but because the pressures upon character, which really intrigued him, were so much greater in the confrontation of Old and New Worlds. He was not a Henry James, lacking that great artist's refined psychological perceptions, but he helped light the path that James and others like Edith Wharton shortly traveled.

The Lady of the Aroostook was a skillful portrait of an innocent soul in contact with potential evil, and surrounded by sham conventions and false sentiment that corrupted innocence. Lydia Blood was a heroine because she resisted falseness. Her journey was a tribute to the virtues of common sense and basic decency, resting on regard for others. The book abounded with discussions of the old puritan mores of Lydia's Maine homeland, their shortcomings, their decay into stultifying rules. The story was a major statement on the condition of the New England conscience and culture in general. But the novel was essentially a story of growth and emerging consciousness. As Lydia said: "All that seems over forever. I couldn't go back there and be what I was. I could have stayed there, but I couldn't go back." [30]

In these formative novels published between 1872 and 1880, Howells, at first gropingly and then with the assurance of experience and deepening perception, stated the themes of a new American fiction. His ambivalence toward the American scene clarified, pointing toward the great "economic novels" of the early 1890s. He developed the international theme. He stated the formula of Realism. More than any contemporary, he began the treatment of man in his total environment that became the touchstone of American fiction in the twentieth century. He did not invent these things, but he stood above other American novelists concerned with flights from reality. He drew compelling portraits: the bittersweet awakening of Lydia Blood from rural slumber to social consciousness; the violated tenderness of Kitty Ellison in *A Chance Acquaintance;* the miseries of the fatally touched priest, Don Ippolito, in *A Foregone Conclusion,* whose inventions were "the stunted fruit of a talent denied opportunity, instruction, and sympathy," and whose destruction through his infatuation with an American girl illustrated the tragic element present in all men and situations.[31] And through all these separate pieces of the mosaic he was building ran the muted colors of social protest, dislike of inhumanity, and a conviction that the economic and social structure would have to change.[32]

These early novels, in both American and foreign settings, carried Howells toward the completion of two minor masterpieces, *The Undiscovered Country* and *A Modern Instance* (1882). On the surface, *The Undiscovered Country* was merely an excursion into the world of spiritualism that always fascinated Howells. It concerned Doctor Boynton, a spiritualist medium, and his clairvoyant daughter Egeria. The Doctor's impatience and willingness to believe in absurdities was offset by his daughter's frailty, patience, and languid goodness. Through her suffering, she redeemed both herself and her father by releasing them from the slavery of his false idea that a supernatural grace could save him in his present situation. The cynical Ford, moving through the novel to comment on human folly, and to court Egeria, typified doubt. Behind and over all wandered the Shakers, isolated in a Massachusetts utopian colony, steeped in spiritualism, acting as a Greek chorus to highlight the Doctor's delusions and final redemption.

Boynton was a study in failure, which fascinated Howells more than success, since it exposed character and sharpened morality in crises. The book's theme was the thread that now unified all Howells' work, the violation of one individual by others. "I seized upon a simple, loving nature, good and sweet in its earthliness, and sacred in it," the Doctor said, at last perceiving his true sin, "and alienated it from all its possible happiness to the use of my ambition. I have played the vampire!" [33] It was the first of Howells' books to be filled with darkness and tension. From the Boyntons' original flight from Boston, across the bleak landscape of personal failure and physical isolation, to their rescue by the Shakers, the Doctor's death, and Egeria's salvation through a newly awakened consciousness of both her limitations and the need of others, it held the reader despite loose construction. The secret of its success was character analysis. It showed men and women in the grip of tragedy, which however hard, was compelling.

It contained the tensions Howells refined in another decade into his greatest works: the conflict of city and country, the presence of natural forces that determined man's conduct, the tragedy inherent in the train of every day's events. Its psychology was both perceptive and true. "The origin of all our impulses is obscure, and every motive from which we act is mixed," he noted, proceeding to the book's central truth: "We grind upon each other in the encounter of life, and a spark of light is evoked by the attrition." [34]

The Undiscovered Country is one of Howells' unrecognized masterworks and was an important link in the chain of Realism. His figures here moved in a larger context than in his previous books. Their search for the mind's undiscovered country was a search for the sources of life itself. The book's point was as simple as the social theory toward which it looked: No man violates another without penalty. And the Doctor's plea that the Shakers "shake off this drowse of prosperity, this poppied slumber of love and peace, and buckle on the armor of action" forecasted the call to social action that Howells made after 1885.[35]

These years of growth climaxed in *A Modern Instance,* a novel with divorce and personal degeneration for its theme, that both shocked and fascinated its readers. The book introduced Marcia and Bartley Hubbard, who wove their destinies in and out of several future novels, polarizing around their tastes, ideals, and failures the principal themes of Realism. Bartley Hubbard, cynical, flippant, immersed in himself, interested in the sensational details of modern journalism, symbolized the decay of the old American standards. His wife Marcia, innocent and weak, symbolized the conflict of new and old moralities and standards of conduct. The story's tragedy lay not in Bartley's actions, but in their effect on his wife, who was less able to bear them than he was to inflict them. Though a victim of her husband's deterioration, Marcia was vain, vapid, jealous, and ignorant; only the impact of his desertion and the divorce forced her to examine her situation.

The book was a fine statement of the decline of old American ideals, whose ruins littered the landscape of a Gilded Age too often concerned with money and power. Bartley and Marcia came from rural America, whose people always fascinated Howells in "the keenness of their starved curiosity"; they disintegrated in the big city's impersonal whirl.[36] The novel also mocked Boston's social snobbery and its growing hollowness as money made inroads on its old cultural ideals. It was also a major statement of social responsibility, for Marcia finally defended herself against Bartley's charge of desertion in a spectacular divorce trial on the urging of her crippled lover: "In a matter like this, which seems to concern yourself alone, you are only to regard others." [37]

Good realist that he was, Howells gathered material for the story by personally attending a divorce trial and by weaving into its text his own knowledge of the lower depths of life. Many a man saw a short, pleasant figure poking down a Bowery street or among the refuse of humanity in the police courts without realizing that it was William Dean Howells, the essence of respectability. The book shocked his generation, for divorce, like sex, was taboo. But in its wealth of detail, fine style, and glimpses of the nether side of every man's conscience, it was a powerful statement of human interdependence. It also vividly illustrated the potential tragedy in all men. Bartley's decay came not from any romantically spectacular event, but from a procession of small and petty crises that gradually wore down his protective covering of ethics and morality.

As he verged on middle age, with a growing reputation, Howells took pride in having created an audience for what he called Realism in writing. That Realism, or fidelity to life as he knew it, was the core of all his work in these years of early development. He distrusted all things foreign as artificial to American culture. He patterned his thinking after Hawthorne, who lamented that "the damned shadow of Europe" had fallen across America. By the 1880s, a decade crucial in Howells' development and in all American literature, he said with some pride: "It seems to me that we are in a fair way to have a pretty good school of really native American fiction." [38]

This last generation of the nineteenth century changed all aspects of American life. In the economic and social spheres it profoundly influenced Howells and all American artists. Howells now saw around him a rich if often unnoticed flowering of American letters. The dime novels and sentimental paperbacks did not hide the vital ferment beneath the surface of American letters. New tensions, a new sense of life and its potentialities seemed to burst upon the scene in the 1880s and 1890s.

Regional writing prospered in the products of lesser masters. Sarah Orne Jewett spoke of New England in sharp, moving stories of the land and its people. George Washington Cable spoke for the South, often in hard tones. In the West, Bret Harte, Mark Twain, and lesser men illustrated that section's vitality and earthiness, as well as its occasional melancholy. In the Midwest, Hamlin Garland, Edward Eggleston, Joseph Kirkland, and Ole Rölvaag showed life's harshness and grandeur in a section of the country that always led the van of protest and change.

By the 1890s, Stephen Crane, Harold Frederic, Frank Norris,

and Theodore Dreiser mined the veins of Realism and Naturalism. No man recognized these new trends earlier or welcomed them more heartily than Howells. Nor was any established author ever more generous, helpful, and considerate in dealing with younger talent, even when he disagreed with their works. Nearly every American writer of any stature in the whole generation that closed the nineteenth and opened the twentieth century owed something to Howells for encouragement and recognition.

Whether they admitted it or knew it, these men built upon the foundation of Realism that Howells laid. He came to Realism from a negative direction, out of opposition to false romanticism. Like all esthetic theories, his grew with use and sharpened with time. He disliked romantic fiction because it was a kind of opiate, inducing hallucinations about life. He thought literature too important to be an escape vehicle, feeding the distorted imaginations of scullery maids and swooning schoolgirls with fatuous stories of costumery and absurd situations in which no normal man or woman ever found himself. Romance behaved as if life consisted of extremes, fortuitous accidents, and sweeping climaxes. In its pages and from its point of view, people were acted upon by external events, rather than growing to wisdom and richness through experience.[39]

His Realism was neither pretentious nor hard to define. As the name implied, it insisted on fidelity to life as it really was, not as it might be in some cuckooland. As he told a friend, if all the people in a boarding house rushed into the street at the cry of "Fire!" they would not appear costumed in elegant ruffles, bearing jaded fans, and plying passers-by with witty or magniloquent speeches as they did in many novels. They would be disordered, disarrayed, and distracted; so it was in life, and so it ought to be in literature.[40] His formula was simple, for "what is unpretentious and what is true is always beautiful and good, and nothing else is so."[41] For the realistic novelist, concerned primarily with values, "The novel ends well that ends faithfully."[42]

The romantic literature he attacked rested on a false and dangerous notion. It separated literature from life, setting the artist and his work apart from the mass of mankind whom it should benefit. Literature always had a social purpose, and "good art . . . is never anything but the reflection of life. . . ." [43] That social purpose was not transient reform, though Howells thought the novel could sometimes also serve that purpose. The deeper social purpose lay in creating an awareness of life's demands and responsibilities as well as its rewards. The idea that innocence bred selfishness, which in turn corrupted other people, was inherent in all of Howells' fiction, showing a profundity even in his early work which many critics have ignored.

Precisely because literature was central to mankind's progress, the normally retiring Howells could become angry at his adversaries, as when he passionately exclaimed:

> But let fiction cease to lie about life; let it portray men and women as they are, actuated by the motives and passions in the measure we all know; let it leave off painting dolls and working them by springs and wires; let it show the different interests in their true proportions; let it forbear to teach pride and revenge, folly and insanity, egotism and prejudice, but frankly own these for what they are, in whatever figures and occasions they appear; let it not put on fine literary airs; let it speak the dialect, the language, that most Americans know—the language of unaffected people everywhere—and there can be no doubt of an unlimited future, not only of delightfulness but of usefulness, for it.[44]

This insistence on truth was but a means to the larger end of all the arts—the true portrayal of man's character and his relations to his fellows. The measure of his consistent humanism rested on this insistence, a point that clearly showed his subtle understanding of the changing life of his middle years. "There's the making of several characters in each of us; we *are* each several characters, and sometimes this character has the lead in us, and sometimes that," he noted in *A Hazard of New Fortunes* (1890).[45] The fascination for the novelist lay in finding the source of that character and its reaction under life, both happy and tragic. His frank insistence that the novel be didactic in showing life's unity, and the interdependence of all men, raised eyebrows among both romantics and estheticians. "Men are more alike than unlike one another," he insisted; "let us make them know one another better, that they may be all humbled and strengthened with a sense of their fraternity." [46]

This did not mean that fiction should preach. He thought it should "be the novelist's business to keep out of the way" of his characters; to present them in a compelling light and allow the reader to judge their conduct himself.[47] But the very presentation of reality would be a kind of lesson.

Howells best stated his critical and esthetic theories in 1891 in his celebrated book *Criticism and Fiction,* pasted hastily together from his occasional editorial writings. It contained the unfortunate statement that haunted his reputation when a younger generation of realists and naturalists accused him of squeamishness: "Our novelists, therefore, concern themselves with the more smiling aspects of life, which are the more American, and seek the universal in the individual rather than the social interests." [48] Quoted out of context, "the smiling aspects of life" suggested a certain old-maidish avoidance of brutality, crassness, and tragedy. In context, however, Howells was merely stating a fact without necessarily approving it and was comparing the morbidity of European letters with the vividness and vitality of American writing. He wrote the remark in the late 1880s, before the impact of economic dislocation and social disaster shook his own faith in these "smiling aspects of life" and produced his best work that easily belied any such facile criticism of his work or purpose.[49]

The one obvious exception to Howells' insistence upon realism and fidelity to life was the treatment of sex. His fastidiousness in sexual matters grates on the modern reader, accustomed to the most clinical details as a matter of course in his reading. "I am a great admirer of French workmanship, and I read everything of Zola's that I can lay hands on," he wrote John Hay in 1882. "But I have to hide the books from the children!" [50] The afterthought may seem both laughable and hypocritical.

Howells faced manfully the charge that his omission of sex distorted the Realism he preached. He insisted that young people should not read "smutty" literature, classing as smut many things which bore rather than titillate later readers. He criticized Robert Herrick for making a sexual episode the theme of his novel *Together* (1908). He held that such matters were taboo because emphasis on sex was not natural. "At the end of the ends such things do defile, they do corrupt." [51]

The modern reader finds Howells' attitude toward sex prudish. He often seems like the proverbial maiden aunt, anxious that no body function be named, that no breach of an unreal etiquette be permitted, insisting perhaps that there is no sex drive at all. But his "prudery" must be understood in its context. It is hard to remember that as late as his own manhood, genteel company never discussed such matters. As is often noted, it was an era when men were men and women were single-breasted. A fictional heroine might have a bosom, but she never had breasts. Ladies had no legs, but "extremities" or "limbs," and polite company had no occasion to note any of these appurtenances. Women at bathing beaches did not enter the water and wore costumes only slightly less restrictive than street clothes. Pantaloons were attached to piano legs lest some helpless young man compare them to another kind of leg. None of Howells' contemporaries dealt with the clinical aspects of sex. Twain did not, nor did James, though both, like Howells, treated the moral aspects of life between the sexes.

Howells dealt with sex in the context of morality. It is easy to overstate his own oft-quoted remark that he never wrote a book he would be ashamed to have his daughters read. Most modern novelists could say the same; daughters, after all, have changed. His failure to explore this vein illustrated largely that to his pre-Freudian generation sex was not central. He scored a good point in his attack on the dealers in sex:

> Most of these critics who demand "passion" would seem to have no conception of any passion but one. Yet there are several other passions: the passion of grief, the passion of avarice, the passion of pity, the passion of ambition, the passion of hate, the passion of envy, the passion of devotion, the passion of friendship; and all these have a greater part in the drama of life than the passion of love, and infinitely greater than the passion of guilty love.[52]

He admitted the presence of sexual tension in society. But he thought that the process of civilization in the nineteenth century had reduced its importance, replacing it with more important and acceptable conventions.[53]

Though he usually skirted the issue, he did deal with it explicitly once in his work, but then only to suggest his characters' awareness of it. Two young lovers in *Silas Lapham,* exploring an unfinished house, come upon some wood shavings. The young lady blushes when her young man puts the point of her parasol through the curl of one.

Howells was both contradictory and characteristic on sexual themes. He saw nothing wrong in opposing the theme in American literature while sustaining it in European fiction. European life differed from American, and therefore justified the subject in the works of Zola, Flaubert, Turgeniev, and others. An older, more settled, cynical society might profit from these themes, but America would not. Since these emphases did not apply to the American scene, they were not merely unnecessary, but unreal. Writers emphasized them only to be sensational.

Yet he defended Stephen Crane, Frank Norris, and Harold Frederic when they were attacked for their frankness. He recognized that the way of these writers, while not his, was that of the future, and was content in his old age to remark with a touch of sadness: ". . . but I am still very Victorian in my preference of decency." [55]

Though Howells was proud of his role in emphasizing literary Realism, he knew that "no one invented realism; it came." [56] His method and subject captured an audience that remained loyal throughout his career. His readers found his novels often like eating peanuts. Once started it was hard to stop, until the last small fact had been digested to become part of a larger and often familiar picture. Precisely because it dealt with ordinary things, Realism was new to his generation.

It had its enemies, and later many who once supported Howells turned against him, condemning his works as did Ambrose Bierce to "fibrous virgins . . . and oleaginous clergymen. . . ." [57] Such criticism irritated Howells, but it never slowed him, for he distrusted critics, though he was one himself.

The realist wrote of what he knew, but Howells was no mere cataloguer. A man knows more than the facts of his existence. Once within his mind they take on a separate identity, clad in the qualities of his own imagination and his view of life. To this charge, Realism was true. The very acceptance of realistic writing lessened its force, but Howells knew that it differed from romanticism not in material, but in point of view. It was concerned with humanity and character; romanticism was concerned with incident.

The great success of Howells' work, his well-defined theory of literary Realism, and his own warm and human personality easily made him the leading American novelist of his generation, a man with friends of all varieties everywhere. He praised the work of Mark Twain, so unlike him, yet who was perhaps his best friend. He marveled at the westerner's vitality, falling victim to it himself on his lavish and frequent visits. Twain's humor and universal appeal captivated Howells, who also judged him with a shrewd eye. "It is such a book as *I* would expect from you, knowing what a bottom of fury there is to your fun, . . ." he wrote of *The Prince and the Pauper*. He collaborated on the plays, publishing ventures, and proposed lecture tours that poured from Twain's fertile imagination. Though he did not accept Twain's pessimism, he always thought him a great figure, "the Lincoln of our literature." [58]

Henry James could not abide the mention of Twain's work, but that did not prevent Howells from sponsoring the genteel expatriate's novels and making him a warm personal friend. As with Twain, he judged his man shrewdly, saying enthusiastically in 1866 that James was "gifted enough to do better than anyone has yet done toward making us a real American novel." And he could add a year later a perceptive postscript: "I cannot doubt that James has every element of success in fiction. But I suspect that he must in a great degree create his audience." [59]

In 1881, exhausted by editorial labor, Howells resigned the editorship of the *Atlantic* to travel and devote himself to freelance writing. In the moments of calm before the storm of social discontent that changed his outlook, he produced his most popular novel, *The Rise of Silas Lapham* (1885). In this rich work, set in a changing Boston in the midst of a changing America, full of an affectionate humor and warm style, Howells created his most lasting characters, Silas and Persis Lapham, their two daughters Irene and Penelope, and Tom Corey. On the novel's canvas, Howells painted the changes that had overtaken and replaced the America of his own youth.

Silas Lapham, "raised on the simple virtues of the Old Testament and Poor Richard's Almanack," symbolized the era's self-made man in all his glories and shortcomings. "I believe in my paint," he said honestly. "I believe it's a blessing to the world." Lapham was not a robber baron. He never lost sight of the rustic virtues that enabled him to make a fortune from a paint mine in Vermont and build an elegant new house in Boston's most fashionable district. He was coarse, unlettered, and often clumsy. But as Bromfield Corey noted: "He isn't to my taste, though he might be ever so much to my conscience." [60]

Ostensibly the book dealt with the Laphams' invasion of settled society, using their newly acquired wealth as a lever. Silas and Persis wished social recognition only for their daughters, who felt little need of it themselves. The girls opposed the new house because it was too far from the horsecars, not thinking of fancy carriages or social advantages. On the level of mere social criticism, the novel abounded with sharp comments on business practices, relations between the sexes, and a growing consciousness of the gulf between society's haves and have-nots.

But the book's real point lay elsewhere, for in it Howells extended his old idea of the violation of one individual by another. The innocent young Irene, supposedly the target of young Corey's courtship, was in fact unworthy of him. The jolting discovery that he loved her plain, studious sister, Penelope, shook her from "her normal state of innocent selfishness" to a condition in which she served others for her own reward. She learned of life's burdens as well as its pleasures.[61] The real theme was the community of men's interests, "for each one of us must suffer long to himself before he can learn that he is but one in a great community of wretchedness which has been pitilessly repeating itself from the foundation of the world." [62]

Silas Lapham lost his fortune by refusing to bilk innocent buyers of his property. His fancy new home, symbol of his new status and fruit of his hard work, burned accidentally. Broken with advancing age and faced with poverty, he seemed to have lost everything. Everything but honor, for he clung to his old standards of conduct. As Howells said, trying to explain "the rise" of Silas Lapham, "I did not think it my part to point out that I had supposed the rise to be a moral one. . . ." [63] And as Silas himself said when asserting that he would do it all again: "Seems sometimes as if it was a hole opened up for me, and I crept out of it." [64] A hole, Howells might have noted, leading from the darkness of brutal riches and selfish ignorance to the light of wider life and care for human welfare.

Silas Lapham reflected Howells' deepening concern with social problems and his sharpening talent at portraying humanity. This in turn partially reflected his own reading in Continental literature in the 1880s. He read with special zest and reward the Russian novelists whose impact on America was just beginning. Turgeniev especially impressed him. "Life showed itself to me in different colors, after I had once read Turgeniev; it became serious, more awful, and with mystical responsibilities I had not known before. . . ." [65] Turgeniev's observation of his characters without moral judgment, "letting the characters work the plot out," influenced Howells' own style. [66]

Tolstoy, whose works and life were then attaining popularity among liberal groups, moved Howells with his sense of humanity and fine writing. Though Howells could not follow the Russian's simple socialism, Tolstoy influenced the American realists. [67] Howells' own natural development, his reading of Continental realists, and the social tensions in America which he now began to feel sharply, focused his concern with daily life and literary realism into a general philosophy of life. Realism must now move beyond recording daily life to be a positive force for moral reform and advancement.

In the midst of his own personal literary crisis came the specific event that crystallized his social thinking—the Haymarket Riot in Chicago on May 4, 1886. The city, tense with labor trouble, and filled with the kindling of discontent among the unemployed and foreign born, blazed into near revolution when a mysterious bomb killed and injured almost seventy-five policemen who attempted to break up a meeting being addressed by anarchists. Though the identity of the assailant remains a mystery, the eight anarchists at the meeting were convicted of incitement to murder and were sentenced to die. Of the eight, one committed suicide in prison, four were hanged, and three received gubernatorial commutation of their sentence to life imprisonment.

Whatever the degree of their complicity in the crime—and they were at most "accessories" to murder—the anarchists did not receive justice. The judge and the jury were prejudiced and public hysteria prevented a fair trial. The liberal element rallied to the defense of the civil liberties violated in the case, if not to the anarchists or their doctrine, and in a celebrated series of legal appeals, lost the case in the U.S. Supreme Court. Repelled by the spectacle of public blood-lust, convinced that the men were unfairly tried, and seeing in the whole event stark evidence of the inhumanity of the law, Howells issued a famous public letter in the New York *Tribune* in 1887 urging clemency for the convicted men. Public indignation for a time focused on him, a most unlikely source of social radicalism, but he stubbornly opposed the executions. When the men were hanged, he wrote from deep gloom that the executions were "an atrocious piece of frenzy and cruelty, for which we must stand ashamed forever before history." [68]

History has judged Howells' view correct and has condemned the proceedings against the anarchists. He lived to see Governor John P. Altgeld of Illinois pardon the remaining prisoners in 1893 at the risk of his own public career. But the immediate results for Howells' work were profound. He now turned to the "economic novels" of the late 1880s and early 1890s that climaxed his career. He cast his lot with social change and reform, for as he noted in *Harper's Magazine* in 1887: "Art, indeed, is beginning to find out that if it does not make friends with Need it must perish." [69]

Howells had been chiefly concerned with individual morality and character in crisis. "But isn't the real dramatic encounter always between two persons only? Or three or four at most?" he insisted in 1875.[70] However, his view broadened, and he set the works that followed against a background best defined in his insistence that "the world is what it must be from the selfish motives which underlie our economic life." [71] Fortified by the prestige of his position in American letters, sustained by deep convictions of justice and truth in real as well as abstract senses, Howells moved into a new school of writing, Critical Realism. He defined it himself as ". . . dispersing the conventional acceptations by which men live on easy terms with themselves, and obliging them to examine the grounds of their social and moral opinions." [72]

Though Howells elaborated social themes in *A Woman's Reason* (1883), his first impressive statement of his conversion to reform came in *Annie Kilburn* (1889). Left wealthy and purposeless at her father's death, Annie returned to her New England home to participate in the "good works" so popular in her social set, having no idea of the extent of social need or her proper role in it. "She found she had fancied necessity coming to her and taking away her good works, as it were, in a basket. . . ." [73] She failed to grasp the teachings of the dreamy reform-minded minister, Reverend Peck, or the inebriate but brilliant lawyer Ralph Putney, and thought a musicale sponsored by the town's sophisticates with the proceeds to help the poor a suitable deed. Yet she heard an echo of an older and deeper wisdom and humanity in the Putney family's "pathetically old fashioned" beliefs that culminated in their crippled son's simple prayer: "Our Father, which art in heaven, help us to remember those who have nothing to eat. Amen." [74]

Annie was torn between Putney's radicalism, Peck's impracticality, and the clichés about self-help and progress peddled by Mr. Gerrish, the town's dry goods tycoon. Mr. Gerrish saw progress in technical terms, boasting of the employment his stores provided, the sidewalks and gasworks he built, the wages he paid. Putney and Peck insisted that these were not enough. In their long colloquy, Howells showed clearly that unlike many theorists he understood the magnitude of the problems confronting his America.

Annie's redemption lay in her perception that good work applied to the poor without feeling for them as people was not only an insult but "a peace offering to [the giver's] guilty consciousness of his share in the wrong." [75] Her determination to devote her wealth and life not to alms but to real social progress symbolized the awakening of all honest men and women.

Howells wrote the book "to set a few people thinking . . ."; and that it did, for it was edged in a darkness and set in a somber theme new to his fiction. The sunny realist, filled with wit and wry observations on the human landscape, was gone, replaced by an astute social commentator.[76] *Annie Kilburn* suffered from the defects of its purpose, for it was a social tract. But it was also a powerful statement of Howells' beliefs and a signpost on the road that led now to his most impressive book, *A Hazard of New Fortunes* (1890).

This lengthy, serious novel produced some of Howells' best characters, each symbolizing an aspect of the America which their creator now sharply criticized. The Basil Marches, now middle-aged parents, are reintroduced. They settle in New York to edit a stylish literary magazine that was managed by the curious Fulkerson, a kind of cultural robber baron, and backed by Orville Dryfoos, a typical businessman of the Gilded Age, rich from gas wells and speculation. There was also old Lindau, embittered German anarchist and radical, who gave an arm in the Civil War to free the slaves, only to wonder now if he had freed them all. Conrad Dryfoos, "Coonrod" to his illiterate if well-intentioned mother, the baron's son, spoke for social consciousness and artistic sensitivity. His innocent sisters, raised like hothouse plants in the garish surroundings of sudden wealth, revealed the cruel innocence Howells always feared. Angus Beaton spoke for art in Philistia, and despite his brilliance, succumbed in the end to cynicism and selfishness. Mela and Colonel Woodburn stood for an old South of slavery and magnolias, now disappearing before the smoke of factory chimneys and the steel of railroad tracks. And behind all, punctuating the action, was the presence of the city and its people.

Dryfoos himself was the centerpiece. He was no Silas Lapham, though his background was similar. He thought first of money, rather than the human welfare that saved Lapham. Dryfoos mouthed the platitudes so common to rich men who had been poor, thinking that "laziness and drink and dishonesty and foolishness" ruined men rather than economic and social forces beyond their control.[77]

Dryfoos understood what had happened to the old America that produced him. "There's no farm any more to go back to," he snapped to his wife, who wished to escape the burden of their riches by returning to their earthy beginnings. "The fields is full of gas-wells and oil-wells and hell-holes generally; . . . If I was to give all I'm worth this minute, we couldn't go back to the farm any more than them girls in there could go back and be little children."[78]

The tragedy of Orville Dryfoos was his fall from grace. Until money scarred him, he lived the fruitful values of the Old American Way, caring for others, and working for community service as well as private gain. Money changed that. Now in middle age he drifted pointlessly on ever-mounting waves of wealth, saddest of spectacles, the useful man condemned to idleness. His besetting sin was homage to money, which "bred its unholy self-love in him. . . ." [79] The sensitive March, who challenged Dryfoos and his money on a matter of simple integrity, summed him up best: "He has sharpened but he has narrowed; his sagacity has turned into suspicion, his caution to meanness, his courage to ferocity. That's the way I philosophize a man of Dryfoos' experience, and I am not proud when I realize that such a man and his experience are the ideal and ambition of most Americans." [80] Howells distrusted his era's self-made men, because they were self-made in an economic rather than humanistic mold.

The novel's denouement was a microcosm of the labor strife, social tensions, and hidden war between the rich and poor that plagued the generation of the late 1880s and 1890s. A streetcar strike caused Conrad Dryfoos' accidental death and killed old Lindau, who had already broken with March and Dryfoos over their tainted money. The strike was also a moral climax for March and Fulkerson, and even for Dryfoos. His pathetic dumbness at his son's death, and subsequent flight to Europe after abandoning the magazine on favorable terms to March and Fulkerson, revealed his emptiness. The book's themes and character analysis were not altogether new, but the impersonal canvas of the city against which the strike unfolded brought Howells to the edge of Naturalism. "He interested himself in the apparent indifference of the mighty city," March noted, "which kept on about its business as tranquilly as if the private war being fought in its midst were a vague rumor of Indian troubles on the frontier. . . ." [81]

The novel's economic and social message was clear: Those who produce should share. The book abounded with sharp contrasts of heedless wealth and grinding poverty, indifference and want, the bigness that had already devoured so much of the individualism Americans cherished even as it disappeared. Howells outlined a simple economic environmentalism, based on the general notion that wealth must be more evenly shared to gain progress and security. This required every man's self-sacrifice and attention to these problems. Though Lindau's anarchistic remarks shocked Isabel March, her husband accepted them as a matter of course. They both agreed that the provincial, undisturbed Boston they left was a kind of "death-in-life" to which they could not return even if they wished.[82]

In his preface to a new edition of the book in 1909, Howells referred to *A Hazard of New Fortunes* as "the most vital of my fictions, through my quickened interest in the life about me, at a moment of great psychological import." [83] The book's principal merit was the author's portrayal of tension in his characters. March, committed to art and freedom of thought, upholding Lindau's right to anarchism, nonetheless felt slightly debased. Did not Dryfoos and his breed have much to recommend them? Had they not built America? In the strike that followed, labor had honest claims, but did capital not also have its rights? Did the tenement dwellers deserve something for nothing; could taking from the rich make the poor better? Could art be art if it served social ends, risking eternal verities for temporary gains? Should March morally risk his family's future and livelihood for the sake of what might be selfish, his own principles?

A Hazard of New Fortunes was not Howells' best constructed novel. It was overly long, occasionally melodramatic, and some of its characters, like Angus Beaton, were not fully realized. It lacked the wit, grace, and fine finish of *Silas Lapham,* and the concise brevity of *The Quality of Mercy* (1892). But its passionate involvement in human problems, its description of the varied layers of life in New York, the intense concern with mankind that colored it everywhere, made it powerful and often moving reading. Howells gave full vent to his disgust with the imbalanced American economic and social structure that produced both tramps and millionaires. From the opening pages when March and Fulkerson looked up at the awesome buildings that symbolized the power and impersonality of wealth, to the scenes where morals dissolved in the acids of materialism, to the book's end when humanity triumphed over impersonality and selfishness, a sense of brooding darkness permeated the novel. Not even Fulkerson's flippancy, March's humorous comments on the people around him, or the irrelevancies and charming conversation of the young ladies involved alleviated this darkness. And everywhere a sense of impersonal destiny pervaded the action, pointing the road to the Naturalism of Crane, Dreiser, and Norris.

There followed in quick order *The Shadow of a Dream* (1890), Howells' most acute psychological study, whose chief lesson was "the solidarity of human affairs from the beginning to the end, in which no one can do or be anything to himself alone." [84] In 1892 came *The Quality of Mercy,* a sharp study of an embezzler at the mercy of personal flaws and the power of the economic system that controlled him. The flaw of materialism, so vividly stated in *The Quality of Mercy,* was the same as the flaw in slavery: it blunted the owner's sensibility to all things but possession. Northwick, the embezzling rogue who fled with his company's funds to Canada, leaving his two bewildered daughters behind to salvage their lives, had no taste and no standards except those of money. He knew nothing of art except its cash value. He had no social ideals but those associated with "good works." He pursued no ambition but wealth until his personal crisis and sickness in the frozen wastes of Canada forced a total evaluation of his morality and ethics.

The irony of it all was the indifference with which Northwick's neighbors greeted his embezzlement. It was common among men of wealth and to be expected in a system that rewarded greed. Money spread its corrosion through all levels of society, Howells said, in the form of cynicism and indifference to moral codes. "There must be something rotten, he said, at the core of our civilization when every morning brought the story of a defalcation, great or small, in some part of the country, . . ." the reporter Maxwell noted.[85] But Howells preached a broader message, and Northwick slowly realized that his crime lay not in having stolen money but in having violated the confidence of others. He saw the principle that tempered the fiction of Critical Realism: ". . . when you have suffered, even for a rogue, you begin to feel some kindness for him." [86]

This rich outpouring made Howells a center of social controversy, and it climaxed in his utopian romance, *A Traveler from*

Altruria (1894), cast in a form derived from Edward Bellamy's immensely popular *Looking Backward* (1888). The book was simply a walk through American society, in which Mr. Homos, the traveler from the socialistic and egalitarian island of Altruria that had solved its problems with Christian socialism, commented on American social issues. In Altruria, needs determined status and wealth, and all men were naturally as well as legally equal. No class consciousness but that of intelligence clouded Mr. Homos' vision, and his fellow Altrurians had long since abandoned competition in favor of cooperative Christianity.

The book was a clear statement of the Christian socialism that arose from Howells' own work, and on which he now pinned his hopes for a rejuvenated and free America. His active reforming was no surprise, for he had never been a closet philosopher. Even as a young man he questioned Thoreau's retreat to Walden Pond as an answer to the world's ills.[87] The climactic decade after the Haymarket Riot produced no new theories in him but focused the compassion and latent equalitarianism that flowed originally from his own background. He rejected Herbert Spencer's notion of automatic progress as foolish. "We shall not have fraternity, human brotherhood, without trying for it. From nature, it did not come; it came from the heart of man, who in the midst of nature is above it."[88]

Howells saw how hard it was to awaken Americans to the inequalities and crises around them, ensnarled as they were in the clichés and platitudes whose application had imbalanced his society. At a time that cried out for flexibility, rigidity was the order of the day. To Howells, America clung to outmoded ideals at the very time it needed social collectivism. He noted sadly that in his youth the great statesmen and writers were popular heroes: in his old age public recognition went to captains of industry.[89]

His thinking led Howells to a simple economic environmentalism as unsophisticated as his view of the crisis. "He was a mere creature of circumstances—like the rest of us!" he noted of Northwick in *The Quality of Mercy*. "His environment made him rich, and his environment made him a rogue. Sometimes I think there *was* nothing to Northwick, except what happened to him."[90] He talked easily of "the economic war in which our people live . . ." and supported the radical reform measures of the Populist party.[91] He had no faith in the old parties, but believed that an aroused people would "make this a country where no man who will work need want."[92]

The basic fault was competition, which set man against man and measured his brute strength rather than his needs. It created unequal wealth, "and wherever there is unequal wealth there will be the world, the flesh and the devil."[93] This brought him to the mild socialism he advocated the rest of his life. He treasured individualism but preached its responsibilities as well as its rights. Man in organized society must regard his fellows. This required the surrender of some free will. The agency that protected the remainder and used the common energy must be society, or in action, the state.

Howells never spelled out his socialism as a formal doctrine, adhering merely to the basic principles of cooperation. He referred to himself and Mark Twain as "theoretical socialists and practical aristocrats" in admitting the vagueness of his socialism.[94] But he never thought the theory foreign. Had not the government always entered into the economy, building roads and canals in his youth, railroads and public works in his manhood, pursuing policies in taxation and tariff protection favorable to business? The Ohio of his youth had abounded with utopian communities. He had been weaned on Swedenborg's doctrines of love and mutual respect and could hardly find formal socialism either alien or impractical.

He did not gloss over the faults of the groups he defended. He had walked through too many tenement sections and seen human nature at play under too many suns to think the problem simple or altogether one-sided. He could not believe that charity and help given in the spirit of understanding rather than patronizing would pauperize the already poor or undermine their moral fabric, as opponents of socialism argued. Nor could he believe that they were "the better men and women for being insufficiently clothed and fed, though so many of us appear none the better for being housed in palaces and clad in purple and fine linen and faring sumptuously every day."[95] But he could also warn that "we must not romanticize the poor, or imagine that they are morally better than the rich; we must not fancy that a poor man, when he ceases to be

a poor man, would be kinder for having been poor." [96] Perhaps
the last remark best indicated the contradictions in his own thinking, and the subtle convolutions of a mind that while filled with a
sense of human brotherhood also recognized the dangers involved
in attaining it.

Radical critics often called him a "slowcialist" or "parlor pink."
He trusted to the ballot not the bullet to enact over a long period
of time the cooperative society he outlined in *A Traveler from
Altruria* and one last utopian romance, *Through the Eye of the
Needle* (1907). In *A Hazard of New Fortunes,* he condemned
Lindau's preaching of violence, and when the strikers at the Homestead Works in 1892 used violence he suggested that their cause
would have been better served by martyrdom for themselves.[97]
He was firmly in the American tradition of democratic reform
through representative government. He thought the problem simpler
than it was, believing that "the thing we call mercy is the divine
concept of justice." [98]

Howells' disposition did not permit him the luxury of retirement
into Mark Twain's morbid pessimism. His often bitter view of public problems did not send him to cynicism or despair, for he still
believed that an enlightened people could correct these conditions.
He did not make his quarrel a philosophic principle against the
human race. America was still vital and would reform herself. He
was never a Naturalist. He could not believe in a universe governed
by impersonal laws. He believed that just as bad things resulted
from bad actions, so good things must come from good actions.
Human nature could be changed, if not perfected. America's economic system had bred false and selfish human values. If it were
corrected the values and the people would change. Thinking that
all things tended to natural harmony, he argued that if man removed his artificial rules, social harmony would ultimately prevail.

Personal tragedy combined with widening public responsibilities
in Howells' later years. His daughter Winifred died in 1889 from
a baffling disease. Mrs. Howells was an invalid for many years
before her death in 1910. Inevitably, a man of his longevity saw
a mounting list of friends die. This did not end his tireless battles
over public issues, that even caused him, along with Twain, to

oppose American acquisition of Hawaii and the Philippines after the war with Spain in 1898.

After a five-year absence from editing, he accepted the "Editor's Study" in *Harper's New Monthly Magazine* in 1886. Always a shrewd bargainer as well as tireless worker, Howells never lacked economic security, and his employers quietly sustained his iconoclasm even under threats of financial loss. In 1892 he resigned and again wrote free-lance, resuming as a contributing editor to *Harper's* in 1895. In 1900 he assumed the "Editor's Easy Chair," which he conducted until his death in 1920 and which he made a powerful force in American letters. He disliked editing in old age but confessed that he liked its financial security. He knew what editorial work had cost him, frankly writing Thomas Bailey Aldrich in 1900:

> It might have been wiser for me to have kept out of that place [the "Easy Chair"], but at 63 one likes a fixed income, even when the unfixed is not bad. Essaying has been the enemy of the novelist that was in me. One can not do both without hurt to both. If I could have held out fifteen years ago in my refusal of the Study, when Alden tempted me, I might have gone on and beat *Silas Lapham*. Now I can only dream of some leisure day doing better.[99]

His editorial position carried the great advantage of contact with all spheres of the literary world, and he used it as a lever to promote the fortunes of young writers. Though his wife's invalidism made him almost a social recluse, he was a convivial man, charming and witty, droll in his storytelling, which often seemed surprising in view of his dignified nature. The young Edith Wharton reported that he was "full of a quiet friendliness," and he often sat through tedious plays and read countless bad novels to find the wheat among the chaff.[100] "Kindness and gentleness are never out of fashion," he once said, and he appreciated a small talent as well as a large one.[101] "Your voice is like a thrush's in the din of all the literary noise that stuns us so," he wrote Sarah Orne Jewett.[102] Though many novels remained in his inkwell, the 1890s brought his career to its climax. In the twenty-five years remaining to him, he played well the role of literary elder statesman. Academic

honors, including an Oxford degree, came his way. He was the
first president of the American Academy of Arts and Letters in
1908. His voice counted for much even after his public had
dwindled. In the years between 1895 and 1920 his sure touch was
evident in works like *The Kentons* (1902), *Their Silver Wedding
Journey* (1899), *The Son of Royal Langbrith* (1904), and *The
Landlord of Lion's Head* (1897). But with one exception none of
them held the force of his "economic" novels.

That exception was *The Leatherwood God* (1916). The book
was a striking evocation of pioneer life in the Ohio of the 1830s.
Existence there rose in extremes and darkness mingled with light
in every human soul. Isolation bred loneliness and provinciality a
yearning for some larger ideal and greater promise than daily life.
Into this background strode the majestic figure of Joseph Dylkes,
charlatan, humbug, sorcerer, possessed as much by his followers
as they were by him, first proclaiming himself Jesus Christ and
then God. Working miracles, mapping the road to a promised land,
he shone like a beautiful light ringed with darkness and captivated
rational people until the community's unbelievers rose and drove
him and his followers "Over the Mountain."

Brief, lucid, tautly written with a compelling honesty of dialogue
and situation, filled with themes of hate and love, kindness and
violence, the book is Howells' undiscovered masterpiece. Its gothic
tale is unearthly, yet vividly real. Perhaps it was his *Mysterious
Stranger*; or perhaps it was his answer to that book, for in *The
Leatherwood God,* the gentle, unassuming Squire Braile triumphed
through rationality over the hysteria that Dylkes symbolized.

The story displayed Howells' dislike of the abnormal, whether
religious, moral, or esthetic. But the book was more than an old
man's fairy tale. It warned of man's frequent lapses into romance.
There was no easy or supernatural path, as Dylkes proposed. Man's
problems must be faced and met in this, not the next life. As
Dylkes' career proved again, there was no evil but that of violating
another soul, and *The Leatherwood God* was Howells' finest late
statement of that theme.

His declining years did not end the literary wars in which he
had fought so long. As others elaborated the theories he first announced, carrying Realism into Naturalism and changing the novel's

form and subject matter, the once radical Howells seemed old-fashioned. He became instead of a firebell in the night the Good Gray Dean of American letters. He sometimes helped his opponents by upholding from time to time the tenets which they thought outworn. He seemed naïve and limited in defending authors like Hamlin Garland because they offered "stirring adventure without bloodshed," "love which is sweet and pure," and a belief "in man's perfectibility. . . ." [103]

He felt the neglect that overtook him and his works, and complained quietly to his good friend Henry James: "They bray at my flowers picked from the fruitful fields of our common life, and turn aside among the thistles with keen appetites for the false and impossible." [104] He thought rampant Naturalism as distorted as romanticism. He had no taste for the new "realistic" fiction that all too often was merely a sociological or clinical discourse on the baser aspects of life. Not even his family spared him occasional humorous criticism. His grandniece, caught in the exciting toils of newer fiction, complained that his writing seemed dull. She wanted manliness and virility in her reading, "very strong, don't you know; and masterful; and relentless; and makes you feel as if somebody had taken you by the throat; and shakes you up, awfully; and seems to throw you in the air, and trample you underfoot." The uncle only chuckled in mock horror: "Good heavens, my dear! . . . I hope I'm a gentleman even when I'm writing a novel." [105] When he died on May 11, 1920, many Americans justly felt that an institution had passed.

There is much to say for the tradition he built and left behind. American writing, seeming to diverge from Realism in the twentieth century, has in fact merely followed a branch on the path. Without Howells' patient labors the path might not have been there. Much of his fiction lacks reality to modern readers, and much seems tiresome, but in sum it is impressive. Many of his books are as vital today as when they first appeared. He was not as radical as he once seemed, and his shortcomings are obvious. Henry James said that he lacked "a really *grasping* imagination." [106] Perhaps he meant that Howells lacked a sense of basic tension with his world, that he failed to create a separate world of his own, reflecting instead what he thought was a better picture of the one he had. He did too often mistake the apparent for the real. Anger, irritation, indignation—all of these Howells felt, but not alienation. He believed that nothing incurable afflicted America. In this he subordinated art to reform. But even the purists can surely forgive him by assessing the honesty of his effort and the impact it had upon his time and literature.

Realism triumphed so completely that it seemed pallid in his own lifetime. Whatever else may be said of him in criticism, he dealt with human themes, taking as his text the one common to all great art—the human predicament. One may quarrel with his means, but surely not with his aims, or the ends he achieved. The manner of treatment may have changed in modern fiction, but his themes and ideas remain.

He should not be dismissed as a mere pathfinder who prepared the way for others of great talent. If his total work was uneven, his purpose was always the same and always right—to broaden the scope of the American novel as he knew it. That was no easy charge and one to which he was true. Perceiving that valid art reflects the total context of man's life, the good and bad, the dark and light, the unseen and seen, he offered answers not only to old questions but to new ones that rose around his generation. He has been called timid, the producer of surface realism. Yet how many others of his contemporaries challenged popular opinion at a crucial moment like the Haymarket Riot? How many other writers and intellectuals preached a broader social humanism when most Americans seemed lethargic or indifferent? He had the sensitivity and intellect to feel approaching crises of great importance to all men, and to record them in his fiction. He had the courage both to warn and to praise, to demand as well as to reassure, to challenge established rules while telling his generation of the crucial transition era in which they lived. He seemed colorless to some, but he had the integrity and courage of his convictions, and they were right. These are not to be taken lightly. He ought to be well remembered for that as well as for the fiction he wrote.

The modern reader finds much in Howells' work that is quaint, some that is charming, and some that is arresting and vital. A reading of his works is like a tour through a portrait gallery. There is a sameness in many of the pictures, here and there a lack of color and excitement, and time has faded many. But now and then a picture takes on life and excitement, and fills the beholder with a sense of the artist's power and purpose. But one eye is on the guide, that deft and kindly gentleman who seems always to have been elderly, courtly, affectionate, quick of step, and shrewd of glance. The memory holds the picture of the gray head, nodding in agreement, and the gentle eyes lighting with controversy, the voice taking on an edge of authority and the manner of a teacher. So he stands in history, and in the minds of those who read him well.

Hamlin Garland: The Rebel as Escapist

Youth can afford to be a savage realist, for youth has boundless hope and confidence in itself. When a man begins to doubt his ability to reform the world by challenging it, he softens, allows himself to pity.

—1902

THE BUILDINGS rose up like a vision from Scheherazade's Thousand and One Nights. By day they glistened against blue lagoons and spraying fountains. By night they glowed in sparkling contours under the light of electric lamps. Visitors walked the esplanades and pathways around the central Court of Honor to see the exhibitions and marvel at the buildings. It was 1893, and all the world seemed to be in Chicago for the Windy City's exhibition in honor of Columbus' first voyage and to sing America's praises.

The fair symbolized the America of 1893. It was new, vital, dynamic in its mechanical gadgets and productive enterprises. But it was uncertain, gaudy, and derivative in its art and thought. Its Greek and Roman temples, soon to inaugurate an imitative craze that stifled native architecture, had no relation to Chicago or the United States. But the buildings' contents illustrated profound changes in American economics, politics, and social thought. Chicago's fantastic growth itself showed the nation's vital, if sometimes raw, material progress. A country so long agricultural in its economy and rural in its outlook paid homage here to the dynamo, the electric lamp, and the machine. They, not the plow, symbolized America's future.

It was a trifle incongruous even to the visitors, but it was exciting and beautiful. The spectacle drew millions from all over the world, emptying many Midwestern farm communities by the trainload, if only for a few days, as rustic America came to look into the mirror of its future. Among these crowds one afternoon walked an obviously rural family. The father's hands were roughened from toil, his limbs stiffened by the weather's abuses; but he was straight and authoritative. His son, handsomely bearded, stocky, caught the fair's symbolic meaning, and found it artificial and cold. There was too much to see and understand. As he pushed the wheel chair that held his mother, invalided by a slight stroke brought on by a lifetime of hard work, he spoke in low tones, pointing now and then to an especially important object. It was hot, tiring; and the tourists soon wearied, surfeited not merely by physical exhaustion, but by sadness at realizing how little their lives meshed with what the White City meant. At last the woman turned and said: "Take me home. I can't stand any more of it." [1] It was a generation's epitaph, and the young man who slowly turned her chair toward an exit was already its chief spokesman. As they disappeared through the crowds, the White City testified to the passing of their type. They were lost in the throng, but their family name would not be forgotten. The son was Hamlin Garland, spokesman of the Middle Border, pleader for literary realism and social reform, the last great singer from the frontier Midwest who captured both its harshness and sweetness in a small but rich body of literature.

Though he was a writer almost all his life, Hamlin Garland had only to raise his hand to prove he was a farm boy. It was thick, heavy though soft, obviously shaped by the plow and harness traces. He eliminated his country accent, improved his dress and manners, traveled to Europe, and knew most of two generation's famous writers; but he could not belie his country origins. He is remembered not for elegance, but for his delineation of a vanished America. He lived in Boston and New York, dined in London and Paris; but his sharpest memories came from the hinterland of a youth spent in frontier America, where he was born near West Salem, Wisconsin, on September 14, 1860.

He was the second of four children, named after Lincoln's first running-mate, Hannibal Hamlin of Maine. His father typified the restless, vigorous, and often brooding frontiersman in search of the sunset, undaunted by backbreaking labor, scorning the "back trail" of ease and security. A man of deep though quiet convictions, like many others when war came in 1861 he left his family to fight against slavery and for the Union. Years later his son caught this silent heroism and the whole flavor of his father's type in "The

Return of a Private," a moving testimony to both courage and idealism.

Free of war's burdens, Richard Garland moved his family west in search of fresh land, a new start, and the pioneer's freedom. They left Wisconsin, a land of green valleys and rolling hills, for the raw and isolated Iowa countryside. The elder Garland was a village representative for the Grange organization but after a short time returned to farming. He raised his family amid isolation, hard labor, and natural elements. It was a grim existence, and the sensitive Hamlin, put to work young not through parental cruelty but unthinking necessity, early resented his prospects. What could the bleak weather offer but a maddening sense of frustration? What good was the back-breaking labor if storms or drought or insects ruined a crop? What chance had he or anyone else to fulfill ideals and aspirations when labor filled every moment from dawn to dark? The loneliness, isolation, and paucity of intellectual stimulation that seemed inevitable to his neighbors and fellows sparked rebellion and bitterness in Hamlin Garland.

His rustic home, whatever its physical privations, was not without both charm and beauty. His father liked music and poetry and revealed a strain of oratorical prowess common to his Celtic origin and frontier life. Young Hamlin's uncles loved music, finding in it a secret fulfillment and escape. Filled with the pride of youth and joy of strength, they loved their nephew and his mother, Isabel McClintock Garland, later famous as "A Daughter of the Middle Border." Young Hamlin thought they represented the best of frontier manhood. They might wrestle jovially, or work 14 hours a day during harvesting, or merely turn cartwheels in the yard for sheer fun; but they were also mystical. "A deep vein of poetry, of subconscious Celtic sadness, ran through them all." [2] Their musical taste was not the best, but the tunes scraped from their battered violins stirred the sensitive young Hamlin as he brooded by the fire and saw genii in the flames. At those times his mother's face, so often covered with the veil of tiredness, relaxed into smiles and contentment.

Hamlin's childhood was uneventful, but steeped in the lore, geography, and spirit of both the Midwest and the pioneer type. Like any farm boy, he often rose at dawn on cold mornings and

ate a heavy breakfast before doing his "chores." As he grew older
he plowed furrows, pulled stumps, cared for animals, cleaned
stables, mended fence, and pursued the farmer's life for which he
seemed destined. A husking bee, a country dance, or a traveling
circus, aflame with gilt and glamor, offered a "brief season of
imaginative life"; but for the most part his youth was the story of
manual labor.[3]

But winter evenings afforded leisure over books, and he soon
discovered the romance of print. "My body was captive in our
snow-bound little cabin, but my mind ranged the golden palaces
of Persia," he recalled.[4] He often lay on his stomach under a large
stove, savoring both the welcome warmth and the adventures of
magazines and newspapers, "for I was born with a hunger for
print." [5] He appreciated the grandeur of his own environment, and
nature's glories as well as her harshness easily moved him. The
great oceans of green and golden corn, the undulating prairies and
forested valleys, the magnificent arc of sky, and the sweep of view
often carpeted with spring flowers made him seem part of the
whole. Fortunately for his later writing he never forgot the land's
magic power. Even as a child he felt the heroism inherent in the
type of men his father represented. ". . . I count myself fortunate
in the fact that my boyhood was spent in the midst of a charming
landscape and during a certain heroic era of western settlement,"
he wrote in middle age after devoting his youth to a bitter chronicle
of frontier life's limitations.[6]

He also knew, as the era's sentimental fictionists apparently did
not, that farm life was neither easy nor pleasant. It was all very
well to talk of rural virtues, nature's bounteous harvests, the freedom and ease of rural living; but the men who did the work knew
better. "Most authors in writing of 'the merry, merry farmer' . . .
omit the mud and the dust and the grime, they forget the army
worm, the flies, the heat, as well as the smells and drudgery of the
barns." [7] His father never understood Hamlin's literary inclinations,
but he was not tyrannical, and his mother tacitly supported his
ambitions to "make something of himself." On his fifteenth birth-
day, her small savings bought him a copy of *Paradise Lost,* which
he declaimed to a captive audience of plow mules until they bolted.

Restless motion was the frontier's history in a nutshell. The

Garlands moved on to homestead a claim in Dakota Territory, where at the mercy of fierce weather and rude isolation, young Hamlin did his best to please his father and beat the elements. After a howling blizzard that almost killed him and made life seem futile and unrewarding, he vowed to leave the frontier and "backtrail" to the settled and civilized East. He was "eager to escape the terror and the loneliness of the treeless sod. I began to plan for other work in other airs." [8] But how to escape? It seemed hopeless that an almost uneducated farm boy could make the golden journey to Boston or New York. A chance encounter with a traveling minister brought letters of introduction to Boston ministers. Grasping at this hope, Garland left home in 1881 to wander through New England for almost two years. Joined for a time by his younger brother Franklin, later a well-known actor, he moved through the mountains and valleys of what seemed a very old civilization. The penniless brothers worked at shingling, farm labor, and whatever came to hand. In seeking work he faced much hostility from farm people. His restless bitterness began to focus in a realization of the rootlessness, intellectual poverty, and actual want of much of mankind. Life was his school, and this was its chief lesson.

He returned to Dakota, where his family still wrung a living from the grudging land, but soon left home again to teach school for a year in Illinois in 1882 and 1883. Realizing the meagerness of his education, furnished by country schools and the Cedar Valley Seminary at Osage, Iowa, he read voraciously in his spare time. His hopes were myriad, his prospects few. Though he dreamed of a career, he did not yet know that it lay in writing. As always through his life, he sought to escape the reality he knew. He felt guilty at leaving his family, especially his uncomplaining mother. But he felt destiny stir within him and in 1884 left for Boston, the nation's intellectual symbol.

William Dean Howells came upon Boston as it entered its cultural twilight; Garland came at its sunset. He lived to see Chicago and New York finally triumph as America's artistic arbiters. But in his youth Boston's appeal was still awesome. What other city could boast such Brahmins as Holmes, Emerson,

Longfellow? Its name echoed greatness in the nation's past. Its
size baffled Garland, still the country youth in spite of his travels.
"By contrast with Ordway, it was appallingly splendid." He walked
from the train station because he had no money for carfare and,
clutching his cheap valise, innocently asked directions of policemen
and passers-by. "I was a bewildered plainsman, a scared rustic in
the midst of a gigantic metropolis. With but two clear ideas in my
head, one to make my money go as far as possible, and the other
to get all the learning I could while it lasted, I settled into place." [9]
It was a brave if rash attempt, for he had only a hundred and forty
dollars to last the winter.

Under the sympathetic eye of a kindly landlady in a cheap
boardinghouse, he carefully saved his strength and money. He ate
little, and his robust frame grew weak, his brown skin pallid
under a regimen of enforced study that tried to make up for his
lost youth. In the public library he "read with desperate inten-
sity," running the gamut of disciplines in his assault on learning.
He savored "the sea of song" that was Walt Whitman's verse and
devoured sociological and historical treatises with both ease and
confusion. Like most young people, "I learned a little of everything
and nothing very thoroughly"; but he was on the right road. He
stood shivering in his thin coat and worn shoes at the library doors
when they opened, and was driven from the reading rooms at the
last evening hour, resentful of losing even a minute in his self-
education. As a nonresident he could not take books home, nor
could he audit classes at Harvard. But he approached Edward
Everett Hale with the combination of awe and brass that later
brought him introductions to almost every important writer of his
time. With that worthy's endorsement, he checked out books and
redoubled his efforts, devoting evenings to reading. [10]

His life was not all reading. Surrounded by the city's bustle,
vitality, and glamor, the names of celebrated statesmen and artists
on every hand, Garland also attended symphony concerts, the
theater, and public lectures. Alone in the evenings, or brooding
somberly on his poverty, he desperately sought a focus in his life
and half-formed abilities. He wrote, putting into his first crude
short stories the saving grace of reality and a tough-minded grim-

ness at once fascinating and painful. He poured out "an insistence on the painful as well as the pleasant truth, a quality which was discovered afterwards to be characteristic of my work." [11]

Always gregarious, as well as frankly ambitious, he contrived in various ways to meet his idols and people who might help him. In the next few years, as he clung tenaciously both to his emerging literary ideals and his educational regimen, he went to Camden to see Whitman, who received him kindly, sitting "majestic as a stranded sea-God . . ." in a clutter of books and papers.[12] Mixing humility with brashness, he met the editors of New England's great quarterlies and published small bits of poetry and prose in some of them. His real hero was Howells, whose work he had first condemned but now admired. If he wrote he could only be a realist. He presumed upon a faint friendship, and a card of introduction from an editor who had printed some of his reviews of Howells' work. He disturbed the novelist at lunch, and as he waited in an anteroom had no idea of his reception. "The curtain parted and a short man with a handsome head stood before me," he remembered years later. "His face was impassive but his glance was one of the most piercing I had ever encountered. In that single instant, before he smiled, he discovered my character, divined my state of mind, and probably inventoried my clothing." [13] With his usual kindness and interest in young people, Howells encouraged Garland's writing, recognizing in him a potential voice from the West. "He was as poor as he was young," Howells himself recalled of their meeting, "but he was so rich in purpose of high economic and social import that he did not know that he was poor." [14]

Knowing firsthand the rich literary resources of the Midwest, Garland found its lack of treatment in contemporary fiction surprising. In his reading, Edward Eggleston's *The Hoosier Schoolmaster* (1871) and *The Circuit Rider* (1874) showed the potential that rural life on the frontier offered the fictionist. Though crude and only partly realized, these works held a fascinating grimness and fidelity to life that made them pioneers. Combined with E. W. Howe's more artistic *The Story of a Country Town* (1883) and Joseph Kirkland's *Zury* (1887) and *The McVeys* (1888), they opened a field for fiction in a region not yet prominent in the local color movement. These stories of the life Garland knew so well deeply touched him, and Kirkland became a close friend and supporter. Late in life, Garland referred to Eggleston as "the father of us all" when dealing with his region's fiction.[15]

Literature fascinated him, but economics and politics seemed more vital at the moment. He read Henry George's *Progress and Poverty* and became a single-tax advocate. "The trumpet call of the closing pages filled me with a desire to battle for the right," he remembered, and he moved steadily into the emerging Populist movement.[16] Herbert Spencer's doctrine of evolutionary social progress fascinated him, not because he thought it good, but because he thought he saw it at work in his own life. The evolutionary design offered a rational explanation for the grimness, hard work, and occasional despair he knew on the farm and in the city. It also promised that progress would come from man's struggles. A mind that admired the work of Whitman, Spencer, Howells, Twain, and the local colorists revealed confusion as well as range. But it also showed his efforts to find a pattern in life's meaning, and to write realistically for social as well as artistic ends.

Endowed with an alert if not original mind, easily absorbing his milieu, Garland quickly worked his way into Boston's intellectual grooves. Though still poor and struggling, he socialized a great deal. ". . . although a colossal bore when preaching the single tax or defining the local-color school in fiction, I had moments of being companionable." [17] With hard work and study, he made important social and intellectual contacts. Slowly his reviews, reports, and occasional articles and short stories printed in local newspapers and magazines mounted up. Destitute and despairing at one point, he thought of abandoning his studies. Friends made him a "Professor of Elocution and Literature," and he lectured to attentive audiences. Despite nervousness and self-consciousness about dress, speech, and manners, he spoke confidently, impressing listeners with an innate vigor and native talent. Whether talking on the art of Edwin Booth, Howells' fiction, or local color, he was forceful and appreciative. "He struck a deep key and did not sharp or flat at the close," one news reporter noted.[18]

A combination of guilt, curiosity, and homesickness drove Garland back to the family homestead in 1887, with stops in Chicago to see Kirkland and other writers and editors. Traveling from Boston to the Dakotas was a journey between worlds. Pity, remorse, and outrage welled up in him as he walked among his old neighbors and saw the pathetic little towns strung along the railroad tracks. The drab houses, attended by worn and listless women who only a few years before were young beauties, made him wince. He saw friends of his own age scarred by farming, hands roughened, frames stooped, minds arrested by brute labor. The isolation and endemic loneliness of farm life appalled him, for they stood in sharp relief against his experiences in Boston. Tragedy lay over the whole picture, and in his bitterness he resolved to do something about it. "The essential tragedy and hopelessness of most human life under the conditions into which our society was swiftly hardening embittered me, called for expression, but even then I did not know that I had found my theme." [19]

His mother's physical condition shocked him, for she had aged terribly under her burden. His father seemed impervious to the change and was as restless and hard-working as ever. Garland suddenly saw that romantic notions of farm life were false. He returned to Boston determined to crusade for economic reforms and to help himself and his family escape their toil. His indignation became purpose. Having lived in two worlds, he had standards of comparison:

I perceived little that was poetic, little that was idyllic, and nothing that was humorous in the man, who, with hands like claws, was scratching a scanty living from the soil of a rented farm, while his wife walked her ceaseless round from tub to churn and from churn to tub. On the contrary, the life of such a family appeared to me as an almost unrelievedly tragic futility.[20]

He had found his theme and his method: "Obscurely forming in my mind were two great literary concepts—that truth was a higher quality than beauty, and that to spread the reign of justice should everywhere be the design and intent of the artist." [21]

If Garland did not yet know precisely how to elucidate his theme, he at least understood what was wrong with the current view of rural life:

Up to this time writers on farm life had arranged the weather pleasingly. It was always lovely in June and the haymakers 'tossed the fragrant clover' wearing jaunty, wide-rimmed hats, while the girls in dainty white gowns looked on from the shade of a stately tree. At frequent intervals the toilers gathered about the mossy well curb and sang "The Old Oaken Bucket." Corn-husking was equally social. Laughing lads and blushing lassies gathered in the barn of a moonlit October evening to husk the ears from garnered stalks and the finders of red ears won kisses from the maidens. . . . All our rustic plays contained a male quartet, toilers who spent a great deal of time in the shade leaning on their hay forks and yodeling.[22]

Garland came to his material in a different manner and with a different purpose, for "My mood was dark and bitter." [23] The short stories and novelettes he wrote in the late 1880s and early 1890s formed a central design, the truthful delineation of farm life and the frontier spirit, told in a conversational style without ornamentation that spared no sordid facts or grim tone. He wrote of husking bees where ears of corn made hands bleed. He wrote of the land, never forgetting its glories, but showing nature's harshness, the mercilessness of isolation, the perversity of marketing. The Populist combined with the writer in him to pour out his bitter outrage at man-made laws that made others rich from the farmer's toil. He showed the stultification, ignorance, and desolation of life for the vast majority of farmers.

All these themes and subjects led to his most famous book, *Main-Travelled Roads* (1891), that put him in the front rank of Realistic writers. Its dedication page proclaimed his purpose and in a few lines set the book's bitter tone: "To my father and mother whose half-century pilgrimage on the main-travelled road of life has brought them only toil and deprivation, this book of stories is dedicated by a son to whom every day brings a deepening sense of his parents' silent heroism."

A book that was "so robust and terribly serious," as Howells said, offered no concessions to those seeking romance. The main-travelled road had no glamor for Garland. "Mainly it is long and wearyful, and has a dull little town at one end and a home of toil at the other. Like the main-travelled road of life it is traversed by many classes of people, but the poor and the weary predominate." [24] The book's style made it a major contribution to Realism and bore in it the seeds of a Naturalism that others developed.

Surfeited with rural sentimentality, sick of those who avoided reality, he made one story, "The Return of a Private," a special essay in truth. Based on his own father's return from the Civil War, it told in stark detail the horrors of war and the simplicity of homecoming. To those seeking glamor's sweetness, he offered candor's bitterness in his simple graphic style:

He thought of his chum, Billy Tripp. Poor Billy! A "minie" ball fell into his breast one day, fell wailing like a cat, and tore a great ragged hole in his heart. . . . He tried to recall all that Billy had said and the particulars of it, but there was little to remember, just that wild wailing sound high in the air, a dull slap, a short, quick, explosive groan, and the boy lay with his face in the dirt in the ploughed field they were marching across.[25]

But the land and its people interested him most. Familiar with the West's "boom spirit" and its gift of brag, he saw it with candid eyes, noting its towns on the railroad tracks or along the main-travelled roads for what they were. "How poor and dull and sleepy and squalid it seemed! The one main street ended at the hillside at his left, and stretched away to the north, between two rows of the usual village stores, unrelieved by a tree or a touch of beauty." [26]

Across the countryside, resting like stranded vessels, stood the houses, pathetic clapboarded unpainted affairs, often only one or two rooms. In their yards stood the pump and horse trough; at their backs stretched the barns and animal pens; farther still stood the plumbing. A desolate tree marked a wife's efforts at decoration, but the weeds around it too often showed how little time or strength remained to cultivate beauty. He remembered his own home in all its external drabness when he wrote of a "sitting-room, poor, bare, art-forsaken . . . with its rag carpet, its square clock, and its two or three chromos and pictures from *Harper's Weekly* pinned about." [27]

His indignation and pity rose when he thought of the people trapped within such walls, living lives of toil without beauty's comfort or mental growth. In fifteen years or less, sheer work turned his mother from a woman in her prime to an invalid. His younger sister died. One by one his uncles fell into ruined grandeur, still seeking the will-o'-the-wisp of success on the plains, arrested like men in dreams, moving forever in the same place. What did this life of toil, childbearing, animal-tending, and isolation offer the women in particular? "A few hours in the middle of the day on Sunday, three or four holidays in the summer; the rest of the year, for this cheerful little wife and her patient husband was made up of work —work which accomplished little and brought them almost nothing that was beautiful." [28] Garland caught the aching pathos of this cheer; it reflected a brute existence just as the more common surliness or torpor did. He held his mother's picture in his mind when he wrote in "Up the Coolly": "My God! How little it would have taken to lighten her life!" [29] Most farm women were like old Mrs. Ripley. They harbored the secret dream of escape, just as this stout soul nourished the hope of a final visit to her family in the East. She made her trip and returned without complaint to her accustomed rounds. "She took up her burden again, never more thinking to lay it down." [30]

Though it flashed occasionally with humor, the book breathed pessimism and grim tension, best illustrated in "Up the Coolly." Howard, a famous and prosperous actor, returned home to find his brother Grant trapped in farming, bitter at his own failure and Howard's glittering success. Money, success, and mental development and culture separated them. Howard had taken the lifeblood from Grant in escaping the farm, leaving his brother and mother to toil without profit in the ruts of their existence. Nor could the offer of help restore what the years had taken. "I mean life ain't worth very much to me," Grant said simply. "I'm too old to take a new start. I'm a dead failure. I've come to the conclusion that life's a failure for ninety-nine per cent of us. You can't help me now. It's too late." [31] Howard faced the bitter realization that all men are linked together, and that one draws from another in the scheme of life.

Spoken in grim tones, written in candor, dealing with human types, *Main-Travelled Roads* contains some of the finest short stories in American fiction. Three generations later, when most Americans live in the city, these stories hold the ring of truth. Like some tocsin in the night of the nation's past, they remind all who read them of the toil, sacrifice, and human effort upon which the country's development rests. Somber, grim, but lightened with just enough humor to be real, the book breathes belief in life's value, a love of people, and an outrage at oppression that makes it as real now as in 1891. Filled with the pain of brute labor, the loneliness of rural life, the grimness of existence where there is little light, the characters stand like figures caught forever in pure amber.

Main-Travelled Roads was a major plea for realism in the literary wars, and Howells quickly applauded it. "The type caught in Mr. Garland's book is not pretty," he said; "it is ugly and often ridiculous; but it is heart-breaking in its rude despair." [32] Garland "put in the storm as well as the sun. I included the mud and manure as well as the wild roses and the clover." [33] As a work of art, the book was an outstanding success; as a social document, it aimed frankly at "the comfortable, the conservative, those who farmed the farmer. . . ." [34]

The Middle Border received the book with a shock. Those there who read it often felt outraged; Garland was a traitor for attacking the idea of rural bliss. His work countered Western optimism and expansion. He seemed to repudiate his own heritage. But sometimes he received letters commending his honesty from people like those he wrote about. "You are entirely right about the loneliness, the stagnation, the hardship," one farm wife wrote him. "We are sick of lies. Give the world the truth." [35]

The book was Garland's credentials of admission into realistic writing. "In truth I was welcomed into the circle of American realists with an instant and generous greeting which astonished, at the same time that it delighted me." [36] And his personal satisfaction was even greater, for with its proceeds he moved his mother to Wisconsin where she spent her declining years in comparative comfort. "The pen had proved itself to be mightier than the plow." [37]

The literary wars in which *Main-Travelled Roads* figured were no less severe for their display of words rather than bullets, as Howells had already discovered. It cost something to be a Realist when the high road to wealth and public acclaim was paved with costumery and sentimental escapism. Garland followed the battles with intense interest, heightened by his affection and regard for Howells and the local colorists, strengthened by his firm belief that writing should have a social as well as an artistic purpose. He could not remain silent as the battle raged. "It was a lively contest, and being strong for native art, I naturally took a fist in it." [38]

Armed with youth's vigor, the candor of harsh experience, and the power of a gifted sympathy, Garland did not doubt where or how to begin. In 1894 he issued his manifesto, *Crumbling Idols,* a collection of critical papers he wrote during the white heat of composition that surrounded *Main-Travelled Roads.* Issued in a green binding, heavily embossed with gold corn stalks, the little book breathed truculence and vigor. Taking his stand with Realistic writing, Garland turned west for fresh inspiration and new materials. There the land was new, rugged, and grand. Its people faced nature, life, and each other in dramatic daily confrontations fit for Realism's pen. Cities rose from the prairies to create new problems.

He began first with a condemnation, for the West had not used its raw materials for art, had not produced the geniuses it should have. Its people read imitative writing and thrived on the sentimental in the midst of hard reality. But the land had vitality, life, color; and these were the attributes Garland hoped would make first a sectional and then a national Realistic literature. He was frank in his attack on stylish literature, almost overeager in his assault on the imitative and unreal, calling on the West to embrace Realism. "The West should aim to be wise rather than cultured. Wisdom is democratic, culture is aristocratic. Wisdom is knowledge of principle, culture is knowledge of forms and accepted conditions; the contention is the world old, but necessary." [39]

Garland appealed for a fresh vitality, new themes, a different approach in writing that was grounded in experience common to all men. This could only come from the local colorist, the writer deeply immersed in the customs, people, and physical environment of a given section. In depth studies he could add a fragment to the national mosaic. In England, local colorists and provincial writers "are putting to rout the two-volume British novel, which never leaves anything out and never puts anything in." Pointing abroad to Ibsen in Norway, Kipling in England, Zola in France, the whole Russian group of Realists and Naturalists, Garland saw the local colorist in the van of literary progress. ". . . Art, to be vital, must be local in its subject; its universal appeal must be in its working out—in the way it is done." [40]

Writers should reflect what they know, not what they wished. Garland dubbed his movement "Veritism," that which could be verified in daily experience. But it would not be Naturalism or deterministic; nor did he propose any greater frankness than Howells already offered. Already he betrayed an aversion to sex and the sordid that turned his later work to romance. "This literature . . . will deal, I believe, with the wholesome love of honest men for honest women, with the heroism of labor, the comradeship of men,—a drama of average types of characters, infinitely varied, but always characteristic." [41]

The essays held suspended, in prose too often purple, the dregs of bitterness and tension, and a ringing sense of outrage, that made *Crumbling Idols* a clarion call for political as well as literary reformers. Garland revealed the limitations of his artistic talent with becoming candor in pleading for a native literary realism that would have a social purpose. "The realist or veritist is really an optimist, a dreamer. He sees life in terms of what it might be, as well as in terms of what it is; but he writes of what is, and, at his best, suggests what is to be, by contrast." [42] He was quite honest in selecting themes and styles. He chose to treat those things that enhanced the democratic agrarian tradition, and rejected those which did not. He revealed his reformer's bent, as well as the limits of his artistic design, when he called the artist a voice of the masses, not an individual creative genius:

. . . literary power is not personal; it is at bottom sociologic. The power of the writer is derived from the society in which he lives; like the power of a general which springs from the obedience of his army. When society changes, when his audience dies, the writer's power passes away.[43]

Nothing better illustrated the reasons for Garland's later decline. Always interested in people rather than ideas, he was stranded when the types he knew disappeared. Functioning well only in a milieu of tension, he fell victim to tranquility when that tension evaporated after the climactic events of the 1890s.

Crumbling Idols breathed its author's fervent belief in the social values of art; but it was also superficial in its esthetics, overwritten in style, and imitative in its philosophy. Veritism was little more than Howells' Realism intensified on a local scale. "Mr. Garland's message to the writer is this: Write of what you know. . . . His discovery of so trite a truth hardly justified a cataclysm in celebration," an unfriendly reviewer sneered.[44] While this was unduly harsh, Garland's own reflection in later life was perhaps not all false modesty: "In truth the attention which this iconoclastic declaration of faith received at the hands of critics was out of all proportion to its size." [45]

Though he was young, bombastic in his critical manifestoes, filled with youthful rawness that caused many to discount his unconscious aggressiveness, Garland was a figure in Realism. He had friends in high places, and he had written important books. There was ample opportunity to practice his social and artistic theories, for the decade of the 1890s, far from "gay," was a time of unrest and change in all spheres of American life. The farmers' crusade, known as Populism, that climaxed in the election of 1896, reflecting deep discontent in the Midwest and South, most immediately concerned Garland; for he knew the source of agricultural ills. He campaigned for Populist political candidates and between 1891 and 1893 lectured to farm groups for the radical *Arena*. Falling prices, bad weather, unequal distribution of wealth, and an inflexible financial system penalized the farmer. His remedies were free silver to inflate the currency and ease his debt load, and more government intervention to equalize economic opportunities.

Captivated by the excitement surrounding this political revolt, Garland lent himself to the movement without reservations. *The Arena,* frankly radical, and managed by the sympathetic Benjamin O. Flower, provided a ready outlet for his work. His travels gave Garland new contact with the rural areas he had left. They also instilled in him a vague but potent sense of the tensions inherent in the clash of city and rural life, of the power in the waves of immigrants who swamped Eastern and Midwestern cities, and of the complexity of the whole social problem of human living. Unlike Howells, he lacked the persistence or acuteness to register these feelings in solidly developed and extended work. But like litmus paper, he showed the stresses and strains of his world and time through sensitivity and sympathy.

In *Jason Edwards* (1892), dedicated to "The Farmers' Alliance . . . with its implied hatred of all special privileges," Garland outlined these themes. The book was an essay on environment, opening in Boston's teeming working-class districts, where Jason Edwards, "an average man," was about to lose his job because of factory cutbacks. An aspiring newspaper reporter, Wallace Reeves, strongly attracted to Edwards' daughter Alice, urged the family to leave the city's squalor and disorder. The father was eager to go west, to the land of opportunity. As he walked its streets, much like Garland himself, Reeves saw the city's impersonality, disorder, and dirt. It failed to give intellectual stimulation and mental growth to most of its peoples. It was not so different from the farm in its lower-class quarters. Its chief horror was the ease with which people accepted it. After a while no one seemed to notice the environment. The smells vanished, the noise disappeared, the dirt and filth did not offend the eye. Men whistled and children played ball, girls flirted in surroundings the stranger found repellent until he too became accustomed. "That they could sit and talk with such surroundings was sorrowful evidence that it was habitual, and to some degree unnoticed," he said of the courtship between Alice Edwards and Reeves.[46]

In its honest descriptions of tenement life, and its acknowledgment of the dark presence of sex in the streets, the book anticipated Stephen Crane's *Maggie* (1893). But Garland was not the Naturalist committed to iron laws; the sin here was not of the city, but of the men who allowed it to become tawdry and disordered. As a good environmentalist, Garland argued that society's evils flowed not from nature but from man-made laws.

Driven by desperation and hope born of romantic descriptions culled from calendars and railroad posters, the Edwards family moved west to homestead. Like most Americans, the land of the sunset "was something mythic . . . to these men."[47] Their dreams clashed sharply with reality. They found the land itself not merely wild, but infested with speculators and false promises. Convinced of their freedom from landlords in the West, seeking pastoral beauty and riches, they found instead "A wide-walled grave, arched by a mocking sinister sky." [48] After a violent hailstorm, Jason Edwards suffered a stroke while seeing his crops reduced to stubble, and the family returned to Boston with little hope for a better future.

Jason Edwards suffered from its approach, not its subject. In Howells' hands, the story could have been a major statement on the passing agrarian frontier and the flaws of city life. But Garland made it a lurid Populist tract. He later omitted it from an edition of his works on good grounds. "It is too short, too sour of temper, too drab of clothing, too preachy." [49] Had the story been properly developed, with detachment and reality, all but the last charge could be forgiven. It had its merits; it was new, it suggested broader fields of discovery. But it was ephemeral and was "of value only as an indication of the bitter and accusing mood of that day. . . ." [50]

This sense of heated outrage carried over into his hastily written *A Member of the Third House* (1892), serialized in *The Arena.* Dealing with politics in the atmosphere of bribery and corporation domination so dear to Populist theories, the book indicted public indifference to government. It condemned business lobbying in government, proclaiming proudly: "We can't allow in this republic any corporation, no matter how good its intentions, to dominate legislation or shelter itself under the cloak of bribery." [51] Its time and place were indefinite, but it reflected Garland's belief in the essential wrongness of many American political attitudes. Like its predecessor, it contained undeveloped ideas important to the whole reform movement.

But Garland had left his milieu and could not create believable characters or dialogue. The book was bloated, rhetorical, and unreal. Its chapters bore such titles as "The Rout of the Rats," and the author interposed dialogue like: "The men stared at each other as a nest of rats might, feeling the shock of corn shake over their heads." [52] Against the background of persecuted and oppressed farmers and corrupted public interest, the lobby and its agents ran to and fro like something out of a bad melodrama.

Both these socioeconomic novels lacked development and the sense of reality which Garland took as a trademark, partly because he did not understand the milieu in which he set them, but largely because he was less the artist than the pamphleteer in writing them. He resolved to cover the bare bones of plot with the flesh of realism in the last of a triumvirate of social novels, *A Spoil of Office* (1892), dealing with the rise and impact of the farmers' protest groups in the Populist movement. He dedicated it to Howells, "the foremost historian of our common lives and the most vital figure in our literature. . . ."

The book opened describing a country picnic, where farm problems and Grange business were discussed. It introduced its hero, Bradley Talcott, and offered an impressive start for a chronicle of farm life in protest. Much like *Main-Travelled Roads,* it did not blink at the realities of hard work and rural loneliness. "The sombre shadow of the farm's drudgery had fallen again on faces unused to smiling," he noted of the farmers returning home after the picnic.[53]

Bradley Talcott was the last of Garland's realistic rural characters. Powerful of frame, he also had the endurance and ability to grow mentally that marked the frontiersman in Garland's mind. "He had the mysterious power of self-development." [54] Elected to office, he dared win dramatic reforms, but due to political manipulation was defeated for re-election. But not before falling in love with and marrying Ida Wilbur, feminist and Populist agitator modeled no doubt on the famous "Kansas Pythoness," Mary E. Lease. The book ended with their resolution to devote their married life to reform. Like its predecessor, the novel was a vote for the "new woman" then coming into prominence, and excoriated public indifference toward political and social issues. It also preached a doctrine that Garland elaborated in his old age—the value of an educated and responsible elite and the danger of an uneducated mass.[55]

Garland might have said of all these novels what he wrote of *A Spoil of Office:* "In the writing of it I had remained too much the orator, too consistently the advocate. The book lacked artistry. Too much of it was written on the train. I hurried too fast and I included too much." [56] But despite their lack of development and stilted style, the books reflected the tensions and bitterness of the 1890s. They were major documents of the Populist revolt, and breathed that movement's sense of conspiratorial opposition and simple, striking answers to the era's complex problems. They held occasional glimpses of what Garland might have done, for their plots could have been developed into something as moving and rich as Howells' *A Modern Instance*.

In these novels and his other writings, Garland developed a social theory as simple as the indignation behind it. He believed in honest democratic government, holding that it worked badly only because the people did not reform it. He believed in social equality as he had seen it in his own frontier existence: a compound of neighborliness, consideration for others, and individual work. The era's chief need was equal economic opportunity. This countered all claims for socialism, and Garland was never a communitarian. He cherished the spirit of pioneer individualism too much to believe in socialism. The evils in society and life in general came not from competition, he argued, but monopoly.

Given his belligerence, not without its charm, and his intense convictions, Garland made rewarding social and literary progress in the mid-1890s. This came in part from Howells, who was never open to flattery and who criticized Garland's work with unvarnished truth. Though a basic affinity for literary realism and a strong interest in social justice drew the two men together, they were not artistic peers. Howells' realism reflected his keen observation, which he managed to reproduce in rich writing, carefully shaded and developed, though filled with the same urgent sense of social justice. Garland was grimly determined to reform the system that thwarted progress. His commitment was more personal and less detached than Howells. His impact was more immediate and more emotional, but his writing was thinner and less developed. Howells was a painter, Garland a photographer.

In the mid-1890s, Garland stood at a personal and artistic crossroads. His books added to the swelling chorus of Realism. His stature and ideas fed into the streams of social discontent that eddied about the nation's problems. But while he was something of a critical success, his financial rewards were slender. Many condemned or praised his books; relatively few bought them. He verged on middle age with little to show for all his effort but a modest critical reputation. Always filled with nervous energy, he looked for a deeper, richer theme that might set him in the front rank of American writers. In 1894 and 1895 he worked at an extended novel, *Rose of Dutcher's Coolly* (1895).

Convinced for the moment that he should raise his voice for his section and people, he made Rose Dutcher a symbol of the Middle Border. He showed America in microcosm in her pilgrimage from country to city, from a kind of mental slavery to the independence proclaimed by the whole generation of thinkers and reformers. He took Rose from a rustic coolly in Wisconsin to Chicago, from the intellectual poverty of rural life to an awakening to the city's riches and splendor. In her journey he developed artistically a fine fictional character and showed again, but in subtler form, the social and intellectual problems facing America. ". . . I attempted to embody in *Rose of Dutcher's Coolly,* a picture of Chicago as an ambitious young girl from the Wisconsin farm would see it." [57]

Stolid little Rose, a silent but observing child, gifted with a native intelligence and gentle cunning, was filled with the joy and pain of life. "Sometimes when alone she slipped off her clothes and ran amid the tall corn stalks like a wild thing. Her slim little brown body slid among the leaves like a weasel in the grass." [58] She had only the farm's amusements, and brooded silently on her destiny, feeling within herself forces that could make her exceptional. Not given to flights of fancy, she nonetheless adored a traveling circus performer, taking him as a symbol of the glamor and beauty she longed to have.

Rose of Dutcher's Coolly was filled with the tensions of adolescence, and spoke of sexual matters that Howells and other Realists shunned. Garland did not blink at rural life's seamier side. Rose knew of sex, felt it stir within her, vaguely understood that her compatriots knew it too. But the snickers, scrawlings, and innuendoes that accompanied it repelled her. "She learned early the signs which pass in the country to describe the unnamable and covert things of human life. She saw them scrawled on fences, on schoolhouse doors, and written in the dust of the road. There was no escaping them. The apparently shameful fact of sex faced her everywhere." [59]

Determined to escape country life and the grim existence that awaited most girls, Rose went to the University of Wisconsin.

One year's study showed her the distance between what she could become and what she had been. "I can't stand these little petty things here in this valley," she cried, "these women drive me crazy with their talk of butter and eggs and made-over bonnets." [60] She wanted something better than early marriage to a dull husband, the inevitable brood of children, the isolation of weather and distance. In showing the danger of marriage to the gifted intellect, Garland recalled the tone of vivid imagery of *Main-Travelled Roads:*

Most of the girls were precocious in the direction of marriage, and brought all their little allurements to bear with the same purpose which directs the coquetry of a city belle. At sixteen they had beaux, at seventeen many of them actually married, and at eighteen they might often be seen with their husbands, covered with dust, clasping their wailing babes in their arms; at twenty they were not infrequently thin and bent in the shoulders, and flat and stiff in the hips, having degenerated into sallow and querulous wives of slovenly, careless husbands.[61]

The last half of *Rose* dealt with her problems in adjusting to city life, of realizing that she had forsaken not merely her way of life but her family. Her chief tragedy, like Garland's, was to leave loved ones behind. The old generation fed life into the new, and in a sense destroyed itself. Rose's father, who confidently expected her to return home after her education, cried upon seeing her marry and remain in the city. ". . . he had educated his daughter out of his world." [62]

Toward her journey's end, Rose's ideals underwent a subtle change. Love entered her life, and self slipped into the void of common understanding. By degrees she welcomed life into her heart, prepared to give as well as receive. A rather businesslike marriage completed her circle of development, but she slowly lost her ideas of reforming or changing the world. "She no longer thought of conquering the world; it came to be the question of winning the approbation of one human soul." [63]

Rose of Dutcher's Coolly deserves to be better known. Though it breaks in half and is in essence two novels, its first part contains some finely constructed narrative and well-developed characters. It evokes not only a past America, but a time of life. It is full of the tensions, yearnings, and frustrations of youth and adolescence. It touches upon the force of sex in life, a surprising venture for Garland. When Garland left his milieu in the book's second half, it ceased to be real. His tone became tired and character development faltered. If *Main-Travelled Roads* was bitter, *Rose* was bittersweet. Garland was at the end of his viable career as a realistic writer. As usual, Howells' astute criticism touched the book's weak as well as strong points. While praising the story's truth, even in details he disliked, "there is a strain of sentimentality which discredits it. . . ." [64]

In his work before 1900, Garland touched upon themes whose further development could have made him a major novelist. No one had better delineated the narrowness, terror, and tragedy of rural life. Few had spoken with greater eloquence and meaning of the pioneer spirit ingrained in his country's whole history. His handling of social themes showed a keen sympathy. The mysteries of sex, the demands of genius, the changing face of America in city and country, the revolutionized economy that threatened old concepts of individualism and freedom—these clearly revealed a perceptive if undeveloped talent.

But as the new century dawned, Garland turned to a world of romantic escapism, set in the High Country of the Rocky Mountains, and dealing with cowboys, Indians, forest rangers, and cattle barons. The bulk of this work showed only a residual interest in social themes, and had little artistic merit. His turn to romanticism after so many years of preaching realism was startling but logical. He approached middle age with little to show for his sacrifices. He acquired a wife and family to support. He loved the adventuresome outdoors so much that he joined the Alaska gold rush in 1898 without a second thought. Disappointed at the passing of social issues he had fought for, a trifle bitter that his work had accomplished so little for reform, he turned frankly for a backward look, seeking in nostalgia the comfort and sense of purpose he could not attain in reform or Realism.

Of the adventure novels that followed, *The Captain of the Grey-Horse Troop* (1902) was his swan song to Realism. Dealing with the attempts of cattle barons to seize Indian lands, it praised the vanishing red men who stood for the passing frontier. Integrity, honor, duty combined in the Captain to make him as much a type, if less realistically, as the people of *Main-Travelled Roads*. Garland filled this book and those that followed with glowing and colorful descriptions of western locale; they dealt with battles and intrigues, and added the inevitable love story that made each successive volume an essay in mediocrity. *The Captain of the Grey-Horse Troop* was colorful, exciting, tinged with outrage at mistreatment of the Indians; but its characters were pasteboard and its action stilted. Though it sometimes held the tone of his old outrage and tension, their substance was gone.

That Garland frankly sought commercial success was illustrated in his care in seeking a publisher and his insistence upon the book's promotion and advertising. The novel ultimately drew praise from Theodore Roosevelt, was made into a bowdlerized movie, and sold about 100,000 copies. Critics were quick to see the advantages in his change of theme and tone. "The Indian is not likely to write to the newspapers and object to being championed, as did a Kansas farmer's wife in the days when Mr. Garland was the champion of the oppressed inhabitants of Wisconsin, Kansas, and Nebraska." [65]

Howells had matured in his middle years into the rich Realism of *Silas Lapham* and *A Hazard of New Fortunes,* but Garland followed another trail into the high country of escape. His writing had flowed from the tensions of bitterness and outrage at the inequities of his world. When they passed he lapsed into a natural romanticism. His mind functioned well only in the milieu of external tension; and when the nation prospered, reformed, and took up new political and international problems, Garland became an echo of the past. He had personal reasons for the change, which he readily admitted:

All my emotional relationships with the "High Country" were pleasant, my sense of responsibility was less keen, hence the notes of resentment, of opposition to unjust social conditions which had made my other books an offense to many readers were almost entirely absent in my studies of the mountaineers. My pity was less challenged in their case. Lonely as their lives were, it was not a sordid loneliness. [66]

It would be easy to criticize his decision to take "the back trail" to ease and comfort, but wiser to understand the unrewarded hardships he endured for his art. He was worn down, tired, and above all, felt the task of change hopeless. He could be humorous as well as realistic about his late fiction, noting how he and friends wrote "books of far-off glorious wildernesses and hurry back to Fifth Avenue to sell them. . . ." [67] If "None of them [his books] were sufficiently sensual in appeal to win a large audience," they nonetheless assured him of a steady income.[68] He always sought recognition over wealth, and was content to bask in the glow of stature, attending dinners, making speeches, receiving honorary degrees, as he settled into old age. "Although I filled but a very small place in the world of fiction, I could not afford to lose that," he admitted candidly.[69]

Those who thought his turn from Veritism out of character were wrong. His whole artistic development was logical. His mind never really left home; it merely went upstairs for a clearer view and cleaner air. Howells put his finger on Garland's weakness in 1912, when he wrote: "If I may confess a dreadful secret, I suspected them both [James A. Hearne and Garland] at that time of being unconsciously romantic at heart, and only kept to reality because they did not know unreality." [70]

One great task remained for Garland. If he could not chronicle the present any longer, he could re-create the past. After years of labor, he produced in 1917 *A Son of the Middle Border*. Filled with a sense of life's wonder, written with a rustic charm, spiced with humor, and echoing the compelling call of a whole epoch of American history, the book is a classic of its kind. He knew that the Border was more a state of mind than a place, and told G. B. Shaw that "It lay between the land of the hunter and the harvester." [71] It was gone and would never return except in the nostalgia of an old man's dreams, but he reminded the nation of its existence and importance. From the vantage point of 1917, torn by war and disorder, *A Son of the Middle Border* seemed "a truthful picture of life in a simpler, more unhurried age." [72]

In the long years left Garland produced no significant fiction, but remained a pillar of respectable literature and an institution in American culture. Occasionally he lectured, like some ghost from the past, elegant in his attire, striking in his frame of white hair and elderly geniality. Who would have thought that he who so often then sounded like a lesser Howells and looked like a lesser Twain had once been a fiery radical or the center of a swirling literary controversy? To those who called for his old style he had a simple reply: "I regarded my 'Main-Travelled Roads' as a picture painted." [73]

Though not wealthy he prospered and traveled, mingling with the rich and well-born he had once scorned. Gregarious and shrewd as ever, he fostered younger writers and curried older ones. He became a property holder, dealing in the unearned increment of land speculation in Oklahoma and California, and ended by living off a small income from bonds. His daughters attended a special finishing school; their father disliked the motley array of children in the district school in New York. Impressed by the wealthy men among his latter-day friends, he turned full circle. "We reformers utter a [great] deal of denunciation based upon hearsay." [74] And he could remark with unconscious meaning as he bought a new home in New York: "To the left of us swarmed European peasants, but on our right stood the homes of merchant kings." [75]

He grew to distrust the immigrant, a theme in all his work, for he had praised only the hardy Anglo-Saxon pioneer. Having fought not so much for pioneers as the pioneer spirit, it did not occur to him that the immigrant of Chicago might break new ground as surely as his own father had. He distrusted foreign values as well as foreign immigrants and had no faith in the masses he saw around him. "As a charter member of the Republic I look with disgust on these changes." [76] He bitterly assaulted the new literature that followed the First World War and the mass culture that rode the crest of lurid magazines and sensational movies:

In my life I have seen the ideals of America change from those of a republic almost purely rustic to those of a cynical, pleasure-seeking, crowd-worshipping mob, whose cerebration is dependent on the radio, the machine-made magazine, the tabloid newspapers and the moving pictures.[77]

He seemed to be an aristocrat, but he flavored his changed style of life with humor, often recalling his past. His racism, if that it was, was not virulent, and reflected a sadness at what America had become rather than any desire to persecute. Faced with these dangers to taste and standards, he sought refuge in formal culture, lending his energies and prestige to establishing an American Academy of Fine Arts and Literature. He hoped to pattern it on the French Academy, and with it to halt the deterioration of cultural standards.

Though he never equated money with talent or notoriety with ability, he too often now accepted power and wealth in their own terms. Like a schoolboy, money dazzled him, and he delighted in telling stories of what his rich friends did for him. A ride in a private railroad car, dinner with the socially elite, a speech at an exclusive affair, membership in an elegant club, all the badges of social acceptance and public fame pleased him as inordinately as they did Twain, though he lacked Twain's depth in seeing the hollowness of all mankind's pretensions. Garland had "arrived" in middle age and he intended to stay.

It was easy to sympathize with him. He had endured the rustic life, bleak with the hollow anguish of loneliness, brute labor, and artistic frustration. Why should he now spurn fortune's gifts? As he chatted genially through lavish meals, he remembered the corn pone and fatback that graced an earlier table. When he sipped brandy and smoked cigars in fine clubs, he recalled the bleakness of a Dakota winter and the bitter agony of exile on the plains. Accepting the honorary degrees, gold medals, and engraved scrolls, he remembered the bite of hunger, the shame of shabbiness, the isolation that dogged him as he ransacked Boston's Public Library for the education he had missed. Small wonder that he seemed content to be a literary elder statesman rather than an adventurous innovator. He had paid his price in pain; he had quite simply run down.

He drew fire from former friends:

> Just for a handful of silver he left us,
> Just for a riband to stick in his coat.

It was a trifle cruel, but showed his changed status.[78] To his credit, he was honest in replying:

My position is that of an intellectual aristocrat; I have no confidence in a "democratic art," if by that phrase is meant an art based on popular approval. With due regard for the welfare of the average man, I do not value his judgement upon wall-paper or rugs or paintings.[79]

In the 1920s, which were filled with exuberant optimism, new currents in literature, and experimentation in the arts, Garland seemed hopelessly antiquated. He lived on uneventfully through the Depression, settling at last in California, where he died in 1940.

Garland was a great spokesman in American letters for nineteenth-century agrarian society. His most logical successor was Willa Cather, but her stories of the plains and farms have about them a universal validity lacking in his work. Her steady development, elevated style, and keen insight into universals as well as particulars set her apart from Garland's more reportorial approach. But Garland has his place, and so long as rural life holds a nostalgic or real appeal, he will be read and appreciated. Few writers have so faithfully reflected the death of one standard and the birth of another. His was not a brilliant mind or a great creative talent. However, a natural perception and sympathy forged in the fires of experience allowed him to capture for a while a view of life relevant to everyone. In passing from country to city, from ignorance to culture, from past to future, he carried a double lens to see America's changing face.

His imagination could not make the leap from personal to universal experience, yet few will deny the moving quality of his best work. Out of a nation's agony in a time of change and bewilderment, he wrought a call that still rings clear to men faced with life's full grandeur and tragedy. Was he a talent wasted? Perhaps. But it is wiser to call him a talent undeveloped. How ironic that he who knew it so well left the main-travelled road for a smoother but less meaningful path.

Frank Norris: The Romantic as Naturalist

> *Falseness dies; injustice and oppression in the end of every-*
> *thing fade and vanish away. Greed, cruelty, selfishness, and*
> *inhumanity are short-lived; the individual suffers, but the*
> *race goes on. . . . The larger view always and through all*
> *shams, all wickedness, discovers the Truth that will, in the*
> *end, prevail, and all things, surely, inevitably, resistlessly*
> *work together for good.*

—1901

To THOSE who loved her, San Francisco in the 1890s was as irresistible as a beautiful woman. Fabled with adventures of the Gold
Rush days, her robustness tempered by a Spanish ease of life, re-
splendent in a glorious natural setting, she combined vitality and
sophistication. Her buildings sat upon hills, up whose steep in-
clines rattled the cable cars that were her trademark. From their
top the visitor saw the breath-taking view of a bay untraced by
bridges, perhaps brilliantly clear, sometimes laced with whitecaps,
often blurred in a chill but romantic fog.

The city was historically old but was not much older than the
influx of new men and new wealth made it after 1849. It was
young enough to provide culture, and old enough to want it. After
the Civil War, the city became the western terminus of the trans-
continental railroad, and a focus of fiscal, commercial, and industrial wealth. A group of writers made California's name famous,
and San Francisco was their home. They bore the stamp of her
influence, and she bore the marks of their passage. Bret Harte,
Joaquin Miller, Mark Twain, Edwin Markham, Ambrose Bierce,
and Frank Norris fed color and excitement into the city's literary
life.

Interest in literature, supported by many newspapers and several
"little" magazines like *The Wave, The Argonaut,* and *The Overland
Monthly,* spread through many layers of the city's life. There was
romance in the squalor of Polk Street, the din of Chinatown, and

the elegant richness of Nob Hill. It was a city of extremes and color. One might encounter an inscrutable and beautifully dressed Oriental on the streets, or a finely uniformed soldier in the Presidio. You could talk to a gold miner over a glass of whiskey; or take tea with a railroad magnate. The wharves spilled out the world's goods and peoples. There were men to write these facts into fiction, and their audience was large. Every cub reporter seemed to be at work on The Great American Novel. As Will Irwin recalled: "In those days San Francisco had a literary tradition and atmosphere. The very bartenders were trying their hands at writing. To all of us aspirants, he [Frank Norris] was the local hero. . . ." [1] Small wonder, for no writer brought more lasting fame to the city than Frank Norris, though his life began elsewhere.

He was born in Chicago as Benjamin Franklin Norris, Jr., on March 5, 1870. In their background and fortunes, his parents were storybook characters, and they figured as prototypes in his work. His mother was charming, at ease in almost any company, and had great aspirations for her eldest son, in whom she saw the makings of a famous artist. She was proud, a trifle cold, and was part of the inspiration for Laura of The Pit (1903).

Her husband was a substantial man of the world and successful business tycoon whose history read like something from a Horatio Alger novel. Born on a farm, he started to boarding school at fourteen; but on the way to take up his books, he was attracted by a jeweler's shop, entered, and became an apprentice. In a few years he had his own jewelry concern, with headquarters in Chicago. The fire of 1871 gutted his business, but one of his salesmen saved some of the stock in a wheelbarrow, and Norris rebuilt his fortunes literally on the ashes of the old business with even greater success. He lived well, and though strong, was intellectually a narrow man. He satisfied his wife's social aspirations and insisted only that his sons continue his business. The Norrises lived in a large, elegant house, like the show piece of The Pit, having a carriage with a coat of arms emblazoned on its doors, and several servants. The man whose energy and ruthless drive made this possible also heightened the tensions in a broken marriage. His strength tolerated neither weakness nor delay. When he was over sixty, in a fit of impatience with a builder, he carried home a heavy cornice on his shoulder. If it was like him to become a millionaire, it was also characteristic of him to divorce his wife and never see his sons again, leaving his fortune to a second wife.[2]

Whatever shadowy emotional tensions abounded in the great house, the young Frank grew to maturity in a world without material want. His mother's aspirations were sometimes embarrassing. He disliked being "mama's boy" and fought against fancy suits and dancing lessons at swank academies. Taunted by his friends, he finally ruined his velvet suit by carrying three kittens in its pocket. Like most boys, he was consumed in daydreams and eagerly devoured the novels of Scott, taking for reality the stuff of romance; it was a tendency he never quite outgrew. He loved his lead soldiers and depicted battle scenes and heroic encounters for any patient listener. It was characteristic of all his life and art that he dedicated his last book to his brother Charles: "In memory of certain lamentable tales of the Round (Dining-Room) table heroes, of the epic of the pewter platoons, and the romance cycle of 'Gaston le Fox,' which we invented, maintained, and found marvellous at a time when we both were boys."

The elder Norris suffered from arthritis, and wealth enabled him to ease it by visits to California, where he moved his family permanently in 1884. They lived first in Oakland and in 1885 moved to the fashionable Sacramento Street district of San Francisco. The young Frank's protests did not spare him a preparatory high school, where his schoolmates called him "skinny-well-fed" because of his gangling awkwardness and voracious appetite.[3] He disliked school and found study confining and unrewarding as well as dull. Like his mother, he envisioned a great artistic career and wished to be a painter.

Over his father's silent disapproval, but with his mother's blessings, he attended the Bouguereau Studio of the Julien Atelier in Paris. Between 1887 and 1889, he was an elegant Bohemian, trying rather ineptly to master a style of painting, revealing to those who watched him closely that he had the reporter's eye, not the painter's. Though he had some talent at drawing, the plastic arts did not beckon, and he knew that his impatient father would insist that he become a businessman. But he struggled to avoid that fate. He sketched out a great battle scene, much like the one which so challenged and then disappointed Vandover, but the inspiration flagged. He surrendered in disgust and gave the canvas to friends, who carried it through windy streets to their studio to cut it up into more manageable pieces.

He liked art, but the talent was simply not there. He was more interested in the people he saw than in the pictures they painted. Paris was never more carefree or bizarre than in this decade when new forms and ideas in painting and sculpture triumphed. At the salon he met a Texan who danced in clog boots with a Bowie knife, an Italian hypnotist who mesmerized the models until they fell out of pose, and a Russian who danced in the streets when not painting.

He did not read deeply in the "naturalist" literature that was all the rage. He browsed in the bookstalls along the Seine or near the Cathedral of Notre Dame for lavishly decorated books on medieval armor, special editions of chivalric poetry, and historical romances. He still dwelled on the past's splendor and vivid romance.

He wrote, but neither his words nor paints impressed his father, now suspicious that with his mother's connivance he might escape business. In 1889 Frank returned to San Francisco, where he was captivated by the city he saw with fresh eyes. In a few years he wrote a glowing encomium of the city whose locale and people provided the substance of so much of his work: "There are just three cities in the United States that are 'story cities'—New York, of course, New Orleans, and best of all, San Francisco." [4]

In 1890 he enrolled as a special student in the University of California at Berkeley but never finished his degree requirements. He came there glossed with the elegance of Paris and of the world of art, wearing spats and bright clothes, carrying a gold-headed cane, and sporting a mustache, every inch the *boulevardier*. He affected the fashionable horror of the above-average, the normal, and the respectable. Though never active in sports, he attended football games and cheered with gusto the prototypes of boys who became supermen of his later novels. He was charming, elegant, and often incongruous. He often donned a Sherlock Holmes cap, smoked a pipe which he put lit in his pocket when meeting young ladies, and was very absent-minded.

But he was a curious youth, and something shadowy and undefined remained at the heart of his personality. No matter how many facts rise from his biography, the figure within is curiously hidden. He was deceptively superficial, for no man with an indifferent eye or without values could have produced so much durable work in the decade allotted him as a writer. He gave little promise of becoming a great novelist to those who knew him then, for he often seemed indolent and flashy. As Blix said of her reporter-fiancé: "There *is* that about you, Condy, you like to be too showy; you don't know when to stop." [5] But back of the elegant schoolboy pose, superficiality vanished in the mind of an astute and sensitive observer. As his artist friend Bruce Porter once said, he was "a very dear, a very charming, and a very solitary human being." [6]

College had little appeal for Norris, who hated discipline and the tedium of repeating dead classics; but he seemed certain of his goal at last. "I entered college with the view of preparing myself for the profession of a writer of fiction," he said in a petition for a change of student status.[7] Enthused by action (the sedentary scholarly life was not for him), he already displayed a remarkable vitality in words. Whatever the faults of his English, the structure of his essays, or irrationality of his viewpoint, his stories were exciting. His professors graded him down, and one later explained that his stories often "proved to be a string of unconnected pictures, each excellent in itself, but the whole not forming an adequate treatment of the topic." [8]

Education confirmed in Norris the early suspicion that the academies fostered no vital art and the classroom produced no enduring writing. "The best way to study literature is to try to produce literature," he wrote in 1896. "It is the original work that counts, not the everlasting compiling of facts, not the tabulating of metaphors, nor the rehashing of textbooks and encyclopedia articles." [9]

Disgust with study did not turn him from writing, nor did experience erase the last traces of medievalism in him. In 1891 his mother subsidized the publication of his long historical poem *Yvernelle,* filled with swashbuckling knights and distressed maidens, and a curiously tough-minded social philosophy that pitted the weak against the strong. The three cantos of iambic tetrameter couplets satisfied Norris' romanticism, though he never fully renounced daydreams.

In 1894, his parents were divorced, and a more mature and sensible Norris went to Harvard for a year's graduate study in composition. Though still hating academic discipline, he approved of the Harvard system of independent study that forced each student to do his best work under the fire of merciless criticism. It was all interesting, but not very instructive, for the truth was that Frank Norris learned only from life itself; and that required moving beyond both his youth and environment.

He had a dramatic change in a trip to South Africa, which in 1895 was poised for the Boer War. Formally, he was there as a reporter for the San Francisco *Chronicle*. In fact, he was escaping family pressures and gathering material for the career of serious fiction which he felt lay just ahead. He was disappointed, for the Jameson Raid caught him in Johannesburg; and when the dust settled, the outraged Boers summarily deported him. Racked with fever that weakened his whole system and later contributed to his untimely death, he sailed for San Francisco on passage money wired by his frantic mother.

Recuperation gave him time to reflect on his storybook adventure, so like his daydreams in its color and excitement, and so unlike them in its dangers and drama. He had seen savage natives in revolt, had passed through hospitals filled with sick and wounded, and had seen the bizarre as commonplace and the commonplace as bizarre. He took into his receptive mind the materials for blending romance with realism.

In San Francisco, he recovered slowly, but his restless energy forbade indolence; and he worked as a reporter and editor for the San Francisco *Wave*. In the next few years he wrote dozens of articles, reports, and reviews as well as stories for this small but influential magazine. They revealed his range of interest if not a full mastery of his powers. Vividness, color, vicarious participation marked his factual reporting. But his fiction resembled studio sketches fitted to formulas. His passion for the trick ending, unusual situations, and odd characters died hard. He wrote his stories in bits and pieces, and only when he tied his love for the curious to a system of writing, as in *McTeague* (1899), did these faults fade. He was now frankly derivative, but his fiction had an undercurrent of realism and truth that did not escape the sensitive eye. Like Condy Rivers, his alter ego in *Blix,* his young and impressionable mind had taken too much ink from other men's work.

He had begun by an inoculation of the Kipling virus, had suffered an almost fatal attack of Harding Davis, and had even been affected by Maupassant. He "went in" for accuracy of detail; held that if one wrote a story involving firemen one should have, or seem to have, every detail of the department at his fingers' ends, and should "bring in" to the tale all manner of technical names and cant phrases.[10]

The budding naturalist was groping toward some more substantial base for his fiction, and he realized his faults of style and approach.

While he worked on what became *Vandover and the Brute* (1914) and *McTeague,* he was also busy with a romance, *Moran of the Lady Letty* (1898), serialized in *The Wave.* But all these projects waited upon events for completion. The Spanish-American War erupted, and the correspondent's blood rose in him. He had already moved to New York to finish *Moran* and to write for *McClure's Magazine,* but he left at once for Tampa, Florida, where the invasion army waited in ungainly fashion to assault Cuba.

He had already seen enough war to know its true nature, and he knew that it held more boredom and horror than glamor. But he met Richard Harding Davis, Frederic Remington, and the rising young literary figure, Stephen Crane. Tampa was dull, and the army slow, and like other correspondents he wrote of the people he met and impressions he gathered. He saw Crane as "a very young Personage," and found him an enigma.[11]

Once in Cuba, the fighting fulfilled his worst fears, for there were no romantic charges or glorious assaults on battlements, but only blood, dying, and discomfort. He saw wounded Spaniards and Americans die without care or concern. He came upon the body of a young child, raped and mutilated. He saw a woman of seventy carry a woman of ninety out of the line of fire with supreme unconcern. He made a lean-to for a night's rest from boards covered with blood. Like Crane, he saw war not as glamorous but as a factual essay in the strife and disorder of life.

But he lacked the detached vision and unconcerned observation that marked Crane's war dispatches. His reports and stories bubbled with a sense of involvement. It cost him a good deal, and he pleaded when he returned to New York for rest and forgetfulness. The whole experience "seems nothing but a hideous blur of mud and blood." [12]

Since his personal life remains shrouded and since the appearance he gave to the world is so deceptive, it is difficult to trace the sources of Norris' writing. Concerned with action and "living" rather than study, blessed with a retentive memory and the creative talent's ability to transmute facts into more than one dimension of meaning, Norris began his work early and produced a phenomenal amount of fiction. He recuperated from his South African fever at the Big Dipper Mine in Colfax, California, where he soaked up the milieu that went into both *McTeague* and *The Octopus* (1901). His mind teemed with material, events, characters; but he lacked the discipline or the cohesive philosophy to make much of this glittering ore. He had been writing since his days in Berkeley, and not merely for the newspapers. When he came to Harvard he brought with him the uncompleted manuscripts of both *Vandover* and *McTeague*. Impressed by *Moran,* S. S. McClure, then beginning his erratic career as a muckraker, invited Norris to work for him in New York in 1898. Norris accepted, grateful for the $12.50 weekly salary as well as the experience. McClure left him free to write in his afternoons, and he soon finished his first two books.

Though *Vandover and the Brute* was not published until after his death, and was edited by his brother Charles Gilman Norris, it was his first effort to define the literary Naturalism toward which he groped.[13] Partly autobiographical, it told the story of a young man's degeneration under the impact of events. Endowed with some artistic talent, moving in elegant San Francisco circles, Vandover symbolized the "fast" young set of that day and city. In him lay flaws of personality that turned this talent to ashes, and which made him a pawn in an indifferent universe. *Vandover* lacked focus, was repetitious, and filled with improbable action; but it was a powerful early expression of Naturalism in American writing.

Vandover was the average man, torn between extremes of conduct. He wished to be honorable in his dealings with others, but events and the system of life made him dishonest and degenerate. Sheltered as a youth, he awoke in his teen years to the powers of sex, revealed to him with shock in an encyclopedia article on obstetrics. The event changed his whole life: ". . . the innate vice stirred in him, the brute began to make itself felt, and a multitude of perverse and vicious ideas commenced to buzz about him like a swarm of nasty flies." [14] From event to event—his seduction of a young girl, her suicide, his father's death, his impoverishment at the hands of friends, his failure as an artist, his ultimate lapse into lycanthropy when he thought himself a wolf padding naked on all fours around his dingy room, his death-in-life as a janitor cleaning filth from the wretched tenements he himself once owned—Vandover's degeneration was ruthlessly frank and vivid. The book dealt candidly with such sordid themes that Norris never attempted seriously to publish it in his lifetime.

Though confused, *Vandover* was the first great statement of Norris' method and philosophy. Centered on a character's degeneration under the pressure of events, it was also an attack on the false social and ethical values of his age and class. The young Vandover sneered at the moralistic pretensions of his own class, and of young ladies especially. He maintained they knew that their men frequented bawdy houses, got drunk, and seduced working girls. Yet they held up an artificial standard of conduct because the lie fortified their conviction that they were somehow better. Though Vandover fell, like Lucifer, because of inner faults, society shared in his fall because it made him ashamed of innocence. Its snares, framed in false beliefs and spurious codes of conduct, were everywhere; they, not the human weakness that succumbed to them, were to blame.[15]

The obvious flaw that signaled Vandover's destruction was his weak character that collapsed under events. After his father's death, provoked by the knowledge of his son's seduction of Ida Wade that caused her suicide, Vandover was desolate with guilt and grief. But his easy recovery threw a sharp light on his true self: ". . . his nature was not shallow. It had merely deteriorated." [16] The awful lesson of Vandover's life was simple: ". . . *I can get used to almost anything.*" [17]

It remained for Theodore Dreiser to give a detailed statement of the bewilderment with which the sensitive man met the social, economic, and ethical changes of the late nineteenth century. But *Vandover and the Brute* was an attack on the impersonality and indifference of society that more and more men felt. Vandover's real fault was his inability to master the details of daily living. As long as his affairs passed through the hands of others, he was safe. But when he dealt with property rights, checking accounts, the requirements of daily life, he failed. The system he confronted was too intricate, too nonhuman, too open to manipulation against all but the strongest. The order of things in his increasingly complicated world defeated him, and his flawed character was merely the channel through which this weakness ran.[18] His life was wasted. "Was there any need of suicide? Suicide? Great God! his whole life had been one long suicide." [19]

As a study in determinism and literary Naturalism, *Vandover* was not successful. It contained too many conflicting themes, too much confusion. Vandover was supposedly at the mercy of events, yet "he clearly saw the fate toward which he was hurrying; it was not too late to save himself if only he could find help, but he could find *no* help." [20] However gripping, Vandover's career appeared unreal; the events seemed manipulated to cause his downfall, and the author often intruded to moralize. Vandover seemed an average man at the mercy of misfortunes too pat to be truthful.

Vandover's importance lay elsewhere. It was an early, if often raw and unfinished essay on the dual nature of man. The brute full of greed, bestiality, and cruelty lay in Vandover's heart awaiting its opportunity to escape and dominate him, as it did in the heart of every man. In stating this theme, which ran through his subsequent work, Norris was a literary pioneer. He did not discover the theme of man's duality. But he reaffirmed it in American letters in a radical form that set him apart from predecessors who had dealt with it. Hawthorne and Melville, to mention only two authors, had treated the subtle and profound ramifications of man's duality. But they stated their themes in the context of good and evil of supernatural origins. In *McTeague* and later works Norris put his characters at the mercy of themselves and their physical environment and heredity, dividing their persons between the civilized and bestial amid events that rose naturally from daily living.

Because he was basically a romantic dealing with naturalistic techniques rather than naturalistic ethics, these themes were not always clear in Norris' work. His vitality and eagerness to tell a story often blurred or confused his intentions. *Vandover*'s power lay in depicting man from within himself, and in its clear admission of the gulf between a man regulated outwardly by humanism and social ethics, and an inner but natural brute controlled by heredity and natural drives.

Vandover showed the marks of genius. The steady decline from gentleman to scrubman, told with remorseless fidelity to facts, horrifies even the modern reader. Its last half, cataloguing the brute's emergence, is a walk through hell with reality turned into a compelling unreality.

The reader lived Vandover's own life in the double vision of Vandover's eyes and his knowledge of the total context. One by one the small errors lead to major crises and the endless waste of self-respect's failure. Vandover turned from moral innocence to tainted vice to gratify his inner self; from care for others to consuming selfishness; from a rather innocent ignorance to stupidity and ruin. Life acted on nature's flaws and made him a primeval beast, walking on all fours and snarling, "Wolf! Wolf!" He who once was wealthy and indolent became a handyman, cleaning the appalling refuse from kitchen sinks as if it were his normal occupation, a testament to the ease with which life degraded the weak. He was thoroughly defeated, recognizing a four-year-old as his master in a final horrifying scene in which the child's eyes revealed what he might have been had the good in him triumphed.

As a study in human weakness and as a comment on the increasing complexity of modern civilization, *Vandover* pointed to *McTeague*.[21] Though lesser projects consumed his time after he moved to New York in 1898, Norris' mind centered on the powerful story of "the Dentist" as he called McTeague. He had met William Dean Howells, who recognized the young caller's talents even though he did not always approve of what he said or wrote; and he filled the Good Gray Dean's ears with reports of what this novel would be. "I think it will be called 'The People of Polk Street.' It is as naturalistic as *Moran* was romantic and in writing it I have taken myself and the work very seriously." [22]

Stephen Crane had published *Maggie: A Girl of the Streets* in 1893, a naturalistic analysis of life on the Bowery; but despite Howells' encouragement, the book received little attention. *McTeague* was the first widely recognized American naturalistic novel. It came upon the literary scene with more force and caused greater controversy than Crane's work, for it was told with a raw gusto and lack of stylistic charm that made Crane's work seem almost academic in comparison.

McTeague presented the brute horror of life in the squalid environs of San Francisco's Polk Street. Opening with the famous scene describing McTeague's office, filled with the smell of ether, leather, the sweat of his lower-class patients, steam beer, and dirt, the novel ruthlessly described life's lower depths. McTeague, who had no first name, was too stupid to learn dentistry from books. Spawned and abandoned by his mother in a mining camp, he learned his profession from an itinerant quack. He capitalized on the brute power of "a young giant, carrying his huge shock of blond hair six feet three inches from the ground. . . ." His strength was legendary; he pulled teeth with his fingers and cracked nuts in his elbows. He was ponderous, slow, dull. "Yet there was nothing vicious about the man. Altogether he suggested the draught horse, immensely strong, stupid, docile, obedient." [23] He had a dimly lit better self, for he lavished loving care on a canary in a fancy gilt cage. McTeague's chief disability was his acceptance of whatever fate offered him. He could not grasp life's scheme. This flaw destroyed him, for he "never questioned himself, never looked for motives, never went to the bottom of things." [24]

Into his life came a pretty patient, Trina Sieppe, equally ignorant but possessing a cunning denied the dentist. Etherizing her for an extraction, McTeague was seized by animal desire that marked the presence of a darker nature. "It was resistless, untrained, a thing not to be held in leash an instant." [25] Though he did not ravish Trina, he kissed her coarsely. Why should he be at the mercy of such forces and desires? "Below the fine fabric of all that was good in him ran the foul stream of hereditary evil, like a sewer.

. . . The evil of an entire race flowed in his veins. Why should it be? He did not desire it. Was he to blame?" [26] At the mercy of a heritage that shaped him beyond his control and a world he could not understand that compounded his natural weaknesses, McTeague began his journey into hell.

When his friend Marcus Schouler relinquished claim to Trina, McTeague courted and won her. When she in turn became wealthy by winning a lottery, Schouler's resentment at losing her set in motion the events that destroyed the dentist.

In superficial ways, Trina changed McTeague's life. She bought him a long-coveted gilt tooth sign, an immense symbol that hung outside his office to advertise his profession and bad taste. He gave up cheap beer, dressed better, tore down the bad chromos that decorated his walls, and promenaded in the park with her. But she could not alter the inner man, any more than social conventions could change mankind's basic drives. His blood still rose in a fight until he nearly bit off Schouler's ear. He lapsed into an animal stupor on losing his dental practice. All her improvements were no more permanent than changes on the land between rains.

Trina also bore the fatal flaw of selfishness; nothing she did was to help McTeague, but rather to glamorize herself through him. Her love for him was one dimensional. "She began to love him more and more, not for what he was, but for what she had given up to him." [27] She surrendered herself to his brutal playfulness, enjoying his mastery over her, but she could not give the compassion or love that might have made them both better people.

The mail one day brought a fat brown envelope to McTeague's "parlors" that fell through the slot like an evil animal. It and several successors, instigated by the jealous Schouler, forbade McTeague's practicing dentistry because he had no diploma. Stupidly accepting the verdict, McTeague and Trina moved downward to ever lower depths. Though Trina won five thousand dollars in a lottery, her selfish greed forbade spending it.

Driven beyond desperation, McTeague left Trina, whose degradation now paralleled her husband's, and wandered forlornly through the city's lower depths. Trina lost her fingers after McTeague bit them to torment her, and became a pathetic charwoman, still hoarding her precious gold. Obsessed with money, she took animal pleasure from sleeping naked on her golden coins, running her hands through them piled on the table, tasting and smelling them. Money was the serpent in the jungle of her mind, but it merely symbolized the selfish greed that blinded her to any redemption through love for McTeague or the world at large. Trina's tragedy was her failure to identify with anything beyond herself.

Hungry, homeless, driven to despair in actual want, McTeague begged Trina for part of her money, which was rightfully his, but she refused. In a fit of bitter rage he murdered her and fled with the hoard. Driven by some animal instinct or "sixth sense," he hid in the mining country of the high Sierras, and Death Valley, reverting to the type from which he sprang. But now he was driven relentlessly by fear of discovery so great that he even abandoned a rich gold claim when warned of an encroaching posse. Fleeing aimlessly, he stumbled into the appalling waste of Death Valley, "this hideous sink of alkali, this bed of some primeval lake lying so far below the surface of the ocean." [28]

Desperately clutching the gilded canary cage and its tiny twittering occupant whose presence and fate symbolized both man's entrapment in the world and McTeague's own unwitting kindness, the dentist was caught by Marcus Schouler. The two men confronted each other in the shimmering heat and barren waste, beyond whose vision and behind whose actions stretched a world without mercy or meaning. Deprived of water by accident, they grappled; and though McTeague killed him, Schouler's body was still fastened to McTeague's wrist in handcuffs. The doomed McTeague stared stupidly at his half-dead canary, fluttering helplessly in its gilt prison.

Though essentially the story of McTeague's decline and death at the mercy of impersonal forces, the book was woven with the strands of several minor subplots. Its characterizations made it one of the most memorable of all American novels and revealed the measure of Norris' growth in the years since *Yvernelle*. No reader was likely to forget the vivid portrait of half-mad Maria Macapa, slain by her husband, the Jewish junkman Zerkow, because she would not reveal the hiding place of a nonexistent hoard of gold plate she insanely discussed for years. To balance the essential gloom of the main story, Norris created Old Grannis and Miss Baker, the two aged lovers who communed through the walls of their rooms, too shy to speak to each other, yet deeply in love. Though McTeague and Trina died, these two lived to affirm Norris' belief in life's permanence. Individuals passed, but the race and what it stood for continued. They also bespoke the cruelty of civilization that hindered man's natural expressiveness. The wall between them was emotional as well as wooden.

The novel abounded with great scenes in the manner of Zola and the Continental naturalists. The reader participated in the coarse wedding feast set before McTeague, Trina, and the Sieppes. The picnic in the park organized by Trina's father, a Prussian martinet, was stirringly funny and pathetic. The scenes rose up like images on film: the little boys all primly starched marching at their father's behest, Mrs. Sieppe nervously obeying her husband, McTeague and Trina dutifully caught up in the small battalion, the little toy boat sinking on the park lake and the resulting childish anguish. The sound, the smell, the feel of all the action was there, showing Norris' gifts as a reporter. And who was unmoved by the vaudeville show to which McTeague took Trina, her mother, and little "Owgooste"? Nervously inadequate even before the ticket seller, awed by the tawdry ormolu glitter of the gaudy theatre, cowed into meek submission by the overbearing usher, dazzled by the cheap show, the McTeague party symbolized Norris' belief that a complex life overbore man.

McTeague was a major statement of the Naturalism which insisted that man's actions were determined by hidden forces, but it also protested the artificial inequalities of life that could be rectified. It insisted on the redemptive powers of love, a theme to which Norris returned in his last works. It was a plea for understanding the submerged personality in every man, and a statement of the value of subjects not regularly treated in American fiction.

McTeague suffered from faults that were Norris' trademark: verbosity, repetition, opaqueness, and inconsistency. He had a passion for curious words like "osseous," and described physical features endlessly. When friends chided him for allowing McTeague's canary to survive the hazardous trip across Death Valley, he smiled and answered: "Well, I did say that the canary was *half* dead." [29]

His dislike of discipline and academic purity made Norris rely on his story, character development, and vivid incidents to carry his main points. In *McTeague,* his vitality, color, and his commitment to his subject made the novel compelling and real, despite its structural faults. He made essentially dull people interesting, controlled his crowded background enough to develop individual character, and gave the reader a moving portrait of one man's life that became all men's life.

McTeague came upon the scene in the twilight of the Gilded Age, when readers still pored over historical romance and the sensational press. Howells commanded an audience with his Realism, but it doubtless consisted of the same people year after year. Those who bought novels preferred something "different," something to raise them above their humdrum existence. During the years in which Norris worked, the American public savored *When Knighthood Was in Flower, Graustark,* and *David Harum.* If the public had read "Naturalism," it came from abroad, in yellow paperbacks hidden from polite company and read in locked rooms. Zola's name was akin to the devil's in many minds; for Naturalism dealt with sex, life in the gutter, the sordid, and undecorative. Minds attuned to the principle that the novel should not preach but please offered little welcome for *McTeague.*

Norris expected adverse critical reception and was not surprised to hear the book labeled "McTeague: A Study in Stinks." [30] Nor was he surprised to read one reviewer's comment: "It is about the most unpleasant story that anybody has ever ventured to write." He was not mollified by the sanctimonious injunction to make his future work "not less true but a good deal more agreeable." [31] He was more pleased by the grudging admission from one reviewer that though the story was depraved, "*McTeague* seizes and holds in a vise-like grasp that is almost painful from the beginning to the end. . . ." [32] Most reviewers thought it reflected the French Naturalism that was already dying. It was in fact the prelude to a movement that dominated American fiction for the next generation.

If many reviewers irritated Norris with their prudery and finger-wagging, he at least took comfort in Howells' support. The Good Dean had blazed the way with Realism, and though he chided Norris for omitting the pure and pleasant from his book, he approved its purpose and manner. Norris accepted the quiet rebuke and showed his deepening artistic consciousness in answering: "I believe too, you were quite right in saying that it was not the whole truth, and that the novel that is true to life cannot afford to ignore the finer things." He swept aside criticisms of technical faults, such as the melodramatic ending. "I agree with every one of your criticisms always excepting the anti-climax, the 'death in the desert' business. I am sure that has its place." [33]

The novel caused a stir among Norris' friends and family, as well as genteel literary circles. Charles Norris remembered a friend's remark to his father after reading one of Frank's early stories: "If I had a son who wrote a story like that, I'd have put him out of the world in a lethal chamber." While the elder Norris did not care for literature, he would hardly go that far, though he often wondered about Frank's "thimblehead-bobism." [34] Norris cared little for public acclaim and liked to shock readers and listeners with his ideas, but he wrote seriously and tried to counteract basic misunderstandings of his purpose.

Possessing neither a scholarly nor critical mind, Norris approached the art of fiction with gusto and inconsistency. His occasional essays on the subject, written at varying intervals, were collected after his death as *The Responsibilities of the Novelist* (1903). If he was never quite sure of his philosophy, he was very sure of what he attacked, the sentimentality of the Victorian era's reading matter. He hated the swashbuckling romance that presented Michigan Avenue as "La Rue de la Harpe." "A poor taste, a cheap one," he insisted, "the taste of serving men, the literature of chambermaids." [35] He hated the "love story" that was a standard fixture even in Realistic writing, and insisted in *The Pit* that the novel of the future would lack a love story. Norris' oft-quoted cry that life was better than literature was part of his revolt against this artificiality.

He knew from experience that a successful writer drew material from the world around him. He knew also the dangers and pitfalls that awaited the young writer, so vividly illustrated by his own experience in "smart" circles in New York. Life was not derivative, and neither was the literature that depicted it truly. As he wrote of young Overbeck, a budding writer, in one of his short stories: "He was not literary. He had not much time for books. He lived in the midst of a strenuous, eager life, a little primal even yet; a life of passions that were often elemental in their simplicity and directness." [36]

He was often inconsistent in his approach, but upon the importance of his craft he never wavered. He insisted that fiction was a basic weapon in the war against ignorance and unreality. He hated the sentimentalists largely because they degraded the novel to "a simple diversion, a means of whiling away a dull evening, a long railway journey. . . ." [37] Painting and music were once in the van of human progress, depicting life as it really was, deepening and widening the view of mankind. That task now fell to the novel. So long as fiction refused to depict life, it committed suicide.

Though he could be a magnificent pamphleteer against social injustice, as in *The Octopus*, he did not say that the novel should preach reform. He argued simply that fiction must present a view of life arising from personal experience, applicable to all men. In this manner, and for this purpose, whether he was a naturalist or a romantic, Norris filled his books with a sense of awe and wonder of life that make them as vital and meaningful today as in 1900.

Though Norris was always slightly snobbish, and cared little for petty troubles, preferring in life as well as his work to take the broad view, he had faith in the reading public. In the end they made up the Force or Life about which he wrote, and both to touch and to change them was art's chief purpose. "It is all very well to jeer at the People and at the People's misunderstanding of the arts, but the fact is indisputable that no art that is not in the end understood by the People can live or ever did live a single generation." [38] The public got trash often because it wanted it, and it wanted trash because that was what it got. Habit played its part here as elsewhere in life; give the people better books and they would demand better books. But in any event, "Better bad books than no books; better half a loaf of hard bread than *no* frosted wedding cake." [39]

Though he appreciated Howells and the realists, Norris felt that something more was now necessary in fiction. Realism had the virtue of familiarity. "Nothing much happens," Curtis Jadwin told his wife in *The Pit* as she read Howells to him. "But I *know* all those people." [40] Yet Realism's scope was too small, its shafts into the heart of experience too shallow:

It [Realism] notes only the surface of things. For it, Beauty is not even skin deep, but only a geometrical plane, without dimension and depth, a mere outside. Realism is very excellent as far as it goes, but it goes no further than the Realist himself can actually see, or actually hear. Realism is minute; it is the drama of a broken teacup, the tragedy of a walk down the block, the excitement of an afternoon call, the adventure of an invitation to dinner. It is the visit to my neighbor's house, a formal visit, from which I may draw no conclusions. I see my neighbor and his friends—very, oh such very! probable people—and that is all. Realism bows upon the doormat and goes away and says to me, as we link arms on the sidewalk: "That is life." And I say it is not. It is not, as you would very well see if you took Romance with you to call upon your neighbor.[41]

The judgment was inadequate. Such a charge was hardly fair against the Howells of *Silas Lapham* or *A Hazard of New Fortunes*. But Norris' basic criticism was true. Realism did lack a deep grasp of the full complexities of personality. What was his answer? In a word, Romance—the romance he elevated from a *form* to a *viewpoint*. Just as Howells pledged himself to the normal as the basis of Realism, Norris pledged himself to the nonnormal, in whose problems and situations he found the deeper meanings that eluded realists. "Romance, I take it, is the kind of fiction that takes cognizance of variations from the type of normal life," he said in a famous definition.[42]

Romance was not sentiment; it was not a false view of life. To him, it was the ability to see farther than a mere description of life's surface and to value the unusual not for its own sake but for what it represented common to life and men in general. Above all, it was broad and imaginative. "But to Romance belongs the wide world for a range, and the unplumbed depths of the human heart, and the mystery of sex, and the problems of life, and the black, unsearched penetralia of the soul of man." [43] He was tired of the dictum that literature should not offend the young girl and that some subjects were taboo. Fiction should cease to adorn life and entertain readers. "If there is much pain in life, all the more reason that it should appear in a class of literature which, in the highest forms, is a sincere transcription of life." The cry that the sordid, evil, and depraved should be hidden was "the complaint of the coward, this cry against the novel with a purpose." [44] He tried to practice what he called sincerity not merely to material but to purpose. He wanted always to say of himself what he said of a fictional character: "He had dealt with it [life] honestly; he did not dab at the edge of the business; he had sent his fist straight through it." [45]

There were three kinds of novels, he insisted. The first told something, such as *The Three Musketeers*. The second showed something, like *Romola*. The third proved something, as in *Les Miserables*. He wished his work to fall in the last category, where fiction "draws conclusions from a whole congeries of forces, social tendencies, race impulses, devotes itself not to a study of men, but of man." [46]

His equipment for this task consisted basically of an ability to see the inner core of experience and to portray the extraordinary in the ordinary. He was a fine reporter and filled his writing with the observations of a keen eye. The most remarkable and welcome aspect of his work was its reality. His novels recorded a vanished way of life; for they captured in their fabric the truth, the falseness, the standards, the values, the cheapness, and the greatness of his generation both in the characters and their settings. The modern reader is not likely to forget the San Francisco depicted in *Mc-Teague,* or lose the sense of having participated in something grand when finishing *The Octopus.*

This was a deceptive talent, for he seemed the most inattentive of men. He could be smiling, happy, depressed, and languid all in an afternoon. He could argue knowledgeably about one thing, and ignorantly about another, and take his leave with the impression that he had learned nothing. But with pen and ink he transmuted the details of his experience with unerring accuracy. As his friend John O'Hara Cosgrave said with a touch of awe: "Frank never saw things with his eyes. He had no faculty of physical attention, but after having been to a place, exposed to its stimuli, he could describe it—*on paper*—with complete verisimilitude. I used to say that his pores served him as visual organs." [47] However fine this talent, Norris realized its limitations. Good reporting was not enough. Since reality differed to people, it must be made universal through the creative process. As he said shrewdly: "It's not the things that have really happened that make good fiction, but the things that read as though they had." [48]

His passion for verisimilitude made him hungry for facts, and he wrote best of the things he knew. Preparing for *The Octopus* meant historical research, visits to the area of actual combat. He knew the San Francisco of *McTeague,* and had visited the desert area where McTeague died. Yet he hated study, and no amount of application or facts could have made his work come to life. He clung stubbornly to his belief that "The most brilliant scholarship attainable by human effort is not, to-day, worth nine years of any young man's life." [49] He often placed his characters at the mercy of "instinct," and believed it helped him create. ". . . if a man can be sure of his instincts, I think he has little to fear,—the rest he can work out of his own bowels and brains." [50]

Norris read little and superficially, but the Naturalists' dazzling techniques, combined with their passion for big scenes, captivated him. He liked Zola, Maupassant, and Daudet among the French; Kipling among the English; Twain, Howells, and sometimes Henry James among Americans. He saw promise in Garland, Crane, Frederic, and Dreiser among his contemporaries. Given to easy enthusiasm, he digested much in a glance, and doubtless studied more than he seemed to. Howells once shrewdly said: "By what Frank Norris wrote we might easily know what he read." Norris himself, when asked what he had been reading, often gaily replied: "I'm reading a darn good book by Frank Norris." [51]

Of all the immediate literary influences at hand, none impressed him more than the work of Émile Zola. He often styled himself "the boy Zola." [52] Though he did not especially read Zola's work while in Paris, he reviewed and commented on it when writing for *The Wave* in the mid-1890s. "The world of M. Zola is a world of big things," he noted, "the enormous, the formidable, the terrible is what counts; no teacup tragedies here." [53] The naturalists' emphasis on scope and the details of daily life, combining an essentially scientific approach in a romantic setting, appealed to Norris.

Literary Naturalism grew out of the world and thought of the late nineteenth century. An age of comparative world peace, general prosperity, and scientific investigation, it placed great faith in material progress. It was also a time of deeply profound social and intellectual change and questioning that found science and its promises of unity in an obviously chaotic world especially captivating. If scientific and rational laws governed life's development, the naturalists reasoned that they could be discovered, perfected, and employed not only in economics, politics, and thought, but in human relations.

Naturalism flowed partly from the Realism that took fidelity to observable life as its model. But Realism became Naturalism with the added ingredient of determinism. Realism depicted man as a free agent and was interested in his activities. Naturalism saw him in a much more complex total setting as a creature of heredity and environment, an animal species of an immense earth often at the mercy of impersonal and inevitable forces. Naturalism was scientific in insisting on fidelity to all facts in pursuit of general laws. It tried to place man and his actions in proper perspective. To the naturalists, man had no life apart from his total environment.

It was easily sensational, and the term "French novel" meant something akin to pornography. Naturalism's major themes were the fight for survival, violence and disorder in all men, and biological drives. The major forms into which it flowed were the "slice of life" method, the clinical account, the panoramic novel, and finally the stream-of-consciousness approach. Of all cultures and eras to oppose these ideas while at the same time offering material for their development, none was more logical or more paradoxical than *fin de siècle* America, where ideas of free will, self-help, and progress were ingrained not merely in the culture, but in the hearts and minds of the people.

Naturalism involved a fresh view of mankind's world. It widened the context of human actions, deepened the understanding of human emotions, recognized the complex and often hidden tensions in life, and challenged the apparent order and goodness of life. It could probably have arisen only in countries caught in the midst of profound social and cultural change. It is not accidental that it flowered in Russia, France, and the United States. All these

nations were passing through changes on every level of consciousness. Naturalism made less impact on countries that were more
rigid culturally, socially, and politically, like England, Germany,
and Austria. In America, it faced and came from a generation
caught up in the perils of transition from a rural to urban society,
from an agrarian to an industrial economy, and from isolation to
internationalism.

Norris did not merely reflect his period, nor was he warmed-over
Zola. He brought to the tensions of his era a gifted mind that
transmuted vague feelings and premonitions into the reality of
moving literature. He came to his material, locale, and characters
with a distinctly American attitude. He could not have copied Zola
or anyone else, and have written enduring novels. His work, like
that of all great artists, flowed from his mind and his era and rose
organically from his total being.

Like a potent acid, both Naturalism's forms and its philosophy
ate through Victorian social and moral conventions. That it ultimately questioned man's goodness, rationality, and the idea of
human progress and perfectibility made its proponents controversial. If Howells' earnest Realism offended many American readers, what must the idle bookstore browser have thought of *Mc-
Teague*? The real source of controversy over Naturalism was the
commitment it demanded of readers. Before this they had largely
observed actions while reading fiction, even in Realism; now they
must actively participate. The rich detail, minute description, and
large approach explicit in naturalistic fiction drew readers into the
action. Controversial themes and explicit detail only said that they
must experience what the writer described, however painful. Naturalism involved a major change in human consciousness, for it
widened not merely the subject matter of fiction, but the view of
life itself.

Its determinism darkened it for many. The naturalists hoped
simply to relate without comment the events, character development, and situations they saw. It was not their place to moralize.
The scientific method which they fancied theirs only reported facts.
However attractive or repulsive, this doctrine was never strictly
true. The writer may wish to cast his creation in the mold of dis-
interested observation, but this does not imply either a disinterest

in his subject or a lack of humanism. Life is not scientifically organized, and determinism involves the manipulation of facts and events. The human agent causes actions, and the human eye reports them. The very desire to write is an affirmation of value. If all things were determined, and mankind but a beetle in the sun, why write to prove a point? Though the naturalists were seldom interested in transitory reforms unless they involved a general principle, Zola defended Captain Dreyfus, and Frank Norris condemned the railroad's oppression in *The Octopus.*

Just what Norris owed the European naturalists and how much determinism and Naturalism he adopted is difficult to say. His novels are least effective when they deal with impersonal forces. His frequent lapses into talk of "sixth senses," "Force," "Life," and heredity showed clearly that he borrowed more technique than philosophy from Naturalism. *McTeague* and *The Octopus* do not reveal a simple determinism. Norris' compassion, outrage at injustice, concern for humanity, and belief in life were too great for so simple a label. His inconsistency puzzled and irritated many, and is reflected in his often weak stylistic form as well as his bifurcated attitude. He put man at the mercy of biology and society in *McTeague,* piling clinical detail upon detail, acting like the true naturalist interested merely in observing and reporting. But in *The Octopus,* he also condemned the railroad speculation, selfishness, and inhumanity, that was presumably open to correction.

The duality between romanticism and Naturalism was constant in all of Norris' work. The secret of his growth lay in his broadened experience and deepened vision in handling his materials. He wished to see romance in reality and reality in romance. That he never attained a harmonious balance between these two does not detract from the power and permanence of his work. He argued as a romantic that strange locales, bizarre action, and exotic characters were the stuff of life. But as a realist or naturalist he also argued with deeper insight that truth was a matter of perception, not situation.[54]

Norris groped slowly and chaotically toward a well-defined Naturalism in his late twenties. But while he sought his true medium, he turned aside for three romances, which showed clearly that his love of the exotic died hard. The most amazing of these was

Moran of the Lady Letty, first serialized in *The Wave,* then issued as a book in 1898.

Moran was pure adventure, bearing few obvious overtones of the serious purpose or impressive talent that came with *McTeague.* Set in San Francisco, it recounted the kidnapping of Ross Wilbur, elegant young man about town, by Captain Kitchell's press gang. He arrived on the sailing vessel "silk-hatted, melton-overcoated, patent-booted, and gloved in suedes." A smart blow from the Captain showed Wilbur the futility of protest, and he emerged from the hold moments later "in oilskins and a sou'wester" to begin his career as a shanghaied pirate.[55]

Captain Kitchell was little more than a pirate, and his delight at discovering a salvageable coal barge adrift allowed him to ignore that its chief mate, and daughter of its owner, was a Viking female known as Moran. She was the first of Norris' Nietzschean women, blonde, immense, masculine even to her name, and yet virginal in her prowess. She was "a strange, lonely creature, solitary as the ocean whereon she lived, beautiful after her fashion; as yet without sex, proud, untamed, splendid in her savage, primal independence —a thing untouched and unsullied by civilization." [56]

The adventures that followed combined Robert Louis Stevenson, Rudyard Kipling, and Richard Harding Davis. The capture of a sperm whale, the ship's destruction on the rocks of Lower California, the fight at sea and then on land with Chinese pirates for the valuable whale oil and ambergris—all read like a comic book. In the climactic fight with the pirates, Wilbur discovered his latent strength, as the savage rose in him and he killed an opponent. He exulted for the moment in "the joy of battle, the horrid exhilaration of killing, the animal of the race, the human brute suddenly aroused and dominating every instinct and tradition of centuries of civilization." [57]

Properly tamed, Moran abandoned her career of piracy, swearing, and innocent virginity in a touching surrender to Wilbur. Her destiny lay with him; and love, not battle, mattered most. But it was not to be, for a Chinese man killed the now weakened Moran; and Wilbur last saw her dead on the deck of her ship, gliding noiselessly into the fog beyond the Golden Gate like a fallen Valkyrie in a Wagnerian opera.

One turns from *Moran* as from a hallucination, for however absurd the story itself may seem—filled with impossible people, contrived events, and incredible dialogue—it flashes on the mind and memory like a Technicolor movie. Norris' verbal skill made it gripping adventure. Beneath the romance and absurdity glittered the half-formed themes of all Norris' writing. Moran and Wilbur illustrated the split personality in every man, the dangers of the beast latent beneath the veneer of civilized manners. Civilization destroyed primal innocence. Like McTeague, Moran was at the mercy of a society she did not understand and could not conquer.

The book also attacked the false social values of the time, especially the hollow aristocracy of manners and wealth that ensnared Ross Wilbur. He returned from his experience a changed man, broader in vision for having struggled, fought, and loved. Landing at a fashionable hotel in San Diego, clad in rags and filth, he proclaimed his superiority to the elegant guests, boasting of his exploits, condemning their sterile existence. "As though there wasn't anything else to do but lead cotillions and get up new figures!" [58]

If *Moran* offered any serious theme, it was the redemptive power of love. Moran's emergence from selfishness and isolation into contact with humanity gave the study serious purpose. Norris, like Wilbur, attacked manners and sham morality, but he reveled in participation with, if not love of, humanity. The once brutal Moran, tamed by love, even intervened to save the disgraced pirate captain, speaking the book's ultimate moral: "We've had enough fighting and killing." [59]

Norris knew the novel's faults and justified it as an essay in adventure, a tribute to his love of action and the vital life. "I do not think, though, that I shall ever write another story of adventures," he promised a friendly critic. "When I wrote 'Moran' I was, as one might say, flying kites, trying to see how high I could go without breaking the string. However, I have taken myself and my work much more seriously since then." [60]

The gulf between *Moran* and the youthful memoir *Blix* (1899) illustrated the range of Norris' style and interest. Though it followed *McTeague* in publication, *Blix* was written first, detailing Norris' years as a reporter and his courtship of Jeanette Black, whom he married in 1900. Norris had no purpose in *Blix,* titled after the nickname the young reporter Condy Rivers gave his fiancée, except a kind of reminiscence. "It is essentially a love story," he told a friend. "No sentimentality—everything healthy and clean and natural. 'Blix' does not belong to any 'school' so far as I can see. It's not naturalism and it's not romanticism; it's just a story." [61]

But *Blix* was a parable of innocence in the face of experience, of purity confronting corrosive civilization. Every page was a paean to youth, preaching vitality and innocence. "Cynicism, old age, and the weariness of all things done had no place in the world in which they walked. They still had their illusions, all the keenness of their sensations, all the vividness of their impressions. The simple things of the world, the great, broad, primal emotions of the race stirred in them." [62]

Blix breathed a charm of manner and grace of style that made it seem the work of another hand. It was like a fine photograph of its period, centered on two young people who promise never to grow old. Amusing, light, it was delightful to read and a nostalgic evocation of youth in San Francisco in the 1890s. Only in its subtle interest, easy reading, and cumulative detail did it foreshadow the great books that followed.

There remained one final adventure before Norris turned to the naturalistic veins whose ore filled his last great work. *A Man's Woman* (1900) was part of the fever for Arctic exploration that gripped the world in the 1890s. Expeditions set out from almost all major nations to conquer the poles. Outfitted with inadequate equipment, they often ended in tragedy, offering in microcosm a tableau of man's fight against nature. The subject inevitably caught Norris' fancy. Perhaps because he verged now on a final commitment to Naturalism, or perhaps because at this critical moment he realized the inconsistencies of his philosophy, *A Man's Woman* was his least impressive book. Repetitious, verbose, filled with unreal characters, surprisingly naïve and maudlin, it bore the marks of the hackwork which Norris labeled it.

It presented, however, a strong man, Ward Bennett, whose saga across Antarctica's ice was the only part of the book that caught fire. Bennett was strong of jaw, determined of purpose, physically as rugged as the elements he fought with his doomed expedition. As the Antarctic wind howled about him, "folly-stricken, insensate, an enormous, mad monster . . . pitiless as a famished wolf," Bennett vowed to beat it, and finally saved his party.[63] But not before reverting to a kind of primal savagery, when he and his starving men fought with their huskies "for the privilege of eating a dead dog." [64]

Once saved, Bennett returned to Lloyd Searight, and the remainder of the book dealt with their clash of will. Lloyd, a typical Norris heroine, strong, determined to do things with her life, masculine in name, defied Bennett, but succumbed finally to the realization that strength and growth lay in love. She gave herself to Bennett, offering him also the means of redemption, in another clear statement of Norris' belief in love's power in human relations. "This was only the beginning," he wrote of Bennett's conversion to love; "the breach once made, Humanity entered into the gloomy, waste places of his soul. . . ." [65] Lloyd, "A Man's Woman," subsidized her husband's return to the Antarctic, recognizing the importance of his work, and refusing to capitalize on her femininity.

Though the book deserved Norris' own condemnation—"It is very slovenly put together and there are only two real people in all its 100,000 words"—it was the best statement of his worship of what Jack London called the superman.[66] Though Norris loved action and admired rugged men, he did not set his fiction in London's "blood and fang school." He tempered strength with a respect for life, and endowed his supermen and superwomen with an innocence that set them apart from the ruthlessness of London's Wolf Larsen. Norris believed in action rather than meditation, because movement indicated growth. His strong insistence on action reflected his disgust with Victorian romanticism's passivity and artificiality. Norris used his supermen as laboratories, to study the conflicts of men and life which he handled more effectively in the panoramic settings of The Octopus. At the same time, he insisted on a sense of responsibility for the weak from the strong. Ward Bennett, faced with the chance of survival himself, refused to abandon his party after asking: "Was it not right that the mightiest should live? Was it not the great law of nature?" Norris' answer was an explicit No.[67]

Norris' interest in the life of action stemmed in part from his own personal ill health. It also mirrored a larger belief in what he called "race." He believed in the Anglo-Saxon mission and never surrendered the idea that some peoples were weak and some strong. As a young reporter he said smugly: "In every Chinaman there is something of the snake and a good deal of the cat," in an article that vilified the Chinese and Spanish of San Francisco.[68] In *The Octopus* he contrasted the "pure" blood of Anglo-Saxon stock and the "degenerated" blood of the Spanish settlers. His views were confused, but he equated strength with Anglo-Saxon ideals and origins. He was at first an imperialist, glorying in the spread of English and American ideals in the 1890s, in the acquisition of empires of "lesser peoples." But in this as in other things, he changed with time. Late in life he argued eloquently and stubbornly against British imperialism in the Boer War.[69] As the great trilogy, "The Epic of the Wheat," developed in his last years, he saw the scope and depth of human problems with a clearer eye, and wrote in one of his last articles that "the true patriotism is the brotherhood of man. . . ." [70]

That he could lapse so easily into the pasteboard romance of *Moran*, the superficial if delightful *Blix*, and the unrealized rawness of *A Man's Woman* indicated the still unresolved dilemmas of form and philosophy which he confronted in 1899 with greater maturity and experience. "I am going back definitely now to the style of *McT*. and stay with it right along," he promised in apology for *A Man's Woman*.[71]

Though Norris apologized for the crudities of these books, he had touched on themes that further stirred the waters of controversy surrounding American realistic writing. His rather frank discussions and intimations of sexual conflicts aroused considerable opposition from a generation that preferred not to discuss such things in its literature. Norris' sexual discussions often seemed a trifle raw and brutishly suggestive, as he intended them to be. In *McTeague*, he talked about Trina's joyous yielding to the dentist's coarse advances and "animal" drives. Elsewhere, sex seemed even more disturbing for being more subtly hidden. In *The Pit*, it would seem at times to make both Curtis and Laura Jadwin mere pawns, an atavistic reminder of an animal past, which even the most cultured could not wholly control. In the short stories, and in most of his novels, he hinted at or discussed sexual problems and perversions in terms that showed the emerging importance of sex as a theme in Naturalism.

Only a man of unusual vitality and great purpose could have accomplished what Norris had done by 1899, when he was only twenty-nine years old. In 1898 he left California for New York, where he worked for S. S. McClure, and then as a reader for Doubleday. Dozens of manuscripts passed through his hands for editorial judgment. He helped Theodore Dreiser publish *Sister Carrie* (1900), and was an inspiration to many younger writers. It was grueling labor, highlighted only occasionally by a rather grim jest at the appalling quality of most of the manuscripts he read. "At a conservative estimate there are 70,000,000 people in the United States," he wrote in exasperation. "At a liberal estimate 100,000 of these have lost the use of both arms; remain then 69,900,000 who write novels." [72]

He found New York oppressive and often squalid, a curious view for the naturalist who brilliantly pictured both the decadence and splendor of San Francisco. He longed for the vastness of California, and slowly the outlines of a masterwork settled firmly in his mind, a novel whose sweep, color, and excitement would capture the California he loved and the life that fascinated him.[73] He appreciated the city's artistic facilities, and he enjoyed contact with men like Howells and Garland. He was egotist enough to savor success without mistaking sweetness for its total taste. "I think I am going to 'get on' now, my stuff seems to take pretty damn well, much better than I expected, and lots of people,—big people in a way— have patted me on the head and chucked me under the chin." [74]

He circulated in literary and social circles, impressing those he met with his deceptive personality. Hamlin Garland remembered him as a striking man. "He is perilously handsome, tall and straight, with keen brown eyes and beautifully modelled features. His face is as smooth as that of a boy of twenty, but his hair is almost white. I have never known a more engaging writer. He is a poet in experience, but a close observer and a realist in his fiction." He was not one to "disappoint his admirers." [75]

He now settled into the style that made him famous, projecting a huge naturalistic trilogy based on the growth, distribution, and consumption of wheat, to be called "The Epic of the Wheat." "Now I think I know where I am at and what game I play the best," he assured friends. "The Wheat series will be straight naturalism with all the guts I can get into it." [76]

He wished to pour into the trilogy all his observations on life, and to define the philosophy that had risen thus far only sporadically to the surface of his work. He wanted also to enshrine a passing California, to turn from the one-dimensional local color of Bret Harte to something deeper and more meaningful. "I have great faith in the possibilities of San Francisco and the Pacific Coast as offering a field for fiction," he said.[77]

It was a vast scheme, encompassing a world view. "The idea is so big that it frightens me at times, but I have about made up my mind to have a try at it," he wrote early in 1899.[78] The work had three phases: in *The Octopus* he would grow the wheat; in *The Pit* he would follow its distribution; in *The Wolf* he would see how it carried life abroad to a famine-stricken country. He knew the task's difficulties. "It involves a very long, very serious and perhaps a very terrible novel." [79]

He gathered facts during trips to California in 1899 and 1900. He spent weeks reading accounts of the Southern Pacific Railroad's development of the San Joaquin Valley. He visited wheat farms, ran machines that planted, harvested, and processed the grain. He roamed the docks of Oakland and San Francisco, where ships gorged themselves on grain that fed the world. He drove locomotives and talked with friends and foes of the railroad. He focused his story on the famous Mussel Slough incident of 1880 that pitted angry farmers against the railroad's oppressive policies.

In writing *The Octopus,* Norris seemed little interested in the railroad's specific abuses, which reformers were already attacking. He was never concerned with radicalism, and unlike Garland, stood outside the Populist movement. He had no taste for politics; and though he recognized clearly and attacked specifically the railroad's oppression, he was more interested in its development in the economic and social change that was overtaking the country's old agrarian way of life. Determined now to take the largest possible view of the struggle for life, he used the railroad and its setting to illustrate the impersonal forces that so deeply interested him. He used specific personalities and events to illustrate general ideas.

He could hardly have chosen a more controversial topic. The Southern Pacific Railroad had long dominated most of the western states through which it passed, and most specifically California. Thinly disguised as the Pacific and Southwestern Railroad in the novel, it was the book's symbolic title; for on a map it looked like "a gigantic parasite fattening upon the life-blood of an entire commonwealth," its monied tentacles reaching into every sphere of life.[80] Its agents in Norris' view reflected its greed and oppressive power, caricatured in S. Behrman, railroad agent and chief human obstacle to the wheat farmers. "He was a large, fat man, with a great stomach; his cheek and upper part of his thick neck ran together to form a great tremendous jowl, shaven and blue-grey in color; a roll of fat, sprinkled with sparse hair, moist with perspiration, protruded over the back of his collar."[81] Clad in a vest checked with interlocking horseshoes that might as well have been dollar signs, Behrman was the human villain of the plot. He was imperturbable, sinister yet somehow as impersonal as the economic forces he represented.

Norris cast the railroad's opposition in an equally large mold. The men opposed to the railroad because its rates were high, and because it would not sell them their land at reasonable prices, were hardly embattled farmers. Their leader, the aloof, dignified Magnus Derrick, in whom flowed a vein of ruthless expediency that proved his downfall, farmed vast estates. In many ways they were as greedy as their opponents. "They had no love for their land. They were not attached to their soil. . . . To get all there was out of the land, to squeeze it dry, to exhaust it, seemed their policy. When, at last, the land worn out, would refuse to yield, they would invest their money in something else; by then, they would all have made their fortunes. They did not care. 'After us the deluge.' "[82]

If the railroad was corrupt, so were the farmers who bought a railroad commission, bitter only when it turned against them to do the railroad's bidding. They had more animal frenzy than the forces Behrman symbolized, and between the two Norris saw little to choose. When the railroad announced its exorbitant land prices, the mob erupted in savage denunciation. "It was the human animal hounded to its last stand, at bay, ferocious, terrible, turning at last with bared teeth and upraised claws to meet the death grapple." [83]

Norris developed his story in panoramic manner, using the earth and its life-giving wheat to show the indifferent natural processes that controlled man's actions. In magnificent sweep, he described the plowing, harvesting, and storing of the wheat in a series of famous scenes that gave the grain a life of its own. Men came and went, but the land and its produce remained to nourish generation after generation. "Men, Lilliputians, gnats in the sunshine, buzzed impudently in their tiny battles, were born, lived through their little day, died, and were forgotten; while the Wheat, wrapped in Nirvanic calm, grew steadily under the night, alone with the stars and with God." [84]

The Octopus was verbose and often sentimental, but it was captivating in its vitality and color. The reader participated in the great barn dance, where cowboys, farmers, and businessmen mingled with pretty girls in the gusto of country entertainment as a celebration of animality. The great jack rabbit drive, which harried thousands of destructive pests to a stockade where the men clubbed them to death, was a distinguished piece of visual writing. "The Anglo-Saxon spectators round about drew back in disgust, but the hot, degenerate blood of the Portuguese, Mexican, and mixed Spaniard boiled up in excitement at this wholesale slaughter" across the quaking carpet of furry bodies. [85]

Their wheat harvested, the farmers were enraged at the railroad's excessive hauling charges. When their land itself was threatened, they revolted. Led by Annixter and the younger Derricks, they met a posse of federal marshals and railroad agents at an irrigation ditch. In the ensuing battle, the principal contestants were killed, and Behrman and his railroad triumphed. Even Osterman, who defied the railroad by stealing one of its locomotives for a wild cross-country escape, died. Only the women, an insane Magnus Derrick, and Presley, the ineffectual poet, survived. The railroad's complex triumph did not surprise S. Behrman, who had always preached the futility of fighting its force.

There remained Presley's final realization that only if he participated in the human drama around him, only if he was committed to the cause he saw defeated, could he write his epic poem. Moving in elegant circles in San Francisco, he saw the results of the railroad's wealth in the barons and magnates he knew by sight. In a final, lurid, melodramatic scene, Norris wove the details of an elegant dinner party with the sordid decline and death of Mrs. Hooven, widow of one of the railroad's victims. Her eldest daughter driven to prostitution, she herself reduced to begging, her younger child wracked with hunger and cold, Mrs. Hooven died just as the elegant dessert was served at the dinner where Presley was a guest.

But the railroad's agents were no more free of its control than the farmers. Confident that he had calmed the storm, Behrman saw one of his ships loading grain at a dock in Oakland. He fell into its hold and died in the flood of grain that closed inexorably over his gasping mouth and tortured reach. No man challenged the Wheat and lived.

In its sweep, *The Octopus* seemed merely a series of great set pieces, like an old-fashioned opera. Aware of the limitations of this episodic approach, Norris wove into his narrative a number of subplots whose themes united the action. His minor characterizations were especially fine. His eye for color and distinctive qualities in persons let him subordinate minor characters to the larger plot at no sacrifice of their importance or reality. One remembered with ease the outlines of Magnus Derrick, S. Behrman, or the moody, morose, volatile Annixter. But one also saw clearly the vitality of a lesser man like Father Sarria, "relic of a departed regime, kindly, benign, believing in all goodness, a lover of his fellows and of dumb animals, yet, for all that, hurrying away in confusion and discomfiture, carrying in one hand the vessels of the Holy Communion and in the other a basket of game cocks." [86]

Taking to heart Howells' earlier criticism that just as the sweet was not all of life, neither was the bitter, Norris included the story of the shepherd Vanamee's search for his dead love, ravished long ago by a nameless assailant. She was dead but alive in the daughter born of that tragic union. Endowed with telepathic powers, Vanamee, the wandering herdsman, spoke for the same sixth sense that drove McTeague into the desert.

In Annixter, Norris found a vehicle for his earlier belief in the redemptive power of love. This bitter man, ravaged by fictitious stomach ailments, munching dried prunes, with no time for "feemales," was softened by his love for Hilma Tree. Through the lenses of selflessness, he saw new life in care for others. "This poor, crude fellow, harsh, hard, with his unlovely nature, his fierce truculency, his selfishness, his obstinacy, abruptly knew that all the sweetness of life, all the great vivifying eternal force of humanity had burst into life within him." [87]

But the novel's basic lesson lay in the larger sphere of life's triumph over all man's vicissitudes. "Men were naught, death was naught, life was naught," Norris insisted. "FORCE only existed—FORCE that brought men into the world, FORCE that crowded them out of it to make way for succeeding generations, FORCE that made the wheat grow, FORCE that garnered it from the soil to give place to the succeeding crop." [88] He preached in *The Octopus* of the vastness of life and the need of perspective. "Never judge of the whole round of life by the mere segment you can see," Vanamee quietly told the depressed Presley. "The whole is, in the end, perfect." [89] What did it matter that men died or failed when the natural forces behind them lived on? The ecstatic Vanamee, raising his arms in stunned wonder to the green carpet of wheat that rose from the ground in the light of an apocalyptic dawn, spoke with beauty and vivid power: "Life out of death, eternity rising from out of dissolution." [90]

The Octopus was a moving attack on economic oppression. If Naturalism implied disinterest in its subject, *The Octopus* was not naturalistic. The reader never doubted that his interests lay against the railroad. If Norris did not overly sympathize with the wheat barons or "the people," he uttered in this book a fervent and enduring plea for common humanity.

Stunned at the defeat of his ideals, realizing the shallowness of his own commitment, the poet Presley visited the shadowy railroad builder Shelgrim, modeled after Collis P. Huntington. Surprisingly, he found him a man of artistic taste, honest and forthright, not the one-dimensional monster he expected. Before entering the office he heard the great man intervene to save a drunken clerk's job because he had a family to support. Confronted by Shelgrim, he heard him talk of Power, Life, Force. "The Wheat is one force, the Railroad, another, and there is the law that governs them— supply and demand. Men have little to do in the whole business. . . . Blame conditions, not men." [91] Shelgrim's explanation was a classic statement of laissez-faire economics.

Presley left Shelgrim's office disturbed. He had never seen the struggle, so personal to him, from so great a height. Shelgrim's argument seemed valid: the railroad was but an agent of a vast unseen force; the railroad manipulated men and goods, and the force manipulated the railroad. The system was invincible, blind, inevitable.

Norris passed without comment to the novel's end, leaving the impression that this was also his view. But he was perhaps more subtle than he knew, for the moralist shadowed the determinist in this famous scene. If Shelgrim could defeat these blind forces and save a drunken clerk's family, why could he not also intervene to save the farmers or the public from extortion and oppression? Men were not in fact at the railroad's mercy, for they built it. It was a human machine, run by men, who grew their wheat for it and for other men. Shelgrim's talk was simple rationalization for his and others' sins of omission and commission in their business policies.

Because of its sprawling form and confused philosophy, *The Octopus* remains one of the most complex modern American novels. Though it was not a pamphlet aimed at contemporary evils, neither was it entirely naturalistic. It was pessimistic in doubting the scope of man's effectiveness, but it preached action and was not passive or negative. Norris' confused Naturalism was never more real, for he behaved as if good and evil were supernatural qualities. In fact, they are man-made and not absolute in the world. His handling of the wheat was the key to focusing this inconsistency, for he failed to see that men grow, harvest, and consume the wheat. It reflected a natural force, but that force was also a valid expression of human labor and intelligence.

When indignant, Norris realized the essential artificiality of divorcing man entirely from self-control. The elegantly impersonal Cederquist spoke for Norris when he said that corruption existed *"because the People allow it.* The indifference of the People is the opportunity of the despot." [92] The poet Presley captured the essence of meaning behind the false talk by erupting with the true reformer's zeal in a classic attack on the laissez-faire doctrine:

We know them for what they are—ruffians in politics, ruffians in finance, ruffians in law, ruffians in trade, bribers, swindlers, and tricksters. . . . They swindle a nation of a hundred million and call it Financeering; they levy a blackmail and call it Commerce; they corrupt legislature and call it Politics; they bribe a judge and call it Law; they hire blacklegs to carry out their plans and call it Organization; they prostitute the honor of a State and call it Competition.[93]

Norris weakened and ultimately dissipated the book's determinism by his frequent intervention to explain action and justify characters, saying in the end a simple truth: "Because the farmers of the valley were poor, these men were rich." [94]

The Octopus ranked with *McTeague* as Norris' best work, but its faults could not be ignored. It was overly long, it preached, it bore all the irritating marks of Norris' habitual repetitiousness. Its plot was not fully developed, its continuity was sporadic, and some of its characters were mere pasteboard mouthpieces for the author's preaching. But it remains a deeply moving work, and its achievements far outweigh these detriments of style which are more irritating than damaging. Its central purpose was to show man in nature, to depict some of the struggles of life in a manner believable to all men, and in this it did not fail.

The Octopus made Norris an important American figure, presaging a brilliant future if he could complete "The Epic of the Wheat." Only *The Pit* exceeded its sales. It provoked comparisons with Zola, but Norris worked in his own vein, using his own materials and from a personal viewpoint. Though many reviewers quarreled with the book's message and condemned its stylistic faults, they praised its gusto and vividness. To one it was "the novel of the season." [95]

Though Hamlin Garland warned him of large projects that turned stale or changed design, Norris moved to the trilogy's second volume, *The Pit.* He and his wife went to Chicago to study the mechanics of the wheat exchange. Its trading pit gave the book

its title, and in its action Norris dealt with the men who manipulated the wheat in its journey to feed the world. As in *The Octopus,*
he wove the book's story around an actual event, an almost successful corner of the world's wheat supply by Joseph Leiter in
1897. Then, as with the fictional Curtis Jadwin, the wheat mastered
its masters.

Facts were merely the skeletal framework on which he put the
three themes that united the story. (1) The wheat, or life, was
greater than the men who manipulated it; (2) the American businessman, here reminiscent of his own father, was more interested
in the challenge of building big business than in making money;
(3) the danger of subordinating the personal to the impersonal and
inhuman.

Curtis Jadwin, Chicago's leading financier, symbolized the era's
tycoons, but he was not ignorant or brutal. He attended the opera,
had artistic taste, and thought enough of his fellow men to break
a villain in order to help a wronged wheat broker. Laura Dear-
born, later his wife, lived in the grand manner, like the great
actress Norris' mother could have been, calculating, coolly impersonal, self-centered. These two wills met in fascinating combat,
Laura surrendering to Jadwin because of the power he represented.

"They call it buying and selling down there in LaSalle Street,"
a broker commented of the wheat dealers. "But it is simply betting. Betting on the conditions of the market weeks, even months,
in advance." [96] But Laura saw it in the light that fascinated Norris:

Terrible as the Battle of the Street was, it was yet battle. Only the
strong and the brave might dare it, and the figure that held her
imagination and her sympathy was not the artist, soft of hand and of
speech, elaborating graces of sound and color and form, refined, sensitive, and temperamental; but the fighter, unknown and unknowable to
women as he was; hard, rigorous, panoplied in the harness of the
warrior, who strove among the trumpets, and who, in the brunt of
conflict, conspicuous, formidable, set the battle in a rage around him,
and exulted like a champion in the shoutings of the captains.[97]

Captivated not by the spectacle of making more money but by
the daring, romance, and scope of the project, Jadwin sought to
corner the wheat. Ruthlessly efficient, breaking opponents with his

power, mortgaging his property and his ethics, he drove heedlessly ahead, blind to the estrangement of his own wife, and the effect of his actions on innocent people far from the scene of conflict. The real terror of the scheme lay in its effect on his own morality, for as the corner developed, "a vast contempt for human nature grew within him." [98] He preferred to see the struggle in impersonal terms that justified his deeds and left him guiltless, crying in despair: "I corner the wheat! Great heavens, it is the wheat that has cornered me." [99]

Though he came within sight of his goal, raising the price of wheat even higher, beyond the reach of the world's hungry, he failed; for the wheat was greater than the brokers. Drowned like S. Behrman, though not literally, in the wheat's flood, he was broken though he looked forward to a fresh beginning in the West.

Despite its grandiose theme, *The Pit* was not really a continuation of *The Octopus*. Wrought on an inevitably smaller scale, it was more subtle in its approach. Since it lacked the sweep and reality of *The Octopus,* it was a duller, if more sensitive book. The book's protagonist, the wheat, never appeared except in the sample sacks fed to pigeons on the exchange's window sills. It was an idea, a flood of paper, a gabble of noise, not an army of men. It existed not in earth or silos, but in men's imaginations. The brokers' call slips for thousands of bushels did not make it as real as in *The Octopus.*

Norris' determinism was even more ill-defined here than in *The Octopus*. Despite Jadwin's talk of impersonal forces, and Norris' interpolations about Nature, Life, and Force, Jadwin was broken not by the wheat but by the farmers who grew it. Eager to cash in on the rise in price he manipulated, as Jadwin's partner saw, "all the farmers planted it, and are getting ready to dump it on us." [100] The book's sharpest conclusion was profoundly moral: no man should control the lives of others for selfish gain.

The book's title had a double meaning, for just as Jadwin entered the wheat pit daily to speculate, caught in the madness it symbolized, so his wife dwelled in a personal pit of selfish loneliness. The love between them paralleled the story of the wheat's victory, and was often counted a weakness in the novel. But it was in fact its chief theme. Only gradually Laura understood that she was not whole until she loved her husband for himself. "Laura in that moment knew that love, the supreme triumph of a woman's life, was less a victory than a capitulation." [101] She cared only for Jadwin as he mirrored her own success. Her great house, built as a monument to his love, was filled with servants, passing guests, bad art works, and the great pipe organ on which she played the hackneyed music she knew no better than to like. The novel's central event was the collapse of her selfishness and her stunned question: "Whither had this cruel cult of self led her?" [102] Laura's emergence from the pit of self was as significant as Jadwin's emergence from the pit of his selfish lust for power. Laura learned through the gentle Sheldon Corthell the limitations of her artistic tastes. She also turned from her one-dimensional self to the deeper realization that beauty and meaning consisted of love for Jadwin, and through him for life. "A little good contributed by everybody to the race is of more, infinitely more, importance than a great deal of good contributed by one individual to another," Corthell told Laura in the book's real point.[103]

Cast in the same philosophical terms as Norris' earlier work, *The Pit* offered a final judgment on the values of life as a whole. As Laura and Jadwin left their mortgaged palace, she reflected that the wheat "had passed, leaving Death and Ruin in its wake, but bearing Life and Prosperity to the crowded cities and centres of Europe." [104] The larger view, the larger belief mattered most.

The Pit ran serially in *The Saturday Evening Post* in 1902, and was published after Norris' death in 1903. His view having deepened, Norris hoped to make the trilogy's last volume, *The Wolf*, an epic comment on life in general. He planned a trip around the world with his wife and young daughter to gather facts and impressions for this final effort. He also planned a massive naturalistic trilogy on the battle of Gettysburg, a volume for each day of the conflict. But it was not to be. In 1902 he moved his family to California to plan their world tour, and after resting at the isolated ranch of Mrs. Robert Louis Stevenson, he died of a perforated appendix on October 25, 1902.

His fame and recognition have often come for the wrong reasons. He was the first great Naturalist in American fiction, but he was also the bridge between old and new, combining in his work traditional American values with new concepts. Because of his confusion of purpose and often disordered style, many dismiss him as "a successful failure." Like Thomas Wolfe, of a later generation, critics and readers often either misread his main purpose or catalogue his stylistic imperfections.

Norris took for his subject man in crisis, which differed little from that of Howells and Realism. But if his technique often seemed realistic, his point of view was deeper. He infused fresh vitality, sheer energy, into American letters. He left behind a series of works that catalogue the life of his time. He extended Realism's themes into the dark places of life and man's consciousness. His description of man's duality, probing of the unconscious, interest in all the details of life, and his awareness of the disorder and complexity of his era make him a major figure in American fiction.

It is easy to attack his style; but its faults merely proved the dynamics of his talent, for he raced ahead of the limitations of language as he knew it. These faults showed only that he was hasty, not that he was wrong. His books read like first drafts, but further polishing might have removed their immediacy and vigor. Norris worked the only way he could. The finest structural and linguistic form in a dead situation is not as compelling as the most vital purpose in a flawed form. *The Prisoner of Zenda* is a model of its special *genre,* but who reads it today in preference to *McTeague*?

Norris left behind an aura of youth and genius cut off in its prime, touching upon many contemporaries like a bright light. "To those of us who were destined so long to outlive him, and to whom his fine and free and gallant spirit has become a sort of splendid tradition, Frank never did outgrow his youth," Kathleen Norris recalled.[105] An artist is judged by what he did, not by what he might have become. On that basis, Frank Norris' reputation is secure.

He was often uncertain of his purpose, inconsistent in his thinking, wasteful of his gifts. But these things fade when the heart of his achievement is touched. How much better it is to remember the scenes and people he left behind: Vandover sees in a child's eyes the man he might have been. Consumed by the lusts of acquisition, Trina barters her soul for false gold to symbolize all mankind's weaknesses. McTeague dies in the sun of a universe he dimly understood at the mercy of forces he never fathomed. Vanamee pays homage to the eternal Wheat in the sunrise. Laura Jadwin dances Carmen before her bewildered husband to the empty echoes of a lavish art gallery. The power, the misery, the grandeur of the people Frank Norris brought to life will always move those who wish to see.

Theodore Dreiser: The Naturalist as Humanist

*The world owes me nothing—or little at best. I have not
felt that I owed the world much. My sympathy and sorrow
have been for individuals—never for life itself.*

—1915

*If you are moved to praise anyone or anything from toad-
stool to star, praise life, whose generative compulsions present to you and to me, all that we are, see, feel and do. What
else, which else is there to praise?*

—1938

HE WAS CERTAINLY a very elegant young man, and his vigor and
charm impressed visitors. He was not exactly handsome, but he
had a certain magnetism that offset rather plain looks. He was
over six feet tall, but gave the impression of being larger, even
when seated, because of a heavy build. His eyes were firm in their
glance, and often contained a curious hardness with warmth. He
had poor teeth, set above a receding chin, and his hair was thin-
ning. He had not yet outgrown a youthful feeling of inferiority
about his supposed bad looks; but he compensated for physical
shortcomings with the judgment, courtesy, and energy that had
made him so successful.

For he was successful, accustomed already to giving newspaper
interviews, to talking on art and business at cocktail parties, to
being considered a "figure" in American letters. He seemed contradictory to those who knew his career. He was a powerful editor
for a syndicate of ladies' magazines that marketed "uplifting"
literature. He had worked for Street and Smith Publications, pur-
veyors of dime novels and boys' adventure stories. Yet he himself
was in the vanguard of naturalistic literature. He came from
poverty to the glittering opulence of New York, but he sym-
pathized with life's less fortunate. He moved in elegant circles,

affecting fashionable dress, adorning an impeccable outfit with gold-rimmed pince-nez on a black string. Yet he hated false values and affectation. He was kind and generous, but could be an office tyrant and was a ruthless organizer and shrewd money-maker for his firm. His name was Theodore Dreiser, and while he often wondered just why he was at Butterick Publications, so much had happened to him that nothing seemed surprising.

He began life many times removed from his present world. He came into the world on August 27, 1871, in Terre Haute, Indiana. His birth presaged much of his life, for he bore a strong streak of German mysticism. Legend said that while his mother labored to give him life, she saw three garlanded maidens dancing in her room. She had had visions before, and despite her husband's scoffing at such nonsense, she called on spirits to help in her times of trial.

Theodore was a spindly child, gangling and prey to sickness; but his dreamy air made him his mother's favorite, and that compensated for much of his childhood's harshness. He was taciturn and serious minded, listening solemnly while grownups talked, now and then asking a question to which he expected an honest reply. He loved nature, walked in the woods, admired birds and animals, and was very observant of the life around him. He seemed to reincarnate his mother's pantheism, and thus began the long process that consumed most of his adult life—trying to define nature.

The rather grim and fatalistic view of life that critics later called Naturalism in his fiction sprang organically from Dreiser's own life as well as his personality. It came first from his family— varied, disordered, poor, and ruled by hidden forces, yet full of human sympathy. What he later saw of mankind, as a reporter and writer, editor and traveler, reinforced this early grounding in life's grim aspects.

His father was the center of much of his life and work, despite the son's protests against almost everything the older man believed. Paul Dreiser came to the United States like many other Germans to escape military service and oppressive government. A man of considerable business talent, he prospered in his middle years and raised a large family. But accident and misfortune bankrupted him and robbed him of the will to succeed. Through most of Theodore's life, his father eked out a living as a carpenter, bricklayer, and handyman.

Perhaps to ease this painful failure of nerve, the elder Dreiser turned to religion. He pursued the teachings of the Catholic Church with a ferocity that eventually helped turn all his children against him. He hammered religious ideals into a narrow mold that repelled Theodore. Until the end of his days, the writer-son considered Catholicism one of history's most oppressive creeds; and he never forgave, though he finally understood, his father's religious harshness.

Theodore's mother offset her husband's strictness. Though nominally a Catholic, she seldom attended services, and was lenient with the children. If his father was a negative factor in his development, his mother was the great force for sympathetic understanding in Theodore's life. He thought her beyond good or evil, "A strange, sweet dreamy woman, who did not know how life was organized. . . ." [1] Misfortune, poverty, and a broken home dogged her footsteps. Though she loved her children dearly, and wished success for them, she lived to see almost all desert the rigid moral standards her husband enforced in their childhoods. One of Theodore's earliest memories was playing as a child with her torn shoes until he cried at their poorness.

His older brothers quickly left home, partly to escape the family's rigid moralism, and partly to satisfy a consuming wanderlust. Brothers Al and Rome became continental wanderers, often making their distant presence felt with postcards or letters from exotic ports of call. More often they were silent until they suddenly crossed the family threshold for a prodigal's welcome from their mother and sisters, filling young Theodore's ears with adventure tales.

Then there was brother Paul, hopefully named after his father and exactly his opposite. He changed his name to Paul Dresser and captivated a generation with banal and sentimental songs like "On the Banks of the Wabash." His music made him rich and famous. He grew fat as a *bon vivant* and indulged a rather innocently coarse appetite for pleasure. He moved in the bright lights of show business, surrounded by beautiful women and hangers-on. More than once, his money saved his family from extremity; and he thought nothing of having them live with him and the madame of a bawdy house, who was his current favorite. He had no interest in books or thought, but he often kept Theodore from despair and want.

Theodore's sisters were a curious compound of kindness and weakness, and became models for Carrie Meeber and Jennie Gerhardt. Theodore sometimes thought they combined in their persons all of mankind's faults and virtues, they were so unpredictable and foolish, yet loving and gentle. He remembered his father's raging against their early "walking out" with village boys, and heard neighborhood gossip about "those Dreiser girls." One by one they left home for the glitter of the city, fascinated with fine clothes and the tinsel glamor of a fictitious world to which their harsh upbringing made them doubly susceptible.

His childhood did not seem unusual, except in his love of color and variety. He remembered wanting the figure of Christ on the church altar, thinking it was a doll. He watched spotted cows in a neighbor's yard and heard the chickens gabbling in their search for food. He also recalled the slaughter house near one early home, the cries of dying animals, and the lustful squeals of delight from pigs feeding on their entrails. Life was ugly as well as lovely.

Above all, he remembered the gray color of poverty, for it was his family's hallmark. As a child he lived in Vincennes, Terre Haute, Warsaw, Evansville, and Chicago—usually one jump ahead of foreclosure. In desperation at one point, the family divided. The girls and young Theodore went with their mother to a small town where living was cheaper. They earned money by washing laundry and domestic services. Occasionally money came from the father and brothers, but it was seldom sufficient, and almost never enough to color their drab world. Paul's occasional visits after he became famous brought his vitality and warmth as well as money, and he was always a favored brother.

The family was so chronically poor, yet so patient under poverty's burden, that Theodore felt it colored his whole existence. For the rest of his life, even when he was financially secure, he dreaded winter's onset, because it reminded him of youthful poverty. He and his brothers often stole coal from the railroad yards to warm the house. But there was a strain in all the Dreisers that made them want more—to be somebody, as the current parlance put it. In the midst of such poverty, Theodore often saw his brother Al dressed in his best clothes lounging outside a fashionable restaurant, with a toothpick between his teeth, giving the impression that he had eaten there. It was an amazing milieu, but its dominant theme was oppressive. "What I personally lived through at that time was different—a dour and despondent period which seems to have colored my life forever." [2]

Though Dreiser later exaggerated this poverty and his bitterness toward his father, these two negative forces doubtless formed a great deal of his thinking. Poverty bred in him and his sisters a desperate need for the appearance of wealth. His interest in money both as a reality and as a symbol of man's desires, displayed so vividly in *Sister Carrie* (1900) and the "Trilogy of Desire," came largely from this youthful insecurity. Money not only meant success; it meant color and light in life.

But the young Theodore had his refuges from the real world's grimness. He loved to read, and chance brought him a most incongruous book on which to begin. A traveling agent sold his mother Thomas Edie Hill's *Manual of Social and Business Forms,* a compendium of business and social letters and forms of address. Few things could have been more incongruous on the parlor table or in an enthralled young Theodore's lap. He sharpened his literary talents on imaginary letters to supreme court justices and social leaders, finding this whole mysterious world of power and affluence enchanting.

Between ages seven and fourteen, over his bitter protests, he went to parochial school, and there endured a narrow pedagogy and theology that deepened his dislike of the Catholic Church. He was a dull student. "To myself I seemed little more than a mooning, dreaming youth who was so largely speculative that he could never hope to master details." [3] This was an ironic beginning for a naturalistic writer who reveled in details in his own fiction. He liked botany, zoology, astronomy, and history, but cared little for literature and philosophical speculation.

Drifting, disgusted with his life, torn between a love of the nature he saw around him and stark fear of the poverty he had always known, the young Dreiser emerged into manhood even more confused and uncertain than most adolescents. "Chronically nebulous, doubting, uncertain, I stared and stared at everything, only wondering, not solving." [4]

In 1886, he rebelled against further schooling, which his tolerant mother decided not to pursue, and bravely set out to be a farm hand. One day at backbreaking labor, for which his still slight frame was ill-suited, turned him from the field and furrow. He went to Chicago and promptly fell in love with the city whose color and variety always fascinated him. "Chicago was like a great orchestra in a tumult of noble harmonies," he wrote. "I was like a guest at a feast, eating and drinking in a delirium of ecstasy." [5] He worked at odd jobs, as a dishwasher, a clerk in a furniture warehouse, and as a bill collector. He soaked up the city's color, trying to fathom the purpose behind so vital and discordant a place as the then youthful Chicago.

In 1888, he showed signs of lung consumption, and worn down by hard work and mental depression, he seemed ready to collapse when his high school teacher offered to send him to Indiana University for a year. This generous offer from a woman he knew could ill afford it moved him, and for a time he was determined to profit from her sacrifice. In 1889 and 1890, he attended the University and studied a smattering of most of the introductory curriculum. The intellectual fare intrigued him less than the people. He roomed with a group of boys who represented humanity's spectrum. One was shy, like Theodore himself. One was weak but determined to be a scholar. Another was a lady-killer, Theodore's special envy, for he fancied himself a sexual failure though his sexual drive was very strong. Self-conscious of his poor looks and slight physique, he let his stronger roommates "build him up" by doing early morning push-ups on the lawn, running around the block in his shorts, and taking long walks.

College life heightened his inner tensions, though he presented a rather phlegmatic exterior to the world. He was acutely sex conscious, yet believed himself impotent. He longed to partake of what the world called pleasure, but fear held him back. He wanted to repay his teacher for sending him to school, but it frankly bored him. He was not made for the academic life; he lacked discipline and tended to daydream. A year convinced him that he could never master either himself or his surroundings through study. He would have to learn through doing, in typical American fashion. Order would come to his chaos through experience. In 1890, he returned to Chicago, resuming his rather pointless career at odd jobs, selling real estate, working for a laundry firm. Late in that year his mother died, a central event in his early life. Not only was her understanding sympathy gone, but her death meant a final family breakup. Each member now went his way.

But where was Dreiser to go and what was he to do? He was equipped for nothing but manual labor, and his own personality was still so torn between romance and realism that he seemed unable to train for an academic or literary discipline. His fascination with the passing scene of life was too great to embitter him for long. These youthful experiences and uncertainties fed the sources of his later art by bolstering his two greatest talents: observation and sympathy for struggle.

In the early winter of 1892, he decided to become a reporter. He still had no settled purpose to be a writer, though he wrote a little poetry and wanted to be a playwright, largely because he loved the glittering theatre world. Newspaper reporting had fostered many talents he admired—Eugene Field, James Whitcomb Riley, Finley P. Dunne—and Dreiser thought he could move in the circles of fashion and power as a newshawk. The Democratic national convention that nominated Grover Cleveland for President met in Chicago in 1892, and the Chicago *Daily Globe* took him on as a cub political reporter. By sheer grubbing and brashness, he filed a number of well-written and intelligent stories and quickly won the regard of fellow newsmen.

He had opened what seemed a promising career, but dissatisfied with his situation in Chicago, he moved to St. Louis, where he worked for two major newspapers in succession. In the course of finding or making news, Dreiser moved through the heights and depths of life. His work might take him to a mansion of the newly rich and a sharecropper's shanty in one afternoon. He saw the inner workings of local politics, business, and law. If he had any illusions left about human nature or life's sordid side, they vanished. His newspaper work impressed on him the variety of life, the unpredictable nature of people, and the apparent blindness with which nature showered favors or curses indiscriminately on mankind. He soon saw that his childhood teachings were wrong, or at least incomplete. The good were not always rewarded for being good; the bad were not always punished. He began to think that perhaps badness won the world's favors. He saw no apparent scheme of moral law in the world.

Nothing was more important in his whole life than these few years as a newspaper reporter, for the life he saw and events he reported shook him free from youthful romanticism. He never lost his streak of mysticism, but he now turned to facts and sense impressions as the basis of his future literary work. He saw that he had no life and no art apart from mankind and events.

It may seem provincial or naïve that the young Dreiser dwelled so long on what he called the cruel contrasts of life. That smiles exist in a world of sorrow, that poverty is the frequent counterpart of luxury, that happiness and misery live side by side in an often indifferent scheme of things is no longer news to many people. That critics later condemned Dreiser for dwelling on these things illustrated the era's standards. That such attitudes and facts have long since become a part of American literature should not diminish their importance to Dreiser or his generation.

These contrasts of misery and happiness especially depressed Dreiser because he was imbued with moralistic teachings then undergoing severe criticism. The Indiana of his youth produced both him and sentimentalists like Booth Tarkington and James Whitcomb Riley. With his moral values facing inner criticism, and his hopes for worldly success in the balance, Dreiser's move from the country to the city was almost traumatic. The move threw into relief a source of his fictional art: he saw himself as a typical man who could be rich while others were poor; who would be famous while equal talents rusted in obscurity; who unconsciously abetted an indifferent world by being selfishly absorbed in his own affairs. He began to see tragedy in all of this. *Not that anyone or anything caused it, but merely that it existed and was a basic fact in human life at all levels and circumstances.*

His newspaper work showed him the variability of human nature, with its apparent irrelevance to the scheme of things. He knew many brilliant men who simply disintegrated or ceased to grow, surrendering to some hidden weakness for drink or women or isolation. He saw skilled artists kept from full maturity because of poor persistence, social pressures, or home and family. Why? How could this be? And above all, why did it seem to make no difference to the larger scheme of things? He had been taught all the classic American values of self-help, initiative, enterprise; now he saw that they were at best half-truths.

His newspaper work, growing maturity, and consciousness of his own talents and the world around him revealed the gulf between what men practiced and preached. "People make laws for other people to live up to and in order to protect themselves in what they have," a cynical friend remarked. "They never intend those laws to apply to themselves or to prevent them from doing anything they wish to do." [6]

Still uncertain about his purpose, unsteady in his painfully growing writing talent, Theodore Dreiser worked slowly toward some hidden rendezvous with his future. Though he shook off much of his romanticism, and examined closely all of his childhood teachings, he was not yet sure of anything. To the end of his life he pursued that most elusive of all quarries: the answers to first questions.

He certainly made a striking appearance as a well-to-do and self-important young cub reporter. He combed his hair neatly à la pompadour, wore checked trousers, colored coats and vests, snappy hats, and patent leather shoes. He reported firemen's picnics and drills, prize fights, murder trials, political conventions, and train disasters. He was no confirmed determinist. In these years he read a smattering of fiction and a little philosophy, but decided to let life develop. He would be the observer rather than the philosopher; he would pass few judgments and amass many details. In his heart he still believed that underneath all the apparent surface horror and disorder of life lurked a plan for ultimate harmony. Despite poverty, vice, crime, and brutality, nature would yet provide a balance to elevate man and explain life. He believed in progress of sorts.

These were years of personal growth as well as professional preparation, and though he often brooded and withdrew into himself while trying to digest what he saw, he could be gay and charming. A great favorite with the ladies, he soon discovered that his sophomoric fears about his sexual prowess were fictitious. At about this time, he summed up his own personality: "Spiritually I was what might be called a poetic melancholiac, crossed with a vivid materialistic lust of life." [7]

His work was not always satisfying, for he wanted to do something more enduring than news reporting. But he was not yet ready to focus his talent. These years were both a testing ground and a foundation for later work. If he brought anything of lasting value from them, it was a sense of direction and a tone of life rather than facts themselves. He was turning now toward the larger questions of life and mankind's state that occupied the remainder of his years. His whole system of values came under close examination:

In short, I was beginning to find the world a seething, stormy, bitter, gay, rewarding and destroying realm, in which the strong and the subtle and the charming and the magnetic were apt to be victors, and the weak and the homely and the ignorant and the dull were apt to be deprived of any interesting share, not because of innate depravity but rather because of the lacks by which they were handicapped and which they could not possibly overcome.[8]

In 1894, after drifting from job to job, he met Arthur Henry of the Toledo *Blade,* a novelist and poet. They instantly liked each other, and Henry urged the still confused Dreiser to start a novel. But Dreiser fancied that he could be a playwright, which was about as unlikely as his becoming an operatic tenor. He could not settle down, though he worked briefly for Henry's paper, covering a streetcar strike that later became part of *Sister Carrie.* He wandered to Pittsburgh and other cities trying to find work as a reporter. He even thought of settling down in rural Indiana or Ohio to produce a country weekly. He read Victor Hugo and the writings of the Continental naturalists and realists. But he was still not convinced that he had the talent to write novels.

He at least understood that popular fiction bore little relation to the world he knew, and that masses of people were absorbing a false view of life. By the late 1890s he sensed that he was ready for literary productivity of some kind, and that America was poised

for a change in institutions and values that might make his new
viewpoint acceptable or even fashionable. He knew now that his
basic theme would have to be faithful reporting of what he had
seen. He did not underestimate his opposition; he knew how shallow
and wrong public taste and standards could be:

> We were taught persistently to shun most human experience as either
> dangerous or degrading or destructive. The less you knew about life
> the better; the more you knew about the fictional heaven and hell ditto.
> People walked about in a kind of sanctified daze or dream, hypnotized
> or self-hypnotized by an erratic and impossible theory of human con-
> duct which had grown up heaven knows where or how, and had finally
> cast its amethystine spell over all America, if not over all the world.[9]

"You couldn't write about life as it was," he recalled, "you had
to write about it as somebody else thought it was, the ministers
and farmers and dullards of the home." [10]

In 1899, he spent the summer with Henry at Maumee, Ohio,
in "The House of Four Pillars," a stately reminder of the canal
town's more prosperous era. Under Henry's relentless nagging,
which Dreiser thought worse than a fishwife's, he started to write
in his halting, turgid manner. He wrote a series of short stories
and passed off Henry's lavish praise as flattery. When magazines
actually bought them, he decided that a more ambitious project
was in order. In these pleasant, quiet surroundings, relatively
penniless but free from immediate worry, Dreiser one day picked
up a sheet of paper and idly wrote two words at the top: SISTER
CARRIE. He did not exactly know what he would say or how the
story would develop, but he wrote methodically, with several
breaks, until he produced the manuscript of his first novel. Though
Dreiser could hardly take seriously the idea that he was now
ready to enter American letters as a full-fledged novelist, he was
poised at the beginning of a long and rich career, and at the
threshold of a famous literary controversy.

The modern reader often finds in *Sister Carrie* a certain antique
quality, and it is difficult to understand the criticism it aroused. It
offered none of the lurid physical descriptions now *de rigeur* in
the novel. It dealt with no social or sexual perversions. It did not
openly discuss any controversial themes. It was not shocking, but

it was nonetheless a major milestone in American literary history, both for its techniques and its contents.

Like any effective writer, Dreiser wrote of things he knew. He modeled Carrie Meeber on one of his sisters, and took her from small-town America to the tantalizing new metropolis of Chicago. That city's wealth, variety, and apparently endless growth fascinated him and many intellectuals of his generation. It seemed to show in its complexity what could be done with new ideas in the arts, economics, and politics. In Dreiser's youth and middle years, the Windy City was a place of ferment.

But this dynamic growth was not its only fascinating quality. The city boasted a polyglot population that reflected nearly every aspect of life. The rush for wealth produced mansions for the rich and shanties for the poor. Poverty rubbed elbows with grandeur. Butchers and ditch diggers became millionaires and social arbiters. In the Chicago of Dreiser's mind, nearly every force that motivated or controlled men was evident in abundance and in mingled conflict or collusion. Setting down the color of this city, making its life real on paper and in print, was no small accomplishment.

Bored with narrow country life, Sister Carrie came to Chicago to find her fortune. Fine clothes, money, the glitter of attention were her standards of worldly success. "A half-equipped little knight she was, venturing to reconnoitre the mysterious city and dreaming wild dreams of some vague, far-off supremacy, which should make it prey and subject—the proper penitent, grovelling at a woman's slipper." [11] Carrie symbolized America's false values and innocence, for she knew nothing of life but its surface manifestations. She was not evil, or even weak; she was the product of her world. She was innocently selfish in desiring attention and status. A lack of perspective on herself and her world doomed her, for it made her prey to events.

On the train taking her to Chicago, a flashy traveling salesman, or "drummer," casually picked her up. Drouet was a rake, but like Carrie he had a charming innocence. "In his good clothes and fine health, he was a merry, unthinking moth of the lamp." [12] He also spoke for America's all pervasive love of goods and money. His fine outfit clothed an essentially good heart, but it also covered an empty personality.

The first half of *Sister Carrie* detailed her gradual settlement in Chicago. She lived first with a sister, whose dull life she did not like. She sensed faintly that there was more to life than family and "making a living." She was sensitive enough to hate the dull, brute labor in a shoe factory, and to resent the other girls who seemed hard and purposeless. But she lacked the intelligence to define her situation. To escape this routine, she drifted gradually into the orbit of George Hurstwood, married and a father, manager of an opulent Chicago night spot, "Fitzgerald's and Moy's," that catered to theatre crowds and traveling men.

Hurstwood ideally symbolized both Chicago and America and dominated the book's last half. The chronicle of his rise and fall is one of the great works in American naturalistic writing. He craved and had attained a large measure of material wealth and social prestige. He seemed hopeful and vigorous, but his tinsel world fell at the touch of events. Unhappy at home with a nagging wife, he found Carrie captivating and gradually took her from Drouet.

One evening while counting the contents of his employers' safe, the door accidentally locked, and he was left holding a large sum of money. This fatal accident determined the rest of his life. He took the money, fled first to Canada and then to New York with Carrie, and began the progressive decline of personality that made the book's last half so gripping. For a time, Carrie and Hurstwood were happy, and he prospered in business. But through accident and unpredictable events, he lost his business and degenerated physically and emotionally until he bore no resemblance to the elegant man Carrie had first met and so innocently admired.

Carrie did not understand why Hurstwood lacked the vigor and spark of their early days together. For a while she condemned him for being lazy and for allowing himself to go to pieces, worrying over each penny that went to the grocer, finally using the subterfuges of the poor in delaying payment of bills. And yet there nagged at Carrie's heart a certain pity that illuminated the whole book, a confused belief that perhaps neither she nor Hurstwood were ever free agents. Looking at the puffy, unshaven, distasteful man she had loved and married, she pitied him, for "now he seemed not so shiftless and worthless, but run down and beaten upon by chance." [13]

The mutual reward in their relationship was a development of deep emotional feeling. Carrie drew from her new husband not only worldly goods and status, but a sense of belonging to him and his elegant world. He took from her the sympathy and warmth his first wife had denied him in a ruthless search for social status. The inherent tragedy of their situation became a major theme in Dreiser's work: the more they grew and changed, the more their desires expanded. They lacked either the knowledge or intellect to perceive that uncontrollable events dictated their lives.

By accident, Carrie entered the theatre world and became an overnight sensation on the stage. Her fortunes rose, her world expanded as the Hurstwood she abandoned declined grimly to cheap lodging houses and soup kitchens. He became a street bum and finally committed suicide after Carrie apparently forgot and ignored his plight. In a sentimental epilogue, Dreiser left Carrie rocking in a dreamlike state, dimly aware that her world was beyond definition, wondering what the future held. Through Carrie and Hurstwood, he had stated a major theme in modern American fiction: man's basic tragedy is that as he grows, expresses himself, and finds greater fulfillments for needs and desires, the avenues through which he does these things are progressively closed. Every satisfaction creates a dissatisfaction; every freedom begets a frustrating desire for further freedom. To grow, as man must, is to be unhappy.

The book presented no heroes or villains and drew few judgments on its characters' conduct. Carrie was not evil; she was merely weak, as nature and her life gave her false values. She symbolized well much of innocent America. "Not evil, but longing for that which is better, more often directs the steps of the erring. Not evil, but goodness more often allures the feeling mind unused to reason." [14]

Though the philosophy that lay beneath *Sister Carrie*'s words was opaque, Dreiser had touched upon the basic theme of Naturalism. Man was at the mercy of forces within and outside himself that he could not understand or control. The wider implication that man-made laws were therefore often cruel and unjust added a certain shock value to the book for a generation that publicly thought otherwise. Carrie's tragedy was more complex than it appeared. She was not overly intelligent, and longed for the superficial appearance of worldly success—money, fine clothes, and material security. But what she could not reason, she felt through her own personality. She resented life's apparent complexity without fully understanding it. She sensed that the world was indifferent, that people were selfish and cruel. Her tragedy lay in not knowing what to do about it. "She felt as though she should be better served, and her heart revolted." [15] She had no mind for facts or systematic thought, and was doubly at the mercy of events and people.

In *Sister Carrie,* Dreiser combined a rich flow of facts with a logical narrative structure and dreamlike tone to make the book engrossing despite many faults of language and structure. Personally, the book was a means of working out, if only haltingly, many of his confusions. Carrie partly represented the childish Dreiser in her desires and values. He wanted her to rise in the world, yet sensed that it was futile. Hurstwood symbolized what Dreiser feared he might become, a man at the mercy of events, thrown back into an atavistic existence by fate and chance.

The book's central theme was the process of development. It was a history, dealing with people and events without passing critical judgment upon them or their acts. Carrie was a sympathetic woman, yet she was not tragic. It was hard to sympathize with her, since everything that happened seemed logical. Tragedy involves bitter struggle against fate, and Carrie did not fight. Everything that came to her seemed predestined, and she moved through events without touching them. Hurstwood was the book's focus, illustrating the power of the theme of poverty and determinism upon the young Dreiser.

The affairs, especially the love affairs, of the lower classes were news to the *fin de siècle* reading public. Stephen Crane had made a small beginning by detailing the life of his Maggie, "a girl of the streets." Frank Norris had carefully detailed a sordid world in *McTeague,* complete with powerful sexual undertones and lurid descriptions of the brutal sides of existence. But these and other naturalists had a small reading public. They were still pioneers when Dreiser wrote *Sister Carrie*. No other American novelist had turned to the lower classes with as much sympathy and compassion, or in as great detail.

This largely explained the critical reception his book met. Dreiser sent his manuscript to the new and supposedly progressive firm of Doubleday, Page. Frank Norris read the book and enthusiastically recommended its publication. He remarked that it was "the best novel I had read in MS since I had been reading for the firm, and . . . it pleased me as well as any novel I have read in *any* form. . . . I shall do all in my power to see that the decision is for publication." [16]

Though Doubleday accepted the manuscript, the fate that Dreiser feared intervened. Because it dealt with a "fallen woman," whose sins were not apparently punished, and because its whole tone of determinism and man's helplessness countered the optimism by which most Americans lived, the firm refused to issue the book. The company printed copies and stored them in a warehouse, abiding by the contract technically. Dreiser was too inexperienced to sue and compel the book's distribution. Instead, he lapsed into a long period of despondent brooding, and *Sister Carrie* remained virtually unread until reissued by a new publisher in 1911.[17]

But Norris managed to send out review copies and advertised the book among his friends and associates. Dreiser faithfully collected and read many of the newspaper reviews, finding a certain solace in those that favored or understood what he tried to do. While most reviewers disliked and condemned the book's supposed grimness and candor, one summed up the grudging acceptance accorded the book and Dreiser's view of life: "The impression is simply one of truth, and therein lies at once the strength and the horror of it." [18]

Though the book remained virtually unread, Dreiser made some impression on the reading public. He was recognized as a spokesman of the painfully emerging literary Naturalism. He even gave newspaper interviews, in which he outlined his purpose and philosophy. "The infinite suffering and deprivation of great masses of men and women upon whom existence has been thrust unasked appalls me," he said. "My greatest desire is to devote every hour of my conscious existence to depicting phases of life as I see and understand them." [19]

Dreiser was not yet able to put this theory into further practice, and his dreams of artistic success and acceptance disappeared under events. The abortive issuance of *Sister Carrie* made him despondent. For the following three years he lived in seclusion in New York, seeing a sister and his brother Paul from time to time, writing in a desultory fashion, and doing odd jobs and hack work. His life now took on the quality and direction of Hurstwood's, as he sank ever lower financially and emotionally. Filled with the sense of hopeless struggle that killed Hurstwood, he wandered down to the East River one evening to kill himself. A passing ferry-boatman cheerfully and unwittingly offered him a job, thinking that he was fleeing from his wife. Dreiser laughed and broke the spell of hopelessness.

He first thought of building himself up physically by working outdoors, and secured a job as a laborer on a New York railroad. But before he began the task that provided material for *The "Genius"* (1915), he encountered his brother Paul, who immediately sent him to a sanatorium. Under the rigid regimen of a former wrestler and prize fighter, "Culhane the Solid Man," as Dreiser later called him in a fine short biography, he regained his physical and emotional stability. He worked for a time on the railroad, further strengthening his body and outlook on life, and then began the years as a fashionable editor that brought him a great deal of money and prestige.

In 1904, he worked at Street and Smith, editing adventure novels, as he recalled later, by adding an ending to their first half and a beginning to their second, making two books from one. Between 1907 and 1910, he was an editor at Buttericks, and during all these years enjoyed to the fullest his new-found distinction and wealth. He circulated in the worlds of power and fashionable success he had thought so glittering from afar. He had a fashionable Riverside Drive apartment, complete with avant-garde paintings and statuary.

But this life was only partly satisfying. His conscience told him he ought to return to writing. He was often unhappy, and still confused about his purpose in life. The meaning of nature, man's place in the universe, the value of life, the contrasts of practice and preachment all still nagged him. His personal affairs steadily worsened, as the wife he had taken in the mid-1890s slowly moved away from his viewpoint. His sexual dalliances did not endear him to her or his associates, and he finally left his editorial job under a cloud of censure after a tempestuous affair with the daughter of a major stockholder. True to his own literary honesty, Dreiser later portrayed these events in The "Genius."

Cut loose from his editorial work, and determined to be an independent writer, Dreiser returned to the themes that had occupied him in Sister Carrie. That book's reissuance in 1911 heartened him; though it made slow headway in sales, it steadily gained critical approval. He had already returned to the themes of sex, nature, family life, and the conflicts of wealth and poverty in a second novel, Jennie Gerhardt, published in 1911.

Like Carrie, Jennie was modeled after one of his sisters, and the novel was a kind of biography not only of her but of his family life. Dreiser now softened the bitterness he had earlier felt toward his father, and with patient care he put some of his best writing into Jennie. The woman's story was briefly told and was familiar to any student or product of the rural America of Dreiser's youth. In the course of supporting her family by working in an Ohio hotel, Jennie had an affair with that state's leading citizen, Senator Brander. Over her father's strong objections, she continued to see her illicit lover, and became pregnant; the Senator's untimely death robbed her child of a name. After his death and after she left her family, Jennie fell in love with Lester Kane while working in his father's home. The Kane family, manufacturers of world-famous wagons and other implements, represented the newly rich America, whose sudden wealth and social stature fascinated Dreiser.

Jennie became Kane's mistress and filled his life as he gradually drifted away from the company business. Disowned by his father, Kane entered abortive business ventures that finally ruined him. Though he recognized Jennie's goodness, he could not resist other sexually attractive women, and his career as a lover began a long series of similar conflicts in Dreiser's work. His business ventures hinted at the "trilogy of desire" in which Dreiser soon detailed the career of a tycoon. Kane died, leaving Jennie to raise another man's child of whom he had become fond.

Within this rather prosaic story, Dreiser developed the major themes of his early work. Like Carrie, Jennie was not wicked. He did not condemn her lapse from the era's moral standards, and though society labeled her "fallen," he was more interested in the process of her fall than in judging her. Like Carrie, but with greater clarity and more certain development, Jennie grew under the impact of experience. Her isolation from much of society bewildered her, as did the artificial barriers that threatened to mark her child. She did not feel unclean or immoral. Throughout the book her innate goodness, expressed in thoughtful attention to others' needs and deep love for her father, Kane, and her child, offset any question of her morality. She was a victim, never a strumpet. "She was not a cheap, ambitious, climbing creature. She was a big woman and a good one." [20]

Jennie Gerhardt was a long indictment of society's false values. Jennie's tragedy was not that society condemned her but that the world did not recognize her goodness. She was in but not of a world that trammeled her own limited but nonetheless meaningful method of self-expression. For one mistake, and that committed innocently to better herself in the world's own terms, society ostracized her. Dreiser argued that the loss was not hers, but society's.

The conflict of wealth and poverty, and the innocent yet destructive desire for material goods, imbued this book as much as they had *Sister Carrie*. Dreiser's fascination with money and the force of false material values was slowly leading him to an acute examination of the structure of his whole era. "We live in an age in which the impact of material forces is well-nigh irresistible," he noted in a telling insight into the conflict of innocence and evil; "the spiritual nature is overwhelmed by the shock." [21] He argued in essence that personality formed in a process unknown to him; the false, nonhumanistic values of the world abetted human weakness and a tendency toward self-destruction. He spelled out with greater force and clarity the rather fuzzy determinism of his first book. *Jennie Gerhardt* discussed love and human understanding, a theme often buried under the sheer weight of details in Dreiser's

books. Jennie's travels abroad with Kane showed her the tran-
sience of even the greatest civilizations. While she lacked the information or intellect to articulate her feelings, she felt that little
of what one did in life had permanent value. Only love, regard for
others, endured. "Did anything matter except goodness—goodness
of heart?" she asked herself. "What else was there that was
real?" [22]

Dreiser wrote *Jennie Gerhardt* with a care and attention to
nuance that he seldom lavished on his books, illustrating the depth
of his feeling for this favorite sister. The book was well rounded,
carefully constructed, and logical. It lacked the scope and color
of *Sister Carrie* and the settled purpose of his later work, but it
had a warm personal tone and clear characterization. Dreiser mel-
lowed in his attitude toward his father. The son paid a rather
belated homage to the man he never fully understood. Old Gerhardt, so full of the world's standards, so unable to understand
what his daughter felt, answered every question with a supernatural response. If this life was cruel, that to come would be
better. If tragedy struck, it was all part of an omnipotent God's
purpose. If life and the world were a jungle, why not cling to the
promise of a heavenly reward? But as age, disillusion, and ill
health closed in upon him, he questioned his carefully fashioned
morality. Life was more complex than he had imagined, for was
not Jennie, despite her "fall," the soul of kindness? Though the
world stamped her "bad," and though he himself condemned her
actions, could he really say that she did not deeply love him and
her child? "He believed that the just would be rewarded in
heaven," Dreiser noted in an illuminating comment on the theme
of worldly conflict. "But who were the just?" [23] If Dreiser had
thought his father harsh and unfeeling, he had also failed to understand what made him so. Within his own developing scheme of
Naturalism and determinism, he now saw that life and nature had
made his father what he was.

Though *Jennie* was marred by the Dreiserian tendency to preach
—a tendency that outlined the limits of his determinism—the
book marked a significant stage in that determinism's development.
In *Sister Carrie,* the pointless struggle and the play of blind chance
in men's lives seemed overwhelming. In *Jennie Gerhardt,* Dreiser

turned to the broader belief that if the struggle was ultimately pointless, it was still fascinating to watch. *Jennie* marked a widening if not a deepening of Dreiser's view.

His second book showed Dreiser's interest in nature and the total scheme of existence. He began the long process of drawing back from his scene to see its full context; this process culminated in *An American Tragedy* (1925). It also showed the beginnings of his long struggle to find harmony in the natural order, and to place man in his proper relation to all of life. Jennie and Old Gerhardt saw that love, harmony with other people and nature, was the essence of life. If they could not always rise above what fate willed them, they could at least feel a significant part of the larger process that produced them. Old Gerhardt took his granddaughter for walks, and they watched the birds and flowers, the wind and sky. Both the child and the old man sensed a kinship with the natural process that gave their lives meaning. Jennie saw that the total outline of life mattered more than individuals. This did not prevent pain and suffering. But it offered her and Dreiser an explanation and a reassurance that though they might falter, the total scheme of things endured. "Nature was so beautiful!" Jennie thought. "If at times life seemed cruel, yet this beauty still persisted. The thought comforted her; she fed upon it in her hours of secret loneliness." [24]

Dreiser was a laboriously steady if not always careful worker, and in five years after leaving editorial work he produced four large novels and many pieces of memoir, criticism, essays, plays, and short stories. Hoping to support himself by writing, he pursued his task steadily. *Sister Carrie* and *Jennie Gerhardt* seemed formidable works in their scope and wealth of detail, but the project upon which Dreiser now entered dwarfed them by comparison. He decided to create the fascinating interior world of finance and business, of wealth and power, in a "trilogy of desire." He would detail the rise and fall of Frank Algernon Cowperwood, an international tycoon and business builder modeled after Chicago's traction magnate, Charles Tyson Yerkes. Dreiser hoped not merely to show the workings of finance capitalism in a historical setting, but to let Cowperwood elaborate his own ideas on sexual conduct, the artistic impulse, the individual in society, and determinism.

After months of research, during which he traveled to the scene of Yerkes' last transactions in building the London underground, Dreiser had a thorough working knowledge of finance, stock-jobbing, and the inner connections between business and politics. He began Cowperwood's story in pre-Civil War Philadelphia, as the promising son of a moderately rich banker with a sharp eye on the main chance. By stages, the boy fulfilled his promise as a moneymaker, and worked in commercial selling, banking, and stock promoting. He quickly made money his polestar, deciding that in life the strong preyed on the weak. In one of naturalistic fiction's most famous scenes, the young Cowperwood watched a fish tank where various species ate each other. It was life in a microcosm. "Things lived on each other—that was it," the boy thought. "Lobsters lived on squids and other things. What lived on lobsters? Man, of course! Sure, that was it! And what lived on men? he asked himself. Was it other men?" [25] Dreiser's Naturalism was never that simple, but its germ lay in that vivid scene.

In *The Financier* (1912), the trilogy's first volume, Dreiser traced his magnate's rise to fame, and ultimate bankruptcy, leaving him on the threshold of greater things in a new city, Chicago. Cowperwood's vision and daring let him dominate lesser men, breeding a contempt for weakness and caution that momentarily halted his upward progress when he was jailed for technically misusing public funds in a stock scheme. Powerful political enemies imprisoned him, fearing that his vision and ruthlessness might dominate their affairs.

Dreiser wove into his narrative the emerging outlines of Cowperwood's complex personality. Apparently happily married, the financier nonetheless found other women attractive and had an affair with the daughter of a powerful rival. Possessing a fatal magnetism toward women, and being above conventional morality, Cowperwood accepted sex as a major part of his personality. He convinced himself that he was "chronically promiscuous, intellectually uncertain, and philosophically anarchistic." [26] To add force to the story's total impact, Dreiser excepted Cowperwood from the normal workings of social law. Since he had so much to give, and was so extraordinarily talented, why should rules made for lesser men bind him? "There seemed to be certain general

principles—or people assumed there were—but apparently there
were exceptions." [27] "That braided symphony of mere sex attrac-
tion which somehow makes up that geometric formula of beauty
which rules the world" was merely the most obvious of these
exceptions.[28] Cowperwood illustrated Dreiser's belief in the dominant individual asserting his will in the face of natural indifference.

Cowperwood fancied himself a free agent, a kind of colossus
astride a petty world that hampered his design for wealth and
power out of spite and ignorance. But he was, in fact, a creature of
his impulses. Frank Cowperwood, the man, disappeared gradually
into the thing he built. The total picture became more real than
the man around whom it supposedly revolved. He was the led
rather than the leader, for he was at the mercy not only of his inner
force, but the outer structure of what he built. The more money
he made, the more he had to make. The greater his empire grew,
the more his enemies multiplied. The larger his effort, the greater
his defenses. Like Sister Carrie, the more he "succeeded," the more
he *had* to succeed and the more difficult it became for him to
triumph.

Dreiser did not make Cowperwood's life a study in mere money-
making or business building, but tried to make him symbolize
life's trials to those who do not fit social law. A strong streak of
mysticism redeemed Cowperwood's ruthlessness, for like life he
seemed to be working for a larger purpose than smaller minds
could see. At first, the financier seemed interested only in making
money, not in answering the riddles of the universe. Power, not
poetry, fascinated him. But as he grew rich and arrogant in *The
Titan* (1914), business intrigued him less than the things his work
symbolized.

He became interested in art, and like the *nouveaux riches* of
all eras, built lavish houses, maintained yachts, bought paintings,
became "social." He realized the hollowness of these pretensions.
At the heart of his desire for fame, money, and power lay a finer
if unattainable urge. "Life rises to a high plane of the dramatic,
and hence of the artistic, whenever and wherever in the conflict
regarding material possession there enters a conception of the
ideal." [29] Cowperwood fancied himself an artist, seeking the harmony of order and the beauty of lasting accomplishment. Weary

and bitter in old age, realizing that most of what he did would pass with him, he remarked: "I have tried to bring into my life . . . the beauty which is entirely outside of cities and business." [30] This quality explained, if it did not excuse, many of Cowperwood's faults and the kind of talent he symbolized.

This lust for order, the desire to make a permanent mark on the face of apparent chaos and indifference, drove Cowperwood to Chicago, where he planned to dominate the emerging traction system that would bind the city together and make him its master. "Street-cars, he knew, were his natural vocation. Even more than stock-brokerage, even more than banking, even more than stock-organization he loved the thought of street-cars and the vast manipulative life it suggested." [31] He saw in the nets of rails and cars a mystical force equal to Curtis Jadwin's wheat in *The Pit*. In the trilogy's second volume, *The Titan,* Cowperwood rose to dominate Chicago's traction and banking systems. "The Wrecker" his enemies called him, but his forceful personality overrode them. He contributed a famous observatory to science, bought great paintings, built a Renaissance palace in New York, and disdained society's disapproval.

Dreiser made Cowperwood the story's narrator, if there was one, and saw his world unfold from his own eyes, rather than stand aside and judge what he did. This technique emphasized the story's development as a whole rather than its component parts. When finished, the first two volumes comprised a fascinating character study and an inside history of American finance capitalism from the 1850s to the end of the century. Though Dreiser did not finish the trilogy until his last years, and *The Stoic* (1947) was published posthumously, Cowperwood and his world were very tangible in these two volumes.

His fascination with personality and the forces that made men differ, as well as his desire to define life's struggles, led Dreiser to compose this extraordinary work. Its fact-laden pages were an encyclopedia of his own times. If his story often faltered under the weight of detail, and if characters receded into the background of events, the persistent reader who fell into the rhythm of his prose made of the books a world apart from normal existence. Their sum total was their power; and digested as a whole their sometimes stilted language, verbosity, and awkward structure did not detract from Cowperwood's reality as a figure or the impact of what he did.

In the largest context of Dreiser's naturalistic writing, the trilogy was an indictment of society. Without its false values, the shark-man of business could not pillage and loot his way to apparent public acceptance and power. Much of Cowperwood's life, revealed in such logical detail, indicted crass materialism. The Titan's ostentatious wealth, tinseled women, and high living made him seem more shallow than arrogant of the world's values.

Dreiser shrewdly left the impression that what the man proposed to do was greater than what he did. His dreams of order, his applications of power, were the source of whatever greatness he had. The rest was symptomatic of man's crasser nature, showing vividly and subtly that so great a man as Frank Cowperwood was at the mercy of desires and drives he did not control.

Dreiser told reporters that he wished to portray Cowperwood "unidealized and uncursed," and he retained a fairly steady amoral attitude toward him.[32] He chose Yerkes as his model rather than John D. Rockefeller or Andrew Carnegie because he thought Yerkes had the saving grace of a larger purpose than money-making. Street railways also touched life more openly than oil or steel. Dreiser had no illusions about the type of man he created in Cowperwood. "In America, the history of our financiers is so full of thievery and selfishness as to appear comic were it not for the mass misery which so many of their deeds involved," he noted.[33]

Yet it was less his purpose to condemn than to understand. His scheme of life had grown so large that he found room for Cowperwood's questionable works as well as for his nobler purpose. While recognizing their ruthless selfishness and moral limitations, Dreiser thought that such financiers paved the way for lesser mortals. The chief flaw in Cowperwood's enemies was their failure to see his larger design. Dreiser thought society ought to allow amorality in the artistically gifted, and permit greater freedom to men like his financier. The builders were "Often humorless, shark-like, avid, yet among the greatest constructive forces imagin-able. . . ."[34]

The contrasts of style and approach in the financial novels of

Frank Norris and Dreiser illustrated the varieties of literary Naturalism. With his sharp eye for color and talent for creating the captivating event, Norris made his narratives bright and compelling. Nothing Dreiser wrote could match the sweep of *The Octopus*. If Norris' story was often thin, the reader seemed not to notice, and his handling of details could be as real as Dreiser's.

But Dreiser could not follow Norris' example. Never given to colorful presentation, with little apparent eye for the illuminating moment that offered volumes in symbols, he lumbered through his novels of finance like an elephant through a rain forest, leaving a trail of details that built up a powerful superstructure. The process of events, the steady construction of a story, fascinated him more than they did Norris or Stephen Crane. If Norris lacked texture and boasted flair, Dreiser lacked flair and boasted texture.

Though he wished to finish the trilogy, Dreiser turned from *The Titan* to an autobiographical novel that dealt with similar themes in a different setting. In *The "Genius,"* he moved from the counting house to the editorial workshop and the artist's life. His hero, Eugene Witla, was the country boy who made good, a familiar character in American letters. He was Dreiser in thin disguise, moving from small-town America through hardship, depression, and self-doubt to the shining lure of New York and the world of art and publishing. The book's first section, "Youth," was by far the best. Dreiser's style and verbal power were always clear and forceful when he discussed individual emergence into consciousness. This and similar sections in *Sister Carrie* and *An American Tragedy* contained some of his best writing. The last two-thirds of *The "Genius"* revealed all of Dreiser's faults. It was turgid, wandering, and endlessly verbose, showing how difficult it was for him to define his philosophy.

Eugene began his artistic life with the urge to unify and to celebrate his own view and talent, and to sing of his country. "What a great country America was! What a great thing to be an artist here! Millions of people and no vast artistic voice to portray these things —these simple dramatic things like the coke oven in the night. If he could only do it!" [35] As long as Dreiser wrote of Witla in this vein, primarily as an observer of his world, *The "Genius"* possessed coherence and power. But when he turned to Eugene the man, attempting to show his individual reactions in the face of his art and world, the book faltered. Witla succeeded as an artist because he observed life without participating in it. He drew "realistic" pictures without feeling their pain. But once the forces that produced pain and beauty attacked him, he no longer had the objectivity to control his inner drives. Surrender to these forces dissipated his talent and turned him into a long soliloquy on life's meaning.

Like Dreiser, Witla broke down physically and recuperated in the outdoors working on a railroad. He encountered a host of earthy characters whom he drew and admired, but he knew that their world was one-dimensional and that he did not really belong there. In the course of his search for power and success, Witla somewhat duplicated Sister Carrie, though with greater consciousness of his goal and purpose. Dreiser vividly described the yearning for money and status that drove him on and which highlighted the feelings of countless Americans in his own situation:

It is difficult to indicate to those who have never come out of poverty into luxury, or out of comparative uncouthness into refinement, the veil or spell which the latter comes eventually to cast over the inexperienced mind, coloring the world anew. Life is apparently striving, constantly, to perfect its illusions and to create spells. There are, as a matter of fact, nothing but these outside that ultimate substance or principle which underlies it all. To those who have come out of inharmony, harmony is a spell, and to those who have come out of poverty, luxury is a dream of delight.[36]

Eugene's great problem was not money but sex. He sacrificed his art for money and position in the art world, but in a sense he sacrificed his whole being to an abnormally strong sex drive. His intelligence told him he should not tempt his enemies by creating scandal. The remnants of his morality told him that he should not hurt his wife by taking other women. But he could defeat reason, and surrendered to his uncontrollable inner forces. Like Cowperwood, he thought that since he was brilliant, the world ought to make exceptions of moral conduct for him. He was both the extraordinary man in an ordinary world and the sensitive man at the mercy of uncontrollable naturalistic forces.

Dreiser began to clarify his Naturalism in The "Genius." Witla's sex drive was a means of defining the force and apparent purpose behind it. Dreiser began to see the large outlines of what he called the natural process. He now moved away from fascination with the individual in his world to the forces that shaped the individual. "Love was a lure," he wrote of Witla's conflicts, "desire a scheme of propagation devised by the way. Nature, the race spirit, used you as you use a work-horse to pull a load. The load in this case was race progress and man was the victim." [37] But though Witla did not wish to be the slave of this force, he knew he could not resist it. Nature had endowed him with drives; they must be fulfilled for nature's purpose. Moral law in man's society depended on will, and Witla and Dreiser doubted the power of human will in life. "It is a question whether the human will, of itself alone, ever has cured or ever can cure any human weakness. Tendencies are subtle things. They involved the chemistry of one's being. . . ." [38]

Eugene surrendered to his desires and wrecked his career. He brooded over the meaning of what he did and turned to a kind of Christian Science to order the natural process. Though hurt and bewildered, he began to see the totality of life rather than his own individual being. That totality seemed attractive, though its purpose was not always clear. Witla decided that "life at bottom, in spite of all its teeming terrors, was beautiful." [39]

The search for power as a means of self-expression and human importance dominated the "trilogy of desire." The use of pleasure for the same purpose dominated The "Genius." Neither means was enough, for human wants and needs in both spheres were insatiable. Both the search for worldly power and for pleasure were, at heart, attempts to order existence. Since Dreiser thought this impossible, the devices seemed ultimately useless. As individuals, Frank Cowperwood and Eugene Witla were Dreiser's chief plea for life's special recognition of the unusual man. As stories, both the "trilogy of desire" and The "Genius" depicted the failure of man's search for unity in his life and the world around him. As expressions of Naturalism, both works showed Dreiser's tendency in his middle years to find the individual less and less fascinating. A broader Nature had replaced men in the center of his still emerging philosophy.

Witla learned the painful need of resignation. In the end, he
agreed that it mattered little what he did as a person. Perhaps the
women who badgered him were right after all; maybe the artist's
struggles were vain. Perhaps all of life did reside in a given moment. But the larger lesson of Eugene's career contained the strain
of deep mysticism that became awe of nature in Dreiser's last
years. Eugene sensed the perspective that made him and all mankind small. He wondered at the scope, complexity, indifference of
nature, and saw that man's place in the whole system was his real
purpose.

The "Genius" illustrated the gropings of Dreiser's middle years.
The story never made Eugene's failures quite clear. Did blind
fate ruin him? Or was he not so great after all, as the quotation
marks around the title might indicate? Aside from resignation to
his situation, what purpose was he to find in life? Dreiser could
not answer the questions, but his good friend H. L. Mencken
offered an explanation in another connection: "The truth about
Dreiser is that he is still in the transition state between Christian
Endeavor and civilization, between Warsaw, Indiana, and the So-
cratic grove, between being a good American and being a free
man, and so he sometimes vacillates perilously between a moral
sentimentalism and a somewhat extravagant revolt." [40]

Though his income and reputation among the reading public
were still small, critics now recognized Dreiser as one of America's
new writers. Abroad, especially in England, he was hailed as
America's most impressive new novelist. Always productive, he
sandwiched many books and articles between his big novels. He
traveled, gathering material in England and on the Continent for
the last volume of the Cowperwood trilogy, producing as an aside
his impressions of the world in *A Traveller at Forty* (1913). Showing an interest in social questions that deepened under events in
the 1920s and 1930s, he wrote controversial plays like *The
Hand of the Potter* (1918), dealing with sex perversion. In *Hey-
Rub-a-Dub-Dub* (1920), taking its name from a circus barker's
cry, he wrote on issues of the day and philosophy. He returned to
Indiana in *A Hoosier Holiday* (1916), trying to recapture his
boyhood, and began the fascinating memoir that ultimately produced *Dawn* (1931), and *Newspaper Days* (1922 and 1931).

Though he was seldom idle and always fascinated with social problems and people, Dreiser was really happy only in the midst of controversy or while writing a novel. After *The "Genius,"* he worked doggedly at ending the trilogy, but the writing went slowly. He was caught up in the currents of opinion that surrounded American entry into World War I. As usual, he took an unpopular stand, favoring the Germans and fighting the hysteria that cut off free speech and threatened censorship. He had already waged a national fight for *The "Genius,"* which "anti-vice" forces banned as lewd despite its lack of prurience. He quarreled with most of his friends over censorship, breaking for a time with Mencken, his most devout champion. Though he often allowed others to edit the style of his books, he fought bitterly when their content was questioned.

The war's end and the apparent triumph of political reaction and the nation's consuming interest with making money in the 1920s helped turn Dreiser away from immediate issues into an effort to define his feelings in what he hoped would be his master-piece. Interested in the function of law as an instrument of punishment for social and moral wrongs, and eager to discover the source of moral wrong, Dreiser studied a number of sensational murder cases until a plot for his novel formed. In the early 1920s, he digested factual material, visited the sites of a famous crime in upstate New York, and started to write *An American Tragedy*. Issued in 1925, it was an imediate best seller despite its formidable length. Mencken wryly thought the public liked its bulk; it occupied the average reader a full winter. Other critics damned its sensationalism in dealing with a sordid love triangle. But Dreiser used this setting to state fully his literary Naturalism and philosophical determinism.

Clyde Griffiths began his story in a company of street psalm-singers. His parents operated a mission for the down-and-out and were full of the tenets of fundamentalist religion. The gray tone of the world's indifference toward their efforts and their fate was strong from the first. "As they sang, this nondescript and indifferent street audience gazed, held by the peculiarity of such an unimportant-looking family publicly raising its collective voice against the vast skepticism and apathy of life." [41] Though the adolescent Clyde knew no life but this, he felt a stirring dissatisfaction with his family's poverty. He obediently accepted his parents' religious teachings, but quickly realized the gulf between practice and preaching in both this and the life he saw around him. His own mother talked of God's law and man's morals, yet secretly hid his pregnant unwed sister. Clyde thought his sister's condition less tragic than the bitter tears she shed over social ostracism and disappointment in love. Ignorance and repression of man's natural instincts were the sources of unmoral acts and the villains of human misery. In time, Clyde saw man's true predicament: "Rather, as he saw it now, the difficulty lay, not in the deed itself, but in the consequences which followed upon not thinking or not knowing." [42]

Like many of Dreiser's characters, Clyde escaped into the world of material lushness; he became a bellhop in a fancy hotel. He saw the city's high and mighty, worked in the opulent tinsel glitter of the lobbies and dining rooms, was staggered by the free spending of money and fine clothes. He saw immorality and the world's practice of paying lip service to a public standard of conduct while following another in the privacy of the hotel's rooms. The hotel was life. Dreiser found its business and standards alternately fascinating, repellent, and pitiful.

Clyde fled from an automobile accident in which he was guilty only by his passive acceptance of a whirlwind ride—his life history in microcosm. He came to Lycurgus, New York, at the suggestion of a wealthy uncle who had no idea of his real family relationship. Working in his uncle's shirt factory, Clyde saw a new level of life and fancied that with time and patient care he could enter his uncle's lavish society. But his nature, compounded of weakness and ignorance, abetted by false social and material standards, led to dalliance with a shopgirl, Roberta Alden, who became pregnant. Though he first fancied himself in love with Roberta, Clyde saw her as a threat to his dazzling prospects in the world of high society. After fruitless efforts to find an abortionist, he took her to an isolated lake, determined to murder her.

Dreiser's careful descriptions of motivation, and his painfully constructed characterizations, made the scenes surrounding Roberta's death and Clyde's capture some of the finest in modern

American literature. Clyde's courage failed at the last moment, but when Roberta upset the boat in which they paddled and he accidently struck her face with a camera, Clyde did nothing to save her. He was not technically guilty of murder, but he wished her dead and left her to drown. His own ignorance, nervousness, and indecision left a damning trail of evidence that quickly led to his capture and trial for murder.

The lengthy trial scenes, often overladen with detail and court-room speeches, showed the remorseless web of events in which Clyde was caught. He was defended on the grounds of a specious kind of insanity, amounting to an admission of moral cowardice that prevented his having the strength to murder. He was prose-cuted largely for political reasons so that the county attorney and his machine could be returned to office. His opponents were not above planting false evidence. The trial was a national sensation, a conflict between morality and immorality, religion and godless-ness, slick city life which Clyde supposedly represented and the bitter rural element from which Roberta came. The latter element composed the vindictive jury.

Clyde was convicted and sentenced to die after his new-found society friends abandoned him. His mother's tortuous efforts to save him by running a kind of fund-raising side show, her pain-ful interviews with the governor, the deadly silence from the rest of the world and Clyde's former friends composed the book's grimly remorseless conclusion. Still uncertain of what he did or why, Clyde confessed his religion, implicitly accepted his guilt, and was electrocuted.

Why was this "an American tragedy"? Dreiser insisted that he had told a story and described a way of life typically American because of its false values and repressions of normal instincts. He bitterly objected to Hollywood's portrayal of Clyde as a sex maniac in the first motion picture made from the novel. That film makers considered this necessary only proved to him the truth of what he had said about America.[43]

Clyde was at the mercy of the nature that gave him his desires and drives, but a society of false values motivated him toward crime. These standards heightened his innate weaknesses. Society made him poor, contrived the stultifying religion that warped his youth, set the social and financial standards that made him think money and social status were life's only goals. Society had devised the legal system that persecuted rather than prosecuted him. It fed the sensationalism that insured him an unfair trial.

Loneliness and the yearning for some kind of self-expression were Clyde's salient characteristics. The ease with which he acquired false values, the force of society in manipulating him, the indifference of nature to his fate, were the book's chief themes. To do exciting things without being responsible for them, to rise above humdrum labor and daily living, motivated Clyde and millions of faceless Americans. "It was so hard to be poor," Clyde often thought, "not to have money and position and to be able to do in life exactly as you wished." [44]

Like other of Dreiser's characters, Clyde discovered that his desires were not only ill-defined but insatiable. The more he climbed in society, the greater were his confinements. The wider his identification with life and the greater his personal fulfillments, the more complicated were his restrictions and obligations. Success subtly bred its own end, for as he grew "better" he grew more selfish and blind to enemies and problems. He thought it selfish for his mother to want his money to help his sister. Why should he go without new clothes to pay for her mistake? He thought it selfish of Roberta to cling to him when he had a chance to enter society. The real tragedy was not that men acted so but that their backgrounds and heredity combined with society to make such actions inevitable. Chemistry and false social values, not deliberate will, were the victims. Like Carrie, Clyde was not wicked, but weak.

In *An American Tragedy,* Dreiser combined his monumental scheme of natural and social determinism with a pity for the ensnared individuals that made much of the book very moving. That Clyde found the cheap hotel glitter so fascinating, and the flashy patrons even more impressive, was a telling comment on his human situation. That he unconsciously treated Roberta cruelly and accepted her love as merely his due made his stricken mistress a tragic figure. That he found the empty Sondra Finchley so attractive because of her money, social position, and flirting ways, complete with inane baby-talk, was simply pathetic.

But this pity arose not from authorial preaching or the moralizing asides that marred so much of Dreiser's early work, but from the fabric of narrative. Dreiser fulfilled the promise of his beginning in *An American Tragedy*. "It seemed so truly a story of what life does to the individual—and how impotent the individual is against such forces," he wrote of the book. "My purpose was not to moralize—God forbid—but to give, if possible, a background and a psychology of reality which would somehow explain, if not condone, how such murders happen. . . ." [45]

Dreiser's early concept of nature as an enemy of man now underwent subtle change. He no longer saw it as entirely indifferent or consciously cruel. He accepted its scope and force. He wished now to find a way to join man and his world to the larger process of life in general. Harmony would be his future watchword.

An American Tragedy's sure tone and lack of confusion and preachiness showed how far Dreiser had come since *Sister Carrie* and *The "Genius."* He combined a rather lofty detachment with patient detail to make the book engrossing. But the old defects of style showed through in his tendency to use long sentences, awkward phrases, repetitious wordings, and to include documentary material like courtroom speeches. Though thousands of people read, admired, and defended Dreiser's point of view and subject matter, few defended his style.

In a single page, Dreiser often committed every heresy known to the English language, and whole sections of books like *The "Genius"* and *The Stoic* are labored and unreadable. He brought to his task almost no formal training and often wrote badly because he did not know good writing. He worked into his style the colloquialisms of the speech he heard, which irritated many purists. He depended on an almost oceanic rhythm in his longer novels to produce stylistic and emotional effect. He wrote steadily and grimly, almost as if it were a duty, and he had little sense of selection. Like the self-made man he was, and like so many naturalistic writers, he absorbed masses of detail and had too little judgment in choosing the significant. Mencken often saw him sit stolidly at his desk or table, writing almost without interruption for hours, as if the words came out of him by their own volition.

His faults were obvious. He tended to overwrite endlessly, especially when discussing philosophy, adding to his confusion. He overused favorite and exotic words like "osseous," "oleaginous," "sapient," "trig," and "eleemosynary." The passive voice, indefinite verbs, dangling participles, dependent clauses, all decorated his pages.

But as with many naturalists and realists, Dreiser depended for impact upon total effect and logical development of his characters and situations. He cannot be read hurriedly; one must accept his ponderous gait and develop an ear and a tolerance for his style. The quality of the situations and characters fascinate the reader more than what they are or do. Dreiser seldom carried a reader through a story to show him events, as a guide shows monuments to a tourist. His books do not depend upon great moments, though they are filled with fine scenes. The process of reaching an event fascinated Dreiser far more than the event itself.

Frank Norris tempered his Naturalism with romance and the color of emotional excitement. His works are ideally suited for the Technicolor screen. Dreiser lacked both this talent and desire, and preferred the specific details that composed a total picture. His novels do not lack tension and drama, but they unfold slowly, like a vast portfolio of still photographs, each carefully posed to emphasize the background.

An American Tragedy aroused more discussion over Dreiser's Naturalism than his style. Both his friends and readers found his view of life a curious mixture of sentiment, determinism, and individualism. The man who talked of human helplessness before an iron nature was also a social reformer. Decrying struggle against fate, his characters all struggled. Feeling that man was petty and insignificant, he celebrated many of his exploits. Taking a detached view of sex, he could be a sentimental schoolboy in courting lady friends. He sprinkled his love letters with phrases like: "Little Blue Bird," "Honey Pot," "Do ju lub me?" and "Flower Face." This is hard to forgive in a young man, but Dreiser was nearly forty when he wrote it.[46]

Like Norris', Dreiser's Naturalism fitted into no neat categories. Whatever philosophy he developed grew organically from his background and his struggles for recognition. His own observations rather than reading underlay his determinism. He began writing with little knowledge of literature in general and Naturalism in particular. Among foreign authors, he liked Balzac, Zola, de Maupassant, and the Russians. Among Americans, he admired but never deeply studied many contemporary realists and naturalists like Garland, Crane, and Howells. Lacking any status or gift for socializing as a young writer, he did not move among literary lights, as did Garland. He was a prime example of self-development. What he read tended to confirm what he already believed rather than open up fresh fields of thought.

Dreiser's philosophy of Naturalism and determinism developed with his writing and experience, but his belief in man's essential helplessness was present in all his work. Like the aged Mark Twain, he divided his thinking into two phases, the general and specific. He argued that an individual's struggles against chance or fate might be meaningful to that individual, but in the largest context no man meant much in nature's scheme of life. His development was a steady adoption of broader perspective, moving from the specifics of people and events to the generalities of cosmic order.

This did not make him indifferent to people. Within the scheme of his determinism he saw endless room for variety and interest in living. "If I were to preach any doctrine to the world it would be love of change, or at least lack of fear of it." [47] Life was essentially a process of change, composed of millions of different organisms, including man. Rigid laws and social rules that did not allow for this variety or face the realistic view of man in the total universe penalized the sensitive and creative. This was especially true, Dreiser thought, in America, which fed on optimism and illusions. His country valued the common denominator too highly. "Personally, my quarrel is with America's quarrel with original thought," he said in 1920.[48]

Valuing individual expression despite his deterministic view, he thought that all efforts to prevent original thought hindered the total race's development. The sensitive and creative mind, though often opposing society's established codes, opened up accomplishments for the whole species. Had not Frank Cowperwood and Eugene Witla been penalized by the world's narrow rules? "Art is the stored honey of the human soul, gathered on wings of misery and travail. Should the dull and the self-seeking and the self-advertising close this store on the groping human mind?" he asked.[49]

The variety of human life, so richly portrayed in all his works, balanced his determinism. Though he disliked many of man's antics, the human animal fascinated him. He could not accept Mencken's talk about the "Booboisie," replying only that nature and society made men stupid or ignorant. It was not their conscious wish to be foolish. "I know you have no use for the common man since he cannot distinguish himself," he once wrote Mencken:

But I have—just as I have for a dog, a worm, a bird, a louse or any living or creeping thing. The use I see is *contrast* and so *interest* for you and for me. For without these where would either you or myself or humanity, as a whole, be? Where? The interest and charm of life— where would it be? And for whom? Your unsaved humanity? I do not follow that course of reasoning. For without natural universal interest in all phases of created life this night I would take a sleeping potion that would end the argument for me.[50]

This did not glorify the pretensions of the specific individual or the human race in general. Seen in proper perspective, mankind did not appear important. "What is one man, one organism, one race of organisms, to a thing that produces them by quintillions, age in and age out?" he asked.[51] In his early work he discussed the individual's place in nature's order, trying to define his importance. As he progressed he turned from this specific to the general scheme of nature and finally accepted its vastness and essential indefinability. "As I see him the utterly infinitesimal individual weaves among the mysteries like a floss-like and wholly meaningless course—if course it be," he wrote after considerable scientific investigation of life's origins.[52]

The search for first causes occupied him until the end of his life. In his middle and later years he decided that the human organism was chemically composed. Balance or imbalance in this composition, an act of sheer chance, determined a man's personality. There but for a pinch of potash might go I, he would remark with a smile, referring equally to the local banker or a notorious thug. "In so far as one may judge by chemistry and physics man appears to be in the grip of a blind force or process which cannot help itself and from which man can derive no power to help himself save by accident or peradventure." [53]

It was a bleak view, especially in an America raised on optimism and individualistic behavior. But as Dreiser matured he developed a perspective that encompassed life's total action. Within that scheme, man's work might be meaningful for some larger purpose he could only feel and not know.

The race, representing the totality of active creations and pushed on by dynamic forces from below, may be, and in so far as one can guess is, a huge success. The God or force or forces using men in various aspects here and now (two billion men at the present moment) [1920] may be and no doubt is finding self-expression through and in him and may well be tremendously satisfied with the result.[54]

The saving grace of humor could make man's foolishness tolerable as well as meaningful. "Surely somewhere must be forces of intelligence that look on and laugh, as we do at comic toys," he remarked. "But where, oh where, is the toymaker who makes us? And can it be that he is ashamed to show his face?" [55]

Dreiser quarreled with men like Sherwood Anderson who feared science. He felt that all facts at man's disposal helped determine his true state. Exact knowledge, not moralistic theorizing, might give meaning and direction to existence. He saw nothing innately wrong with science, though he often berated scientists for lacking a sense of mystery in trying to explain nature. If millions of men died for no apparent reason, if pain and death and disease were part of man's lot, if much of anyone's life was mere chance, he preferred to think that nature was ordering her sphere for an unfathomable reason. "Not perfection, but a better balance is all that is really sought or ever attained," he said in a comment that illuminated his interest in social reform.[56]

Dreiser rather quickly abandoned evil determinism in his work. This was in a sense too positive an idea for him, since it implied a negative force at work in nature. He tempered his mechanistic thinking with a sense of mystery toward life and a sympathy toward human beings. His feeling for the human dilemma was not superficial. He was involved with his characters. He believed in the value and the interest of their struggle, though he could never promise them a happy ending. His objectivity was never indifference. His love of color and variety and his sympathy for the weak and the good alike forbade that. "No man I ever met is so sympathetic with weakness," his friend John C. Powys once said.[57]

In an apparent paradox, Dreiser was a great individualist, resisting any effort to censor or control his own ideas. While believing in natural determinism, he could also say in 1940: "I feel that individual initiative and the competitive spirit must be preserved if life is to remain interesting, dramatic, colorful."[58] He did not belittle individual expression; no man prized it more. "What I do decry is immense and wholly unreasonable rewards allotted to individuals." Since these rewards were in essence man-made, stemming from society's rules rather than nature's, they were unnatural and unfair in often enriching the dull and undeserving. Just as he thought harmony was nature's ultimate aim, he thought mankind's laws and society could be better devised to reward honest endeavor:

What I truly believe is that law and all other governing devices and systems can be so calculated, where careful thought is taken, as to achieve the greatest possible latitude for all, consistent with the greatest possible peace and comfort, and each according to his talents. Nature, either necessarily or because spiritually it desires it (and I think the former is the case) is seeking an equation between extremes which would otherwise clash in enormous contests for dominance, the one to the exclusion of the other through eons of time.[59]

Good and evil were variables; one man's wickedness was another's salvation. Moral and social laws froze definitions of conduct and did not allow for the variable man, as Eugene Witla and Frank Cowperwood discovered. Just as no single coat fitted all men's shoulders, no single code of conduct fitted all men's acts. Beyond the minimum controls necessary for preservation, Dreiser saw no reason for restrictive codes against purely personal actions. Laws could not make nature, life, or man good. Just as literary romanticism had bolstered false ethics, so social romanticism and refusal to accept the grim sides of life prevented human development. "My God, if I have one, is dual," he told a friend, "a compendium of so called *evil* as well as 'good' and a user of both for purposes which man as yet may not comprehend." [60]

Dreiser never attained or desired a completely dispassionate observation of his world. He struck a balance between observation and commitment, remarking in a short story, "Nigger Jeff," that "it was not so much the business of the writer to indict as to interpret. . . ." Inevitably, that interpretation involved a judgment. Dreiser's "interpretation" was a compassionate sympathy for man's individual struggles and a sense of wonder at his collective life.

In the 1920s, Dreiser was often the bad boy of American letters; and "humanistic" critics, like Paul Elmer More and Stuart Sherman, condemned his theory of animalistic and deterministic behavior. They attacked his apparent interest in life's sordid side, decried his grim insistence on fate's operations, and thought the whole naturalistic trend unwholesome and sterile. Dreiser's rejoinder that he did not celebrate darkness but merely accepted its existence did not stem this kind of criticism. It is ironic that a man so sensitive to beauty should have gained a reputation for approving the sordid.

Dreiser's stubborn personality intensified his opposition, for as Mencken noted: "You have a positive genius for doing foolish things." [61] He disliked and often disdained the world's badges of success, and made many enemies with his rough language and stubborn refusal to accept supervision. He could never be a Hamlin Garland, reveling in public acceptance. Whatever else he was, he never acted the part of a benevolent elder statesman of letters. If he disliked the tone or purpose of an organization, he said so, and refused to lend his name and prestige to any cause he suspected. "With the pseudos, reactionaries and pink tea and chocolate bon-bon brotherhood of literary effort in charge however, I should prefer not to appear," he remarked in refusing to help urge copyright privilege, a cause in which he had a high stake.[62]

In all of this, nothing seemed more surprising than Theodore Dreiser the reformer, a role he accepted with increasing relish as he grew older. He saw no conflict between his determinism and social reform. "For after all the great business of life and mind is life," he noted. "We are here, I take it, not merely to moon and vegetate, but to do a little thinking about this state in which we find ourselves, or at least to try." [63]

Dreiser was anti-capitalistic, anti-English, anti-Semitic, pro-socialist, pro-German in many attitudes, and pro-communist in varying degrees throughout his life. To his credit, he slowly and painfully worked out of anti-Semitism, though he never quite abandoned other bigotries. Of all these, capitalism irritated him most, for he thought it a great repressive engine. It had produced the false standards of money and status to which his fictional characters were so often fatally drawn. Though he was not a social reformer in his youth—preferring in his confusion to wonder over primal causes—as he grew older he turned more and more to social action. As a novelist, sweeping moral issues deeply concerned him; as a citizen living a day-to-day existence in a world filled with man-made wrongs, he saw no contradiction in demanding greater freedom and comfort for more people. The same hatred of injustice that made him sympathize with the weak before a brute nature made him resent the artificial injustices of rampant wealth and social inequality. He thought that capitalism aided nature's blind selectivity. It gave rewards at random, and despite American mythology, cast many aside without good reason while giving fortune and power to the irrelevant. As he had noted in his youth, the world tended to honor the beautiful and gifted, whose talents were accidents of nature, and to ignore or stifle the ugly or timid, no matter how gifted. And what of his celebrated human sympathy in this context?

Certainly I pity the individual when he is weak, defeated, put upon. But I also cease to pity him when I find him strong, selfish, vain, cruel, or brutal. And I note that to make him into either requires no more than the addition or subtraction of a very little material success—so little that it is pathetic, really.[64]

But he never quite felt comfortable among reformers, talking of confident futures and changing mankind's basic drives with laws, preaching a utopia ruled by love and mutual kindness. He feared most the leveling tendencies of reform in America, for he disliked the common denominators that did not allow for the unusual individual. He was not an egalitarian, especially when it came to moral and intellectual conduct. In the very long run, through acquired behavior, man might soften his brutal tendencies, but for the moment he put small faith in such regulations. "In too many cases the individual is accidentally favored beyond his deserts, in others too horribly denied, and these extremes will never be wholly overcome by social law, . . ." he told a reformer.[65]

It was always difficult for him to accept the idea that man was necessarily good, or would become so once his opportunities in life were equalized. "As a matter of fact humanity as a whole, the human race, no less, is a predatory organism, fighting and killing to not only save but advance and even luxuriate itself at the expense of and as against every other type of organism," he reminded his reform-minded friends. "If you don't believe it walk to the nearest butcher shop or visit the Chicago stockyards." [66]

Yet he found reform programs as fascinating as anything else in life, and this together with his dislike of capitalism drew him to Soviet Russia. For three months in 1927, he toured the country as a guest of the Soviet government, visiting educational and artistic centers, as well as factories, communal farms, mines, and governmental agencies. He came away with mixed impressions, reflected in his book *Dreiser Looks at Russia* (1928). While he admired much of the communist program, he knew that it would not work in America, where different attitudes and institutions prevailed. His report pleased no one. The book alienated the Russians and American communists who thought he was bourgeois to criticize their dogma and program. It displeased most Americans who read it because he accepted part of communism and condemned capitalism.

Dreiser himself disliked the dogmatizing that surrounded communism more than the program. He admired much of the latter for closing the gulf between material want and plenty. But he repudiated the former when it attempted to dictate what he could think and write. He scoffed openly at the communist notion that familiarity with Marxism would make him a better writer, and remained unconvinced that communism would bring its long vaunted utopia. "I can only say that I have no theories about life, or the solution of economic and political problems," he wrote a Russian friend.

Life as I see it, is an organized process about which we can do nothing in the final analysis. Of course, science, art, commercial progress, all go to alleviate and improve and ease the material existence of humanity, and that for the great mass is something. But there is no plan, as I believe, from Christianity down, that can be more than a theory. And dealing with man is a practical thing—not a theoretical one. Nothing can alter his emotions, his primitive and animal reactions to life. Greed, selfishness, vanity, hate, passion, lust, are all inherent in the least of us, and until such are eradicated, there can be no Utopia.[67]

Though he thought the gains were illusory or temporary, he fought inequality wherever he could. When the Great Depression blighted the United States in the early 1930s, he lent his voice and presence to help the miserable and downtrodden. He investigated labor violence in Kentucky coal mines, was interested in justice toward radical groups, corresponded with President Roosevelt on Nazism, the Spanish civil war, and diplomatic neutrality. His book *Tragic America* (1931) bitterly indicted the inequities of the social and economic system. Though he favored most of what Roosevelt did in domestic affairs, he opposed his internationalist foreign policy, largely because he suspected England of manipulating the world for her own imperialistic ends. In 1941 he wrote *America Is Worth Saving*, arguing against intervention in Europe as long as Fascism did not directly threaten the United States, and urging more attention to domestic injustice. He accepted war with resignation and continued to work, though slowed by age, for social causes. On the eve of his death he formally joined the Communist Party, remarking that if the communists did not like what he said they could expel him.

The Great Depression, World War II, and attendant crises and confusion found Dreiser aging and writing little. His talent seemed to dry up progressively as he valiantly struggled to complete the "trilogy of desire," and to write one last statement of his naturalism, *The Bulwark* (1946). In this last novel detailing the temptations and triumph of Solon Barnes in the setting of an early Quaker background and later success in the material world of business, Dreiser came to a final understanding with nature. He had once seen life as overpowering and intangible, and man as an irrelevant member of countless species of organisms. In *The*

Bulwark and his late social writings, he concluded that while man might never know his origin or purpose, he could find peace and a kind of purpose by harmonizing with nature. He could accept on faith the idea that he was part of a vast plan of some purpose. Insignificant in himself, the individual man might be important to this larger scheme of things. Upon joining the Communist Party Dreiser remarked that the true religion was in Matthew. Though some thought he had returned to religion, he offered this thought in the text of human love rather than a dogmatic Christianity.

In middle life he had once remarked, "I catch no meaning from all I have seen, and pass quite as I came, confused and dismayed." [68] He retained to the end that premonition of man's helplessness, though he accepted the possibility of universal harmony. On December 28, 1945, he died in Hollywood, where he had lived for several years.

Dreiser's life almost uniquely illustrated the pain and time which the sensitive mind consumes in seeking meaning in existence. For that arduous task he will always be vivid in American letters. His warmth of character, his probing questions, and the sympathy with which he treated all he touched will make him respected.

As with Frank Norris, any quarrel with Dreiser's style seems petty when contrasted to the questions he asked and the world he created. Few men in our time came upon life so hungry to know its essence and so filled with the conflicts that beset most men. He spurned the sweet falsehoods that often fed his generation, and at great sacrifice created a world of living people and events that ranks with the finest literary achievements. His world was not merely an evocation of a vanished America. It was the shape of life itself—flawed with greed and lust, seasoned with the indifference of vastness and infinity, lighted too with human kindness and much beauty.

He asked for all men the question that became his epitaph: "Oh, what is this that knows the road I came?" His answers displeased or alienated some. They were not always complete or logical. But the fault belongs less to him than to that larger life whose meaning and value he had the courage to seek and cherish.

Notes

MARK TWAIN: THE OPTIMIST AS PESSIMIST

1. *Mark Twain's Autobiography*, 2 vols. (New York: Harper & Bros., 1924), II, 68. Since the pen name "Mark Twain" is more familiar to the world than Clemens' full name, I have used it consistently throughout this essay.
2. *Ibid.*, I, 7-9.
3. *The Innocents Abroad*, I, 230-231. Unless otherwise noted, all quotations from Twain's writings are from *The Writings of Mark Twain*, 25 vols., Author's National Edition (New York: Harper & Bros., 1909-1918).
4. *Tom Sawyer*, 53.
5. William Dean Howells, *My Mark Twain* (New York: Harper & Bros., 1910), 5.
6. *Roughing It*, II, 108.
7. Albert B. Paine (ed.), *Mark Twain's Letters*, 2 vols. (New York: Harper & Bros., 1917), I, 34.
8. See *Mark Twain's Letters*, I, 40.
9. *Life on the Mississippi*, 119.
10. Howells to Clemens (November 23, 1874), in Henry Nash Smith and William Gibson (eds.), *The Twain-Howells Letters*, 2 vols. (Cambridge: Harvard University Press, 1960), I, 42-43.
11. *The Innocents Abroad*, II, 366.
12. *Roughing It*, I, 47.
13. *Ibid.*, II, 30.
14. *Ibid.*, I, 219-220.
15. *Mark Twain's Letters*, I, 22.
16. *Ibid.*, I, 64.
17. *Ibid.*, I, 92.
18. *Ibid.*, I, 127-128.
19. *The Innocents Abroad*, I, 250.
20. *What is Man? And Other Essays* (New York: Harper & Bros., 1917), 214.
21. *My Mark Twain*, 31.
22. *The Twain-Howells Letters*, I, 226.
23. *My Mark Twain*, 29.
24. *The Twain-Howells Letters*, I, 165.
25. *What is Man? And Other Essays*, 275.
26. *Mark Twain's Letters*, I, 43.
27. *My Mark Twain*, 4.

28. *Connecticut Yankee*, 285.
29. *The Gilded Age*, I, 93.
30. *Autobiography*, I, 94.
31. *My Mark Twain*, 113.
32. *Ibid.*, 108.
33. Helen Keller, *Midstream* (New York: Doubleday, Doran & Co., 1929), 51.
34. Bernard De Voto (ed.), *Mark Twain in Eruption* (New York: Harper & Bros., 1940), 202.
35. *The Twain-Howells Letters*, I, 248-249.
36. *Ibid.*, I, 91.
37. *What is Man? And Other Essays*, 130.
38. *The Twain-Howells Letters*, II, 664-665.
39. *Mark Twain's Letters*, II, 541-542.
40. *The Innocents Abroad*, II, 362-363.
41. *Autobiography*, I, 2.
42. *Ibid.*, xii.
43. *Tom Sawyer*, 206.
44. *Mark Twain's Letters*, I, 290.
45. See "Literary Essays," Vol. XII of *Writings*, p. 85.
46. *Mark Twain's Letters*, II, 738.
47. *Life on the Mississippi*, 308 ff.
48. *My Mark Twain*, 49.
49. *Autobiography*, I, 256.
50. *Mark Twain's Letters*, II, 640-641.
51. Albert B. Paine (ed.), *Mark Twain's Notebooks* (New York: Harper & Bros., 1935), 346.
52. *Autobiography*, II, 7.
53. *The Mysterious Stranger and Other Stories* (New York: Harper & Bros., 1923), 51.
54. *Ibid.*, 227.
55. *Mark Twain's Letters*, II, 483.
56. *The Twain-Howells Letters*, II, 689.
57. *Ibid.*, II, 501.
58. *Mark Twain in Eruption*, preface.
59. This question is discussed ably and at length in R. B. Salomon, *Twain and the Image of History* (New Haven: Yale University Press, 1961), 49 ff.
60. *Mark Twain's Notebooks*, 380.
61. See *Mark Twain's Letters*, II, 785.
62. *The Mysterious Stranger*, 140.
63. Albert B. Paine, *Mark Twain: A Biography*, 3 vols. (New York: Harper & Bros., 1912), III, 1552.
64. *My Mark Twain*, 91.
65. These ideas are developed more fully and with brilliant insight

in Gladys C. Bellamy, *Mark Twain as a Literary Artist* (Norman: University of Oklahoma Press, 1950).
66. *My Mark Twain,* 100-101.
67. *Mark Twain's Letters,* II, 787.

WILLIAM DEAN HOWELLS: THE REALIST AS REFORMER

1. William Dean Howells, *Years of My Youth* (New York: Harper & Bros., 1916), 106.
2. William Dean Howells, *Literary Friends and Acquaintances* (New York: Harper & Bros., 1901), 3.
3. *Years of My Youth,* 41.
4. *Ibid.,* 163.
5. Mildred Howells (ed.), *Life in Letters of William Dean Howells,* 2 vols. (New York: Doubleday, Doran & Co., 1928), I, 22-23.
6. *Ibid.,* I, 28.
7. *Years of My Youth,* 141.
8. *Literary Friends and Acquaintances,* 37.
9. *Ibid.,* 76.
10. William Dean Howells, *Venetian Life* (New York: Harper & Bros., 1907), xvi.
11. *Life in Letters,* I, 58-59.
12. *Ibid.,* I, 87.
13. *Literary Friends and Acquaintances,* 181.
14. *Life in Letters,* I, 162.
15. William Dean Howells, *Their Wedding Journey* (Boston: Houghton Osgood Co., 1871), 67.
16. *Ibid.,* 69.
17. *Ibid.,* 69.
18. *Ibid.,* 54-55.
19. *My Mark Twain,* 153.
20. William Dean Howells, *The Undiscovered Country* (Boston: Houghton Mifflin Co., 1893), 322-323.
21. William Dean Howells, *A Chance Acquaintance* (Boston: Houghton Mifflin Co., 1898), 164.
22. *Ibid.,* 45.
23. *Ibid.,* 84.
24. *Ibid.,* 166.
25. William Dean Howells, *The Lady of the Aroostook* (Boston: Houghton Osgood Co., 1879), 95.
26. William Dean Howells, *A Foregone Conclusion* (Boston: Houghton Mifflin Co., 1916), 31.
27. *The Lady of the Aroostook,* 82.
28. *Ibid.,* 55.
29. *Ibid.,* 278.

30. *Ibid.*, 211.
31. *A Foregone Conclusion*, 51.
32. See the bitter remarks on sham religion, *ibid.*, 166-167.
33. William Dean Howells, *The Undiscovered Country* (New York: Houghton Mifflin Co., 1893), 318-319.
34. *Ibid.*, 106, 89.
35. *Ibid.*, 236-237.
36. William Dean Howells, *A Modern Instance* (New York: Houghton Mifflin Co., 1910), 5.
37. *Ibid.*, 487.
38. to James Russell Lowell (June 22, 1879), in *Life in Letters*, I, 271.
39. William Dean Howells, *Criticism and Fiction* (New York: Harper & Bros., 1891), 81.
40. Everett Carter, *Howells and the Age of Realism* (Philadelphia: J. B. Lippincott Co., 1954), 138-139.
41. *Criticism and Fiction*, 3.
42. *Ibid.*, 86.
43. *Ibid.*, 23.
44. *Ibid.*, 104.
45. William Dean Howells, *A Hazard of New Fortunes* (New York: E. P. Dutton & Co., 1951), 540.
46. *Criticism and Fiction*, 188.
47. *Life in Letters*, I, 410.
48. *Criticism and Fiction*, 128-129.
49. Carter, *Howells and the Age of Realism*, 186 ff., discusses this crucial point thoroughly and clearly.
50. *Life in Letters*, I, 311.
51. *Ibid.*, II, 262; William Dean Howells, *My Literary Passions* (New York: Harper & Bros., 1910), 83, 43.
52. *Criticism and Fiction*, 156-157.
53. *Ibid.*, 150, 154.
54. William Dean Howells, *The Rise of Silas Lapham* (New York: Houghton Mifflin Co., 1912), 161.
55. *Years of My Youth*, 146.
56. *Life in Letters*, I, 378.
57. *San Francisco Examiner*, May 22, 1892.
58. *Life in Letters*, I, 290-291.
59. *Ibid.*, 116-118.
60. *The Rise of Silas Lapham*, 4, 22, 91.
61. *Ibid.*, 326.
62. *Ibid.*, 336.
63. *My Literary Friends*, 141.
64. *The Rise of Silas Lapham*, 515.
65. *My Literary Passions*, 231-232.

66. *Ibid.*, 169-170.
67. *Ibid.*, 183.
68. *Life in Letters*, I, 404.
69. *Harper's Magazine*, 75 (September, 1887), 639.
70. *Life in Letters*, I, 210.
71. *My Literary Passions*, 98.
72. *Harper's Magazine*, 112 (May, 1906), 959.
73. William Dean Howells, *Annie Kilburn* (New York: Harper & Bros., 1891), 47.
74. *Ibid.*, 122-123.
75. *Ibid.*, 169.
76. *Life in Letters*, I, 416.
77. *A Hazard of New Fortunes*, 238.
78. *Ibid.*, 254.
79. *Ibid.*, 287-288.
80. *Ibid.*, 244.
81. *Ibid.*, 457, 199-200.
82. *Ibid.*, 339.
83. *Ibid.*, xxii.
84. William Dean Howells, *The Shadow of a Dream* (New York: Harper & Bros., 1890), 81.
85. William Dean Howells, *The Quality of Mercy* (New York: Harper & Bros., 1891), 140.
86. *Ibid.*, 144-145.
87. *Literary Friends and Acquaintances*, 58.
88. See Robert L. Hough, *The Quiet Rebel* (Lincoln: University of Nebraska Press, 1959), 63.
89. *Literary Friends and Acquaintances*, 2.
90. *The Quality of Mercy*, 422.
91. *Impressions and Experiences*, 271; *Life in Letters*, II, 3.
92. *Life in Letters*, II, 9.
93. *Ibid.*, II, 86.
94. *Ibid.*, II, 1.
95. *Impressions and Experiences*, 148-149.
96. *Ibid.*, 234.
97. *Life in Letters*, II, 25.
98. *Impressions and Experiences*, 98.
99. *Life in Letters*, II, 121.
100. Edith Wharton, *A Backward Glance* (New York: D. Appleton-Century Co., 1934), 146-147.
101. *My Literary Passions*, 15.
102. *Life in Letters*, II, 15.
103. "Mr. Garland's Books," *North American Review*, 196 (October, 1912), 523-528.
104. *Life in Letters*, II, 161.

105. *Harper's Magazine,* 113 (August, 1906), 473.
106. Percy Lubbock (ed.), *The Letters of Henry James,* 2 vols. (New York: Charles Scribner's Sons, 1920), I, 30-31.

HAMLIN GARLAND: THE REBEL AS ESCAPIST

1. Hamlin Garland, *A Son of the Middle Border* (New York: Macmillan, 1917), 460.
2. *Ibid.,* 23.
3. *Ibid.,* 137.
4. *Ibid.,* 69.
5. *Ibid.,* 4.
6. *Ibid.,* 5.
7. *Ibid.,* 129.
8. *Ibid.,* 312.
9. Hamlin Garland, *Roadside Meetings* (New York: Macmillan, 1930), 6-7.
10. *Ibid.,* 9, 13; *A Son of the Middle Border,* 322-323.
11. *A Son of the Middle Border,* 351.
12. *Ibid.,* 408-409.
13. *Roadside Meetings,* 58.
14. "Mr. Garland's Books," *North American Review,* 196 (October, 1912), 523-528.
15. Hamlin Garland, *My Friendly Contemporaries* (New York: Macmillan, 1934), 131.
16. *A Son of the Middle Border,* 313.
17. *Roadside Meetings,* 86-87.
18. Quoted in Jean Holloway, *Hamlin Garland: A Biography* (Austin: University of Texas Press, 1960), 14.
19. *A Son of the Middle Border,* 366.
20. *Ibid.,* 375.
21. *Ibid.,* 374.
22. *Roadside Meetings,* 178.
23. *Ibid.,* 121.
24. See Howells' introduction and Garland's preface in Hamlin Garland, *Main-Travelled Roads* (New York: Harper & Bros., 1910).
25. *Ibid.,* 177.
26. *Ibid.,* 70.
27. *Ibid.,* 191.
28. *Ibid.,* 30.
29. *Ibid.,* 105.
30. *Ibid.,* 280.
31. *Ibid.,* 129.
32. *Ibid.,* 4.

33. *Roadside Meetings,* 179.
34. *A Son of the Middle Border,* 415.
35. *Ibid.,* 417.
36. *Ibid.,* 418.
37. *Ibid.,* 464.
38. *Roadside Meetings,* 32.
39. Hamlin Garland, *Crumbling Idols* (Chicago: Stone and Kimball, 1894), 176.
40. *Ibid.,* 34, 131.
41. *Ibid.,* 28.
42. *Ibid.,* 52.
43. *Ibid.,* 184.
44. *The Atlantic Monthly,* 126 (December, 1895), 840-841.
45. Hamlin Garland, *A Daughter of the Middle Border* (New York: Macmillan, 1921), p. 25.
46. Hamlin Garland, *Jason Edwards* (Boston: The Arena Publishing Co., 1892), 30-31.
47. *Ibid.,* 72.
48. *Ibid.,* 142-143.
49. Hamlin Garland, *My Friendly Contemporaries* (New York: Macmillan, 1934), 396.
50. *Roadside Meetings,* 126.
51. Hamlin Garland, *A Member of the Third House* (New York: D. Appleton and Co., 1897), 97.
52. *Ibid.,* 183-184.
53. Hamlin Garland, *A Spoil of Office* (Boston: The Arena Publishing Co., 1892), 24-25.
54. *Ibid.,* 27.
55. *Ibid.,* 256-258.
56. *Roadside Meetings,* 186.
57. *A Daughter of the Middle Border,* 26.
58. Hamlin Garland, *Rose of Dutcher's Coolly* (New York: Harper & Bros., 1895), 15.
59. *Ibid.,* 19.
60. *Ibid.,* 145.
61. *Ibid.,* 70-71.
62. *Ibid.,* 152.
63. *Ibid.,* 292.
64. *Harper's Weekly,* 90 (March 7, 1896), 223.
65. *The Critic,* 91 (September, 1902), 278.
66. *A Daughter of the Middle Border,* 31.
67. Hamlin Garland, *Back-Trailers from the Middle Border* (New York: Macmillan, 1928), 302.
68. *My Friendly Contemporaries,* 2.

69. *Back-Trailers from the Middle Border*, 125.
70. "Mr. Garland's Books," *North American Review*, 196 (October, 1912), 523-528.
71. *My Friendly Contemporaries*, 519.
72. *Companions on the Trail*, 492.
73. *Ibid.*, 73.
74. *Back-Trailers from the Middle Border*, 123.
75. *Ibid.*, 40.
76. *Ibid.*, 81-82.
77. *Ibid.*, 304.
78. Quoted in Holloway, vii.
79. *Back-Trailers from the Middle Border*, 78-79.

FRANK NORRIS: THE ROMANTIC AS NATURALIST

1. Introduction to *The Third Circle*, xii; Vol. IV of *The Collected Writings of Frank Norris*, 10 vols. (New York: Doubleday, Doran & Co., 1928). Unless otherwise noted, all references to Norris' work are from this edition.
2. Franklin Walker, *Frank Norris: A Biography* (New York: Doubleday, Doran & Co., 1932), 9 ff.
3. *Ibid.*, 24.
4. *Ibid.*, 17.
5. *Blix*, 96.
6. Walker, *Frank Norris: A Biography*, 138.
7. Franklin Walker, "An Early Frank Norris Item," Book Club of California, *Quarterly Newsletter*, 25 (Fall, 1960), 83-86.
8. Walker, *Frank Norris: A Biography*, 54-55.
9. *San Francisco Wave*, November 28, 1896; cited in Walker, *Frank Norris: A Biography*, 57.
10. *Blix*, 10.
11. Franklin Walker (ed.), *The Letters of Frank Norris* (San Francisco: The Book Club of California, 1956), 10.
12. *Ibid.*, 18-19.
13. Though *Vandover* was written while Norris was at Berkeley and Cambridge, it was not published until 1914, 12 years after his death. Since, however, it falls logically in his early career, I have chosen to treat it here.
14. *Vandover and the Brute*, 8.
15. See *ibid.*, 187, especially.
16. *Ibid.*, 139.
17. *Ibid.*, 268.
18. See Warren French, *Frank Norris* (New York: Twayne Publishers, 1962), 59 ff.
19. *Vandover and the Brute*, 218.

20. *Ibid.*, 192.
21. Though *McTeague* was published in 1899, it was apparently largely completed by the end of 1897, thus preceding *Moran of the Lady Letty* in composition though not in publication. I have chosen therefore to treat it here, before my discussion of *Moran* and Norris' lesser works.
22. *The Letters of Frank Norris*, 23.
23. *McTeague*, 3.
24. *Ibid.*, 163.
25. *Ibid.*, 23.
26. *Ibid.*, 27.
27. *Ibid.*, 160.
28. *Ibid.*, 360.
29. Walker, *Frank Norris: A Biography*, 232.
30. *The Letters of Frank Norris*, 33.
31. *Review of Reviews*, 9 (June, 1899), 749.
32. *The Bookman*, 9 (June, 1899), 356-357.
33. *The Letters of Frank Norris*, 34.
34. Introduction to *Frank Norris of 'The Wave'* (San Francisco: The Westgate Press, 1931).
35. *Responsibilities of the Novelist*, 15.
36. Vol. IV, *Collected Writings*, 114.
37. *Responsibilities of the Novelist*, 15.
38. *Ibid.*, 6.
39. *Ibid.*, 80-81.
40. *Ibid.*, 205.
41. *Ibid.*, 164-165.
42. *Ibid.*, 164.
43. *Ibid.*, 167.
44. *Ibid.*, 25.
45. *Collected Writings*, Vol. IV, 122.
46. *Responsibilities of the Novelist*, 21.
47. Walker, *Frank Norris: A Biography*, 139.
48. *Frank Norris of 'The Wave,'* 34.
49. *Responsibilities of the Novelist*, 202-203.
50. *The Letters of Frank Norris*, 45.
51. Walker, *Frank Norris: A Biography*, 283.
52. *The Letters of Frank Norris*, 77.
53. Walker, *Frank Norris: A Biography*, 82-83.
54. See Ernest Marchand, *Frank Norris: A Study* (Palo Alto: Stanford University Press, 1942), 43 ff.
55. *Moran of the Lady Letty*, 186.
56. *Ibid.*, 260-261.
57. *Ibid.*, 286.
58. *Ibid.*, 308.

59. *Ibid.*, 296.
60. *The Letters of Frank Norris,* 22-23.
61. *Ibid.*, 30.
62. *Blix,* 123.
63. *A Man's Woman,* 32.
64. *Ibid.*, 24-25.
65. *Ibid.*, 205.
66. *The Letters of Frank Norris,* 48.
67. *A Man's Woman,* 38-39.
68. *Frank Norris of 'The Wave,'* 140.
69. Hamlin Garland, *Companions on the Trail* (New York: Macmillan, 1931), 11.
70. *Responsibilities of the Novelist,* 61.
71. *The Letters of Frank Norris,* 48.
72. *Responsibilities of the Novelist,* 129.
73. *The Letters of Frank Norris,* 31.
74. *Ibid.*, 7.
75. Garland, *Companions on the Trail,* 103-104.
76. *The Letters of Frank Norris,* 48.
77. *Ibid.*, 23.
78. *Ibid.*, 34.
79. *Ibid.*, 35.
80. *The Octopus,* II, 5.
81. *Ibid.*, I, 63.
82. *Ibid.*, II, 14.
83. *Ibid.*, I, 265.
84. *Ibid.*, II, 161.
85. *Ibid.*, II, 214.
86. *Ibid.*, I, 204.
87. *Ibid.*, II, 82.
88. *Ibid.*, II, 343.
89. *Ibid.*, II, 345.
90. *Ibid.*, II, 106.
91. *Ibid.*, II, 283-285.
92. *Ibid.*, II, 20.
93. *Ibid.*, II, 261.
94. *Ibid.*, II, 317.
95. *The Book Buyer,* 22 (May, 1901), 326.
96. *The Pit,* 121.
97. *Ibid.*, 60.
98. *Ibid.*, 335.
99. *Ibid.*, 270.
100. *Ibid.*, 353.
101. *Ibid.*, 194.
102. *Ibid.*, 388.
103. *Ibid.*, 234.

104. *Ibid.*, 402-403.
105. *Blix*, vii.

THEODORE DREISER: THE NATURALIST AS HUMANIST

1. Theodore Dreiser, *Dawn* (New York: Horace Liveright, 1931), 10.
2. *Ibid.*, 22.
3. *Ibid.*, 277-278.
4. *Ibid.*, 589.
5. Theodore Dreiser, *Newspaper Days* (New York: Horace Liveright, 1931), 20.
6. *Ibid.*, 70.
7. *Ibid.*, 106.
8. Theodore Dreiser, *Hey-Rub-a-Dub-Dub!* (New York: Horace Liveright, 1920), 255.
9. *Ibid.*, 254.
10. *Newspaper Days*, 132.
11. Theodore Dreiser, *Sister Carrie* (Cleveland: World Publishing Co., 1948), 2-3.
12. *Ibid.*, 71.
13. *Ibid.*, 480.
14. *Ibid.*, 556.
15. *Ibid.*, 46.
16. Robert H. Elias (ed.), *Letters of Theodore Dreiser*, 3 vols. (Philadelphia: University of Pennsylvania Press, 1959), I, 52, footnote 16.
17. Dreiser always held that Mrs. Frank Doubleday had forced the book's suppression because she disliked Carrie's conduct and morality. While Mrs. Doubleday's voice was potent in the firm, most of the evidence indicates that the directors were eager to seize upon any chance to reject the book.
18. *Newark Sunday News*, September 1, 1901; cited in Alfred Kazin and Charles Shapiro (eds.), *The Stature of Theodore Dreiser* (Bloomington: Indiana University Press, 1955), 3.
19. *The New York Times*, January 15, 1901.
20. Theodore Dreiser, *Jennie Gerhardt* (Cleveland: World Publishing Co., 1956), 290.
21. *Ibid.*, 132.
22. *Ibid.*, 305-306.
23. *Ibid.*, 245.
24. *Ibid.*, 405.
25. Theodore Dreiser, *The Financier* (Cleveland: World Publishing Co., 1946), 5.
26. Theodore Dreiser, *The Titan* (Cleveland: World Publishing Co., 1946), 201.

27. *The Financier*, 500.
28. *The Titan*, 130.
29. *Ibid.*, 485.
30. Theodore Dreiser, *The Stoic* (New York: World Publishing Co., 1947), 256.
31. *The Titan*, 5.
32. Quoted in F. O. Matthiessen, *Theodore Dreiser* (New York: William Sloane Associates, 1951), 131.
33. *Hey-Rub-a-Dub-Dub!*, 77.
34. *Ibid.*, 74.
35. Theodore Dreiser, *The "Genius"* (Cleveland: World Publishing Co., 1954), 100.
36. *Ibid.*, 488.
37. *Ibid.*, 198.
38. *Ibid.*, 285.
39. *Ibid.*, 695.
40. Kazin and Shapiro, *The Stature of Theodore Dreiser*, 19.
41. Theodore Dreiser, *An American Tragedy* (Cleveland: World Publishing Co., 1948), 16.
42. *Ibid.*, 111-113.
43. to Jesse Lasky (March 10, 1931), in *Letters*, II, 510-512.
44. *An American Tragedy*, 292.
45. to Jack Wilgus (April 20, 1927), in *Letters*, II, 458.
46. *Ibid.*, I, 104-106.
47. *Hey-Rub-a-Dub-Dub!*, 19.
48. *Ibid.*, 273.
49. *Ibid.*, 276.
50. to H. L. Mencken (March 27, 1943), in *Letters*, III, 981-982.
51. *Hey-Rub-a-Dub-Dub!*, 161.
52. "Statement of Belief," *The Bookman*, 68 (September, 1928), 25.
53. *Hey-Rub-a-Dub-Dub!*, 123.
54. *Ibid.*, 244.
55. *Dawn*, 448.
56. *Hey-Rub-a-Dub-Dub!*, 209-210.
57. Quoted in Matthiessen, *Theodore Dreiser*, 205.
58. *Letters*, III, 884.
59. *Dawn*, 578-579.
60. to Frank Harris (June 23, 1918), in *Letters*, I, 254.
61. Mencken to Dreiser (December 20, 1916), *ibid.*, I, 242.
62. to John O'Hara Cosgrave (March, 1913), *ibid.*, I, 152-154.
63. *Hey-Rub-a-Dub-Dub!*, 257.
64. to Michael Gold (September 19, 1928), in *Letters*, II, 474-475.
65. to James Bann (September 23, 1902), *ibid.*, I, 287.
66. to Michael Gold (September 19, 1928), *ibid.*, II, 473-475.
67. to Sergei Dinamov (January 5, 1927), *ibid.* II, 450.
68. "Statement of Belief," *The Bookman*, 68 (September, 1928), 25.

Suggestions for Further Reading

While an exhaustive bibliography seems unnecessary, a few recent critical works may interest readers.

MARK TWAIN

THE LITERATURE on Mark Twain is almost endless and nearly every week sees a new study of some phase of his career. This is more a testament to his stature as a great figure in American culture than to his depth or penetration as an artist, for significantly most new works deal with his life rather than his writing. The standard, full biography is still A. B. Paine, *Mark Twain: A Biography*, 3 vols. (New York: Harper & Bros., 1912), which is unfortunate, since it is a pedestrian account. It is packed with information, however, which will help and interest the persistent reader. Twain's own autobiographical writings are interesting, but should be read with care, since he tended to exaggrate and to "disremember" the events of his life. Bernard De Voto (ed.), *Mark Twain in Eruption* (New York: Harper & Bros., 1940), presents some of Twain's suppressed and irascible prose. The most perceptive personal memoir concerning Twain is William Dean Howells, *My Mark Twain* (New York: Harper & Bros., 1910); it is an engaging, shrewd, and helpful work for the lives of both men. Dixon Wecter, *Sam Clemens of Hannibal* (Boston: Little, Brown and Co., 1952), shows the influence of Twain's frontier environment on his work and attitudes. Gladys C. Bellamy, *Mark Twain as a Literary Artist* (Norman: University of Oklahoma Press, 1950), is a brilliant book, filled with common sense and thorough in its coverage of Twain's literary sources, and his development as a writer and thinker. Pascal Covici, Jr., *Mark Twain's Humor* (Dallas: Southern Methodist University Press, 1962), is a good analysis of Twain's humor. Walter Blair, *Mark Twain and Huck Finn* (Berkeley and Los Angeles: University of California Press, 1950), is a thorough study of the development of Twain's greatest character and best book, written in the tradition of modern textual criticism. R. B. Salomon, *Twain and the Image of History* (New Haven: Yale University Press, 1961), discusses Twain's view of history and the development of his attitude toward time and progress. Henry Nash Smith, *Mark Twain: The Development of a Writer* (Cambridge: Harvard University Press, 1962), is a thorough description of the successive stages through which Twain passed as he developed his literary style and technique. The same author's *Mark*

Twain's Fable of Progress: Political and Economic Ideas in 'A Connecticut Yankee' (New Brunswick, N.J.: Rutgers University Press, 1964), studies a crucial work in Twain's career. Smith's thesis that *A Connecticut Yankee* began as Twain's affirmation of faith in man's progress and ended as "a nightmare" of disappointment in modern civilization is logically and impressively developed. Louis J. Budd, *Mark Twain: Social Philosopher* (Bloomington: Indiana University Press, 1962), is by far the most impressive recent book on Twain. Well written, vital, filled with a sharpness and humor reminiscent of Twain himself, it is a penetrating and sustained analysis of Twain's development as a social critic, and shows his interest in the social issues of his day. It is a model of good criticism, honest analysis, and fine writing.

WILLIAM DEAN HOWELLS

THE "GOOD GRAY DEAN" has come into his own in recent years after a long period of neglect, and a number of studies are very helpful for his work in particular and Realism and Naturalism in general. Mildred Howells (ed.), *Life in Letters of William Dean Howells*, 2 vols. (New York: Doubleday, Doran & Co., 1928), is filled with information, though old-fashioned and pedestrian in approach. It remains a basic primary source for his life and work. Van Wyck Brooks, *Howells: His Life and World* (New York: E. P. Dutton & Co., 1959), like most of Brooks' work, is thin and impressionistic, but is a readable introduction to the man and his era. The standard biography is Edwin H. Cady, *The Road to Realism* (Syracuse: Syracuse University Press, 1956) and *The Realist at War* (Syracuse: Syracuse University Press, 1958). Both are readable, informative, and critically sound. Clara M. Kirk and Rudolf Kirk, *William Dean Howells* (New York: Twayne Publishers, 1962), is a good, brief analysis of the major themes in Howells' works, with special emphasis on his social and economic writings. Everett Carter, *Howells and the Age of Realism* (New York: J. B. Lippincott Co., 1954), is a thorough, informative, well-written examination of Howells' influence on Realism. It is perceptive, free from jargon, and admits his shortcomings as well as his virtues. George N. Bennett, *William Dean Howells: The Development of a Novelist* (Norman: University of Oklahoma Press, 1959), traces the stages of Howells' growth and his major ideas toward writing. Clara M. Kirk, *William Dean Howells, Traveller from Altruria 1889-1894* (New Brunswick, N.J.: Rutgers University Press, 1962), effectively discusses the watershed years in Howells' life, when he was a major literary spokesman of economic and social reform. Mrs. Kirk offers a useful and valid discussion of Howells' Christian socialism and reform ideas in general. Robert L. Hough, *The Quiet Rebel: William Dean Howells as a Social Commentator* (Lincoln: University of Nebraska Press,

1959), is a small but perceptive work, dotted with intriguing quotations from Howells' later works, and shows that he was a consistent, logical, and often effective social critic after 1896. Walter Fuller Taylor, *The Economic Novel in America* (Chapel Hill: University of North Carolina Press, 1952), remains one of the most helpful and interesting books in recent American criticism. Its chapter on Howells as an economic reformer is admirable. Robert Falk, *The Victorian Mode in American Fiction, 1865-1885* (East Lansing: Michigan State University Press, 1964) is a concise, perceptive, general account of the rise of Realism, and of its important themes in the general context of American literature in the late nineteenth century. The same author's, "The Search for Reality: Writers and Their Literature," in H. Wayne Morgan (ed.), *The Gilded Age: A Reappraisal* (Syracuse: Syracuse University Press, 1963), is a good, brief summary of and introduction to the literature of the period of Twain and Howells.

HAMLIN GARLAND

BECAUSE HE is a minor figure whose importance lies largely in his symbolic posture as a reflector of major trends, Garland has not been widely studied. His memoirs, comprising eight volumes of retrospective comment on his life and contemporaries, are a mine of information on the whole period of American history through which he lived. Though often verbose, redundant, and trivial, they are a rich source for the cultural as well as the literary historian. Jean Holloway, *Hamlin Garland: A Biography* (Austin: University of Texas Press, 1960), is a thorough account of Garland's life and works. It is balanced and judicious in analysis, and does not overstate Garland's importance. Taylor, *The Economic Novel in America,* has a good chapter on Garland's social and economic commentary and importance.

FRANK NORRIS

NORRIS IS at present undergoing critical rejuvenation and rediscovery after a long dormant period. His work has been catalogued in Kenneth A. Lohf and Eugene P. Sheey (eds.), *Frank Norris: A Bibliography* (Los Gatos, California: The Talisman Press, 1959). Franklin Walker, *Frank Norris: A Biography* (New York: Doubleday, Doran & Co., 1932), is a trifle sketchy, but reflects the lack of material about much of Norris' life. It is nonetheless a well-written and engaging book whose basic viewpoint is not likely to be superseded by the inevitable exhaustive biography. Warren French, *Frank Norris* (New York: Twayne Publishers, 1962), offers a brief, incisive coverage of Norris' works and major themes. It shows the kind of Naturalism he espoused, its origins and impact, and importance in American literary and cultural history. But Ernest Marchand, *Frank Norris: A Study* (Stanford, California: Stanford University Press, 1942), remains a thorough and eminently sound study of the major themes in Norris' work. Charles Child Wallcutt, *American Literary Naturalism, A Divided Stream* (Minneapolis: University of Minnesota Press, 1956), is concerned chiefly with Norris' style, the unresolved flaws in his thinking, and his impact on Naturalism. Lars Ahnebrink, *The Beginnings of Naturalism in American Fiction* (Cambridge: Harvard University Press, 1950), is an exhaustive critical analysis of the rise of European and American Naturalism, and is useful for Howells and Garland as well as Norris. It makes perhaps too much of Norris' similarity to Zola and other Europeans, and minimizes his growth as an indigenous American writer. Maxwell Geismar, *Rebels and Ancestors: The American Novel, 1890-1915* (Boston: Houghton Mifflin Co., 1953), contains a long chapter on Norris, attempting chiefly to show his relation to Freudianism, and emphasizes his attitude toward sexual themes. Kenneth S. Lynn, *The Dream of Success* (Boston: Little, Brown and Co., 1955), has a chapter called "Frank Norris: Mama's Boy," that pursues the sexual theme with fascinating but questionable methods. Though interesting, the essay is more an exercise in how to prove a thesis than a really valid study of Norris.

THEODORE DREISER

THOUGH MANY critics avoided Dreiser for years because of his unevenness, he is now undergoing a critical renascence. Robert H. Elias (ed.), *Letters of Theodore Dreiser*, 3 vols. (Philadelphia: University of Pennsylvania Press, 1959), is a monumental, well-edited, and invaluable source not only for Dreiser but for his whole era. Alfred Kazin and Charles Shapiro (eds.), *The Stature of Theodore Dreiser* (Bloomington: Indiana University Press, 1955), is a good collection of historical and contemporary information, including memoir, self-analysis, and criticism. Robert H. Elias, *Theodore Dreiser: Apostle of Nature* (New York: Alfred Knopf, Inc., 1948), is the only biography, and while incomplete, it shows his relation to Naturalism, and on the whole is perceptive and well written. F. O. Matthiessen, *Theodore Dreiser* (New York: William Sloane Associates, 1951), is an incisive and perceptive critical appraisal of Dreiser's total work. Charles Shapiro, *Theodore Dreiser: Our Bitter Patriot* (Carbondale, Illinois: Southern Illinois University Press, 1962), is a rather uninspired but exhaustive discussion of Dreiser's development as a writer and his place as a critic of American society as he saw it. Dorothy Dudley, *Dreiser and the Land of the Free* (New York: The Beechurst Press, 1946), is an older but still helpful combination of memoir and criticism, originally published in 1932 as *Forgotten Frontiers: Dreiser and the Land of the Free*.

AMERICAN CENTURY SERIES